THE PRABHAKARA SCHOOL OF PURVA MIMAMSA

THE PRABHAKARA SCHOOL OF PURVA MIMAMSA

GANGANATH JHA

GYAN

Published by

Gyan Publishing House
5, Ansari Road
Daryaganj, New Delhi-110002
Phone: 011-47034999, 9811692060
E-mail: books@gyanbooks.com

Distribution Network
gyanbooks.com
India, USA, Canada, UK, Australia

ISBN: 978-93-6920-137-2 (HB)

First Published, 1911

2nd Impression 2025

Printed at: Gyan Press, Delhi.

THE PRABHAKARA SCHOOL OF PURVA MIMAMSA
Author: GANGANATH JHA

THE PRĀBHĀKARA SCHOOL OF PŪRVA MĪMĀMSĀ

THE PRĀBHĀKARA SCHOOL OF PŪRVA MĪMĀMSĀ

MAHĀMAHOPĀDHYĀYA GAṄGĀNĀTHA JHĀ, M.A.

पितुः श्रीतीर्थनाथस्य
प्रभोर्लक्ष्मीश्वरस्य च ।
मातुस्तीर्थलतादेव्याः
पादयोरिदमर्पितम् ॥

LIST OF CONTENTS.

(The paging refers to the number at the bottom of each page.)

PREFACE.

In the course of my study of the *Bhātta* system of Pūrva-Mīmāmsā, I was, in many places, struck by the ingenuity and apparent simplicity of many *Prābhākara* explanations. This led me to the study of this much misrepresented system;—a study which received fresh impetus from the institution by the University of Allahabad of the degree of 'Doctor of Letters,' in connection with which I elected for the subject of my dissertation, the *Prābhākara* School of Pūrva-Mīmāmsā. At the very outset however, I was faced by the difficulty of the extreme paucity of materials available: the *Prakaraṇapañchikā* of Shālikanāṭha was the sole book available from which we could learn anything, directly, about the tenets of the Prābhākara School. By a strange coincidence, however, another work of the same writer, the '*Ṛijuvimalā*' was brought to my notice by Col. G. A. Jacob, through my honoured tutor, Principal Venis; and I at once applied for a loan of the manuscript from the India Office Library; which was granted to me through the kindness of Principal Jennings. When I had sent my application to the India Office, my friend Mr. Govinda-dāsa very kindly obtained for me a copy of the same work from the Travancore State Library. The fact of the *Ṛijuvimalā* being a work dealing directly with the *Sūtras* recalled to my mind the name of '*Bṛihatī*,' which I had come across, ten or twelve years ago, in a list of manuscripts belonging to the Asiatic Society of Bengal, wherein it was described as a work on *Prābhākara-Mīmāmsa*.' I sent an application for the loan of this manuscript also, which was granted by the Society, through the kind courtesy of the President. This work turned out to be nothing less than a commentary upon Shabara's *Bhāṣya* by Prabhākara himself. The temptation to bring out an edition of this unique work was so great that I at once set about preparing the press-copy. But after having done the first eighteen *paṭras*, I was disappointed to find that the manuscript, though good enough to supply first-hand information with regard to Prabhākara's views, was far from perfect, for the purposes of an edition. Baffled in that quarter, I intended to bring out an edition of the *Ṛijuvimalā*; but the two manuscripts of this work which I had obtained from the India Office and Travancore, turned out to be entirely different parts of the work; the India Office Ms. containing nearly the whole of Aḍh. I (the first leaf in the beginning and the whole of the first *aḍhikaraṇa* of *pāḍa* ii being wanting), while the Travancore Ms. contained *aḍhyāyas* III, IV and V complete.

Though unable to bring out a 'critical edition' of any of these works, I found the Mss. of great help; from these I derived much first-hand information on the views held by Prabhākara and by his direct pupil, Shālikanāṭha; and I was also enabled to verify their views as put forward by Māḍhavāchārya in his *Nyāyamālāvisṭara*. This latter work notices Prabhākara's views—calling them '*Gurumaṭa*'—on the following *aḍhikaraṇas* :—

(*a*) I—i—2—'Veḍa is the sole authority on Ḍharma.'

(*b*) I—i—3—'Necessity of enquiry into Ḍharma.'

(*c*) I—ii—19 to 25—'Nature of those Arṭhavāḍas that have the form of Injunctions.'

(*d*) I—iii—10—Dealing with words as used by the Mlechchhas.

(*e*) I—iii—11—Authority of the Kalpasūṭras.

(*f*) I—iii—15—The 'Holākāḍhikaraṇa.'

(*g*) I—iii—25—Dealing with the Grammar-Smriṭis.

(*h*) I—iii—30—'Words are expressive of class-character.'

(*i*) I—iv—2—'Uḍbhiḍ' is the name of a sacrifice.'

(*j*) I—iv—9—'Āgneya' is not the name of a sacrifice, but indicates the Deity.'

(*k*) I—iv—10—The word '*varki*' denotes class-character.

(*l*) I—iv—13—'Vaishvaḍeva' is the name of a sacrifice.

(*m*) I—iv—17—The word '*Aṣṭa*' with reference to the pans used at the Vaishvānara sacrifice is mere *arṭhavāḍa*.

It will be noticed that Māḍhava ceases to notice the '*Gurumaṭa*' after the first *Aḍhyāya*. Nor is there much of a difference, after this, between Bhatta and Prabhākara, directly bearing on the *aḍhikaraṇas*; the other differences being only as regards certain detailed principles involved in the *aḍhikaraṇas*. These we have tried to bring out in chapter III.

When the present work was undertaken, it was intended to deal only with views of Prabhākara, as bearing upon subjects psychological and metaphysical; but later on, in view of the fact that the full details of what is contained in the *Mīmāmsā-shāsṭra* have not yet been presented before the modern reader, * the writer was advised to present a consecutive account of all that is contained in that *Shāsṭra*. This task proved to be more stupendous than was expected. But with the constant encouragement accorded to me by Principal Venis, and the sage counsel of Dr. Thibaut, I was enabled to set to work and to make out a somewhat presentable account of the contents of the *Mīmāmsā-Shāsṭra*. In the actual 'research'—or 'search'—involved in this work, I am indebted to my friend Mr. Govinḍa-ḍāsa, to whose help, most willingly accorded, I owe the unearthing of all those manuscripts which have enabled me to bring together information, which, in one sense, may be regarded as altogether new,—and also *unexpected*, in view of the fact that, in

* The excellent translation of the *Arṭhasangraha*, with its lucid introduction, deals mainly with the subject of '*Viḍhi*.'

the first place, all interest in the *Shastra* had ceased, and secondly, all hopes of ever getting at Prabhākara's works had been given np; and my friend had to hunt ont, and indicate to me, manuscripts lying hidden in far-off corners of India;—one of these manuscripts being the long-lost portion wanting in the *Prakaraṇapañchikā*, which had to be printed in its incomplete form, by two such enterprising publishers as the Medical Hall Press, and the Chaukhambha Book Depôt. *

2. As regards the originality of the present work, inasmuch as nothing has been written upon the Prābhākara School, in any modern langnage, the whole may be regarded as 'original.' On the other hand, as it contains only what has been written by Prabhākara and his followers nothing can be truly 'original.' Bnt what is claimed for the work is that it represents the first attempt in more than one direction, a few of which may be noted here :—

(1) In no work,—not even in the innumerable *prakaraṇa-granthas* in Sanskrit, is the whole *Mīmāmsā-shāstra* found explained in the systematic and connected way in which it is presented here.

(2) No work known to exist is found to contrast the views of the two sister schools on *all points*.

(3) The bearing of *Mīmāmsa* upon legal literatnre is not found brought ont, in the manner in which it is done in this work. †

(4) This is the first attempt at a systematic account of the *Prābhākara* system. There is no work known to the modern world which affords a detailed acconnt of what that system is; the *Prakaraṇapañchikā* confining itself only to a few philosophical points, and a very few of the purely Mīmāmsā topics.

* The Ms. of this portion has been handed over to the publishers of the Shaukhambhā Sans. Series who have now printed it.

† Since writing the above we have received the *Tagore Law Lectures* on the Mīmāmsā Rules of Interpretation,—a book which deals with the legal aspect of the *adhikaraṇas* in the way that only a trained lawyer could deal.

CHAPTER I.

THE BEGINNINGS OF MĪMĀṂSĀ.

1. In the far-off days of ancient Āryāvarṭa when, we are told, the gods moved among men, and received and gave gifts much in the same way as men give and receive among themselves,—matters went on smoothly; each giving as he chose, and receiving when and what he chose. There was no occasion for any rules or regulations on the matter. All that was needed was that the man should sing the praises of the superior being whom he wished to please. This may be regarded as having been the state of things during the period of the 'Ṛigveḍa', wherein,—at least in the 'older' portions—we do not find 'sacrifices' occupying any important position.

As times changed and the gods ceased their friendly visits, and became, by and by, more remote beings, doubts naturally began to arise in the minds of men, regarding the ways and methods by which the offerings should be made in order to be most acceptable. The wisest among men came together and laid down a set of rules as to these ways and methods. So long as these patriarchs lived, the affairs of men went on under their guidance; as whenever difficulties arose, the original framers of the rules were at hand to settle them, by means of explanations and illustrations. This state of things may be regarded as covering the period represented by the 'Brāhmaṇas', wherein we find all sacrificial details laid down, explained and illustrated. In regard to this period it is quite true, that—

'although there is no reason to suppose that the sacrificial ceremonial was in early times so fully developed,......the religious service would seem to have been already of a sufficiently advanced nature' (*Shaṭapaṭha Br.* Trans., Intro. xi); and also that—

'the idea of bringing together the different family collections would seem first to have suggested itself to the priests at a time when the hitherto divided Āryan tribes had moved from the Panjab to the eastern plains, and became consolidated into larger communities, and the want of a more uniform system of worship would naturally make itself felt;—to the same period we may refer the first attempts at a systematic arrangement of the entire ceremonial of worship, and the definitive distribution of the sacrificial duties among four classes of priests. (*Ibid—XX.*)

When a further degeneration set in, further doubts began to arise, for the removal of which no living authorities were available; and thus arose the necessity of collecting and digesting the old rules and regulations; and as each collector and digester had at hand a mass of material all of which could not be bodily adopted by him,—for the simple reason that the greater part of these appertained to the exigencies of particular times and places,—he had to exercise his judgment in the preparing of his compilation. This gave rise to the literature of the '*Smṛiṭis*,' whose professed aim is to clarify what is already present in the Vedas (Samhiṭās and Brāhmaṇas). With the appearance of this literature there came about the necessity also of a regular study of these matters as bearing upon *Ḍharma* or Duty of each man. It was at this juncture that '*Mīmāmsā*' literature stepped in with its 1000 and odd 'rules' for the interpretation and right understanding of what is said in the Veda, in regard to *Ḍharma*.

These rules of interpretation were formulated for the first time by Jaimini, in a systematic manner, in the work that ḥas come down to us under the name of '*Jaimini-sūṭra*' or '*Mīmāmsā-sūṭra*.' This was commented upon by a number of writers, among whom we may mention—(1) Bharṭṛimiṭra (mentioned by the *Nyāyaratnākara* and *Kāshikā* on verse 10, and believed by my honoured teacher, Mahāmahopāḍhyāya Pandit Chiṭraḍhara Mishra to be the oldest commentator on the *Sūṭras*)—(2) Bhavaḍāsa (mentioned by Kumārila in the Shlokavārṭika, 1—63),—(3) Hari (referred to in the *Shāsṭraḍīpikā* X—ii—59,60),—and (4) Upavarṣa, referred to in the *Bhāṣya* as '*Bhagavān Upavarṣaḥ*' (page 13, line 8); and then at a much later date by *Shabara*, whose work is known as the '*Bhāṣya.*' He is believed by the Pandits to have lived about 57 B.C., being described as the father of King Vikramāḍiṭya, as also of Varāhamihira and Bharṭrihari; this fact is believed upon the authority of the following verse current among Pandits; among whom he is also known as having for his real name, Āḍiṭya-ḍeva, the name 'Shabara' being only due to his having disguised himself as a forester for fear of Jaina persecution :—

ब्राह्मण्यामभवद् वराहमिहिरो ज्योतिर्विदामग्रणीः
राजा भर्तृहरिश्च विक्रमनृपः क्षत्रात्मजायामभूत् ।
वैश्यायां हरिचन्द्रवैद्यतिलको जातश्च शङ्कुः कृती
शूद्रायाममरः षडेव शबरस्वामिद्विजस्यात्मजाः ॥*

It was this *Bhāṣya* that formed the basis and starting point for all later Mīmāmsā works; it was at this stage also that there came about the well-known bifurcation of the system into two schools: One of these was headed by Kumārila Bhatta, believed to have been the senior contemporary of the Great Shankara, also known as '*Bhatta*' and '*Bhattapāḍa*'—who wrote an extensive commentary upon the *Bhāṣya*; this is a work in three parts:—the *first* called the *Shlokavārṭika*, dealing with the first, or polemical, part of the

* But Viḍyāpaṭ Thakkura, a writer of the 15th—16th Century A. C., speaks of him, in the Puruṣaparīkṣā as the 'Guru' or 'teacher' of Vikrama.

first chapter;—the *second* called the *Ṭanṭravārṭika*, dealing with the rest of chapter I, and also with chapters II and III. [Both of these have been translated by the present writer, and are in course of publication by the Asiatic Society of Bengal;] the third called the *Tuptīkā*, which contains only brief notes upon the remaining nine *aḍhyāyas*. Kumārila came to be known as the 'Vārṭikakāra' by a host of followers and commentators, chief among whom are Maṇdana Mishra (the author of the *Viḍhiviveka* and *Mīmāmsānukramaṇī* and also of a commentary on the *Ṭanṭravarṭika*, mentioned in the *Shāsṭraḍīpikā* II—i—1), Pārṭhasāraṭhi Mishra (the author of the *Shāsṭraḍīpikā*, the *Ṭanṭraraṭna*, the *Nyāyaraṭnākara*, and the *Nyāyaraṭnamālā*), Sucharita Mishra (author of the *Kāshikā*) and Someshvara (author of the *Nyāyasuḍhā*, also known as '*Rāṇaka*'). The other school had for its founder a writer whose work has not yet come to light, who is referred to by Prabhākara and his followers as '*Vārṭikakārapāḍāḥ*.' That this '*Vārṭikakāra*' is different from Kumārila is shown by the fact that the quotations referred to him are not to be found in any of Kumārila's works; and that Kumārila is referred to by these writers only as '*Yathāhuḥ*,' without any appellation of honour. Following upon this latter '*Vārṭikākara*,' Prabhākara Mishra wrote his *Bṛihaṭī*,* a commentary upon Shabara's *Bhāṣya*; and this again has an extensive commentary, the *Ṛijuvimalā*, by Shālikanāṭha Mishra, who also wrote a digest of the Prābhākara system, called '*Prakaraṇapañchikā*.'†

In course of time as Vedic sacrifices began to fall into disuse, the study of Mīmāmsā lost its hold upon the popular mind, and gave way to the study of the *Ṭanṭra* and other allied subjects. The principles however that had been evolved

* Mentioned on p. 375 of Aufrecht's *Catalogus Catalogorum*.

† Of this work, the earliest Ms. hitherto discovered is one belonging to the sixteenth century.

by the *Mīmāmsaka* continued to influence all literature, liturgical, philosophical and legal. In fact, whenever any question arose as to the interpretation of certain texts, the aid invariably called in was that of the principles enunciated by Jaimini and his followers. At the present day, apart from the intrinsic merits of the *Mīmāmsāshāstra* itself, the chief interest of the *Shāstra* lies in its bearing upon the whole Hindu legal literature; and for this reason, towards the close of our present study, we shall devote a short chapter where we shall show in what manner *Mīmāmsā* principles have been used to settle legal difficulties.

Prabhākara,—or Guru, as he is generally spoken of in later Sanskrit philosophical literature—is found to be referred to by later writers on Mīmāmsā as '*Nibanḍhanakārah*,' 'the writer of a great work,' apparently the '*Bṛihaṭī*' mentioned above. (*See Shāsṭraḍīpikā* II—i—1st aḍhik. where a passage from the *Bṛihaṭī* is quoted.) From this it would seem that *Nibanḍhana* was another name for the *Bṛihaṭī*. In the only manuscript of this work, that has been found in the library of theAsiatic Society of Bengal, we find the following at the end of the chapters :—

(*a*) **इति प्रभाकरमिश्रकृतौ मीमांसाभाष्यविवरणे**—at the end of pāḍa ii of *Aḍhyāya* II.

(*b*) **इति बृहत्याम्**—at the end of *pāda* vii of *Aḍhyāya* III.

(*c*) **इति सर्वविद्यानिधानकवीन्द्राचार्यसरस्वतीनाम् प्राभाकर-मीमांसायाम्**—at the end of *Aḍhyāya* III.

The name 'Guru' is not found in any of the colophons; it would appear to have been a later title given to him, perhaps as deprecatory of his elaborate or complicated (*guru*) views; though tradition assigns a different reason for this title. That Prabhākara's views were regarded as too elaborate or complicated—without much justification however,—is also shown by the following *Shloka* current in South India :—

> गाथा ताथागतानाङ्गलति गमनिका कापिली क्वापि लीना
> क्षीणा काणादवाणी द्रुहिणहरगिरः सौरभन्नारभन्ते ।
> क्षामा कौमारिलोक्तिर्जगति गुरुमतङ्गौरवाद् दूरवान्तम्
> का शङ्का शङ्करादेर्भजति यतिपतौ भद्रवेदीन्त्रिवेदीम् ॥

As regards the time and place where Prabhākara rose we have not been able to obtain any information, except certain traditional stories current among Pandits. According to these, Prabhākara, along with Maṇḍana Mishra, was a pupil of Kumārila. From the very beginning of his studies, he evinced great independence of thought and opinion, and many a story is told in exemplification of his independent spirit. On a certain point connected with the after-death rites, Prabhākara happened to hold with characteristic tenacity to a certain opinion diametrically opposed to that held by his teacher. Having failed to win the pupil to his views, by reasonings, the teacher had recourse to a trick: one morning it was suddenly discovered that the teacher had died; and there arose among the pupils a discussion as to the exact manner in which his after-death rites were to be performed; when the question was referred to Prabhākara, as the exponent of one view, he declared that the view held by his teacher was the right one, and that he had put forward another view simply for purposes of exciting discussion. On hearing this the teacher, who had feigned illness only for obtaining this confession, sat up and expressed satisfaction at Prabhākara having at last been won over to his views; thereupon Prabhākara said—'Yes, you won me to your views, but not while you were living.' Another story tells us how he acquired the title of 'Guru' from his teacher:—In course of their studies, they came across the sentence—'*Atratunoktantatrapinoktamitidviruktam*'; this apparently meant—'this has not been mentioned there, nor has it been mentioned here, thus it has been mentioned twice,' an apparent absurdity. The teacher could not find a satisfactory explanation, and ultimately gave it up and went to attend to his evening prayers. When the class assembled again, Prabhākara suggested that the sentence in question admitted of the construction—'*atra tunā uktam tatra apinā uktam, iti dviruktam*',* the meaning being 'what is mentioned there by means of the particle *tu* is again mentioned here by the particle *api*, and thus it has been mentioned twice.' The teacher was so pleased at the ingenuity of his pupil that he thereupon conferred upon him the title of 'Guru' or 'Teacher.' That the tradition bearing upon the relation of Prabhākara to Kumārila is not a mere lip-story is proved by the following extract from an old Ms. of the *Sarvasiddhāntarahasya* by Shesa, commented upon by his son Govinda, a pupil of the great Madhusūdana† :—

'अस्यां सूत्रञ्जैमिनीयम्, शाबरम्भाष्यमस्य तु
मीमांसावार्तिकम्भाट्टम्, भट्टाचार्यकृतं हि तत् ॥
तच्छिष्योऽप्यल्पभेदेने शाबरस्य मतान्तरम्
प्रभाकरगुरुश्चक्रे तद्धि प्राभाकरम्मतम् ॥'

तस्य भाष्यवार्तिककर्तुः भट्टाचर्यस्य शिष्यः प्रभाकरगुरुः भट्टमतात् उपादानग्राहकग्रहणादिरूपप्रमाणान्तरनियोगशब्ददबलवादार्थे बलवादादिरूपषड्भेदस्वीकारेण शाबरस्य ग्रन्थस्वामिकृतस्य भाष्यस्य मतान्तरम्प्राभाकरनाम ग्रन्थभेदङ्कृतवानित्यर्थः ।

* The modern reader of well-edited texts has to bear in mind that in old MSS. we do not find the system of '*padachheda*'; and thus there would be no such difference in writing as—तत्रापिनोक्तम् (according to the interpretation of Prabhākara) and तत्रापि नोक्तम्(which gave the former absurd meaning).

† Now published at Madras, Edited by Prof. Rangachārya.

Prabhākara's philosophy had to pay a heavy price for its innovating spirit; it never gained a solid footing; and until the publication of Shālikanāṭha's *Prakaraṇapañchikā* in the 'Pandit,' the philosophy was known only under the misrepresentations of its opponents. It is however interesting to note that the author of the Mitākṣarā (p. 181) quotes an entire passage out of the *Bṛihaṭī* of Prabhākara. Even on the publication of the above-mentioned work, the system was not studied; it shared the fate of the whole *Mīmāmsā Skāsṭra* which, by a strange irony of fate, has not found a place in the curriculum of modern *Pāṭhashālās*.

In regard to the relation between Prabhākara and Kumārila as indicated by the above tradition, it may be noted that this is not borne out by the internal evidence available in the writings of these authors.

(A) Prabhākara's *Bṛihaṭī* is a 'comment,' in the strict sense of the word, upon Shabara's *Bhāṣya*; it does not, in any place, differ from the original, which it always tries to support; nor does it attack any opinions of the original; in fact as a rule, it attacks no opinions except those of the avowed *Pūrvapakṣa*. Kumārila on the other hand, in many places' in the *Ṭanṭravārṭika*, rejects the interpretation of Shabara' and offers an entirely different interpretation of his own. We will note a few of these instances here :—

(*a*) I—ii—Aḍhi (1) (*Ṭanṭravārṭika*, translation, page 32).
(*b*) I—iii—Aḍhi (1) (page 116.)
(*c*) I—iii—Aḍhi (4)—(p. 178.)
(*d*) I—iii—Aḍhi (5)—(p. 207.)
(*e*) I—iii...Aḍhi (7)—(p. 227—where more than two interpretations are given).
(*f*) I—iii—Aḍhi (10)—(p. 347).
(*g*) I—iv—Aḍhi (1)—(p. 373).

If Prabhākara had been an innovator, or reformer, or improver of the *Bhātta* system, he would naturally have taken up every one of these deviations from the *Bhāṣya* and tried to demolish it with his wonted verve and vigour. As a matter of fact, however, we find that the *Bṛihaṭī* takes no notice of any of the new interpretations proposed by Kumārila. This would perhaps indicate that it was Kumārila, and not Prabhākara, who was an innovator or reformer. This view is confirmed by the fact that while Prabhākara does not criticise any of the strikingly original interpretations of Kumārila, the latter in many places, takes great pains to demolish certain views, a few of which we find put forward by Prabhākara in the *Bṛihaṭī*. We append a few of these :—

(*a*) I—ii—Sū 31—(*Ṭanṭravārṭika*, Translation, p. 54) Kumārila objects to the question of the *Aḍhikaraṇa* being put in the form 'are *manṭras* meaningless or not?'—the form in which it has been stated in the *Bṛihaṭī* (Ms. p. 31*a*.)

(*b*) I—iii—2—(*Ṭanṭravārṭika*, Trans. p. 112.) According to Prabhākara (Ms. p. 31*b*) the Vedic texts in corroboration of injunctions found in the *Smṛiṭi* are to be *inferred*. This is objected to by Kumārila.

(*c*) I—iv—1—As regards the connection of *pāḍa* iv with the subject-matter of the whole *aḍhyāya* Prabhākara, in agreement with the *Bhāṣya*, puts forward the question in the form—'Are the words (*uḍbhiḍ* and the like) expressive of materials or of names of sacrifices?'—this question bearing upon the authority of *Dharma* (*Bṛihaṭi*, p. 38 *a*). This is objected to by Kumārila (*Tanṭravārṭika*, Trans. 373).

(*d*) I—iv—1—On the same *Adhikaraṇa*, the *Bhāṣya*, and the *Bṛihaṭī* with it, takes *sūṭra* (i) as the '*Pūrvapakṣa*' and *ṣū*. (2) as the '*Siddhānṭa*'; while Kumārila takes the two *sūṭras* as embodying two distinct *Adhikaraṇas*; and objects to the other interpretation (*Tanṭravārṭika*, Trans. p. 373).

The only point where we have found Prabhākara com batting a view propounded by Kumārila is under IV—i—2 (*Bṛihaṭī*, Ms. p. 64*b*, line 9 *et. seq.*). But in this connection also, it is noteworthy that the words in which the view combatted is expressed—which are apparently a quotation—are very different from those employed by Kumārila (iv—i—2). The words of the latter are—'*Kraṭvarṭhe ḍrayārjane kraṭu-vighāṭaḥ syāṭ*'; while those used by Prabhākara are—'*Kraṭvarṭhaṭve saṭṭvameva na bhavaṭīṭi yāga eva na ṣamvarṭaṭe*'; and this is combatted by Prabhākara in the words—'*pralapiṭa—midaṅkēnapī arjanam saṭṭvannāpāḍayaṭīṭi praṭiṣiḍḍham.*' The difference in the words shows that '*kenapi*' of Prabhākara must refer to some one entirely different from Kumārila. It is Prabhākara's very words in this connection that have been quoted by the *Miṭākṣarā* with approval. (see below, chap. V.)

(B) In point of style also, the *Bṛihaṭī* shows distinct signs of being older than the *Tanṭravāriṭka*. The style of the former is very similar to that of the *Bhāṣya* of Shabara, possessing the same natural grace, simplicity and directness; while that of Kumārila becomes rather involved and rich, very much like that of the *Shārīrakabhāṣya* of the Great Shaṅkara. The contrast is best shown by presenting here side by side a few typical passages chosen at random from the two works :—

Bṛihaṭī.	*Ṭanṭravārṭika.*
(a) नायं हेतुः । कस्मात् । शूर्पंहोमेति हेतुः प्रतीयते ।	(a) तथा यद्यप्यन्यदेवत्यः पशुराग्नेय्येव मनोता कार्येत्यूहप्राप्तिदर्शनमेवमुस्राणाम्मेषाणामित्येवमादीनां यथार्थमूहितानामपि विवक्षितार्थम्भविष्यति ।
(b) कथम्पुनरविनियुक्तमसम्बद्धमेवाक्षिप्यते । नैव विनियोग आक्षेपे हेतुः । किन्तर्हि । कार्यम् ।	(b) स्यादेतत् । अर्थस्मरणेन कृतार्थामान्निष्प्रयोजनम्मूलस्मरणमनादराद्भ्रष्टमिति । तदयुक्तम् ।
(c) अथादृष्टार्थमेवेदं सूत्रं वेदमधीत्यानन्तरन्धर्मजिज्ञासेति । एवन्तर्ह्यर्थद्वयविधानम्प्राप्नोति । वेदमधीत्य अनन्तरञ्चेति । यदि च वेदमधीत्येत्युच्यते, अन्यस्यापि कर्मणो ऽनन्तरन्धर्मजिज्ञासाऽवकल्पते । अथानन्तर्यं विधीयते प्रागपि वेदाध्ययनात् प्राप्नोति । न चादृष्टार्थस्य वाक्यस्यार्थद्वयविधानन्द्विधा सम्भवति । उच्यते । नैवेदमदृष्टार्थं सूत्रम्, वेदार्थविचारायैवेदमारभ्यते । कुतः । ताद्रूप्यमित्यादि ।	(c) अर्थवादानाञ्चान्यपरत्वेन गुणवादप्रायत्वात् आदित्ययूपयजमानप्रस्तरस्वर्गाहवनीयवचनवत् कथमपि प्रशंसनाशेषत्वात् संज्ञासंज्ञिसम्बन्धकरणव्युत्पादनव्यापाररहितत्वाच्च न पदार्थप्रतिपत्त्युपयुक्तत्वमध्यवसीयते ।

(d) कथमवच्छिन्नार्थोऽनवच्छिन्नो भवति। कथन्तर्हि प्रतिबुद्धो मिथ्येति जानाति।

(d) तथा य आत्माऽपहतपाप्मा विजरो विमृत्युर्विशोको विघिकित्सोऽपिपासः सत्यकामः सत्यसङ्कल्पः......इति कामवादलोकवादवचनविशेषैर्जिज्ञासामननसहितात्मज्ञानकेवलावबोधपर्यन्तस्पष्टात्मतत्त्वज्ञानविधानापेक्षितवाक्यान्तरोपात्तद्विविधाभ्युदयनिःश्रेयसरूपफलसम्बन्धः स सर्वांश्च लोकानाप्नोति सर्वांश्च कामानाप्नोति तरति शोकमात्मवित् तथा स यदि पितृलोककामो भवति सङ्कल्पादेवास्य इत्यादिना योगजन्याणिमाद्यष्टगुणैश्वर्यफलानि वर्णितानि।

The above extracts will suffice to show—(1) that while Kumārila employs compounds freely,—and these sometimes very long ones—Prabhākara's compounds seldom contain more than two words;—(2) that while Kumārila joins together several reasonings and arguments in a single clause, Prabhākara always employs a distinct clause for each reason;—(3) that while Kumārila almost invariably adopts the distinctive particles indicative of the objection and its answer,—*e. g.* 'ननु......चेत्, न' 'स्यादेतत्.........तदयुक्तम्'—Prabhākara seldom makes use of any of these, except occasionally the *first*; and almost always puts the objection and its refutation in the form of qnestion and answer; which makes it difficult at times to ascertain where the one ends and the other begins; this is the feature that marks all older works, as for instance the *Bhāṣyas* of Paṭañjali and Shabara.

Another feature of Prabhākara's style pointing to the same conclusion is that his work abounds in many of those flashy retorts which one meets with in the older works, and which become rather rare as we descend to the later artificial period of Sanskrit literary style. We shall quote a few of these, chosen from the *Bṛihaṭī* :—

(*a*) अज्ञानकातर्यमायुष्मतः प्रदर्शितम् (30*b* l. 2).

(*b*) अहो ऽनवस्थितनयनीतिज्ञो भवान् (32, l. 3).

(*c*) अनभिज्ञो भवान् वैकल्पिकानाम्पदार्थानाम् (32*b*, l. 2).

(*d*) मूर्धाभिषिक्तम्प्रामाण्यम् (b 32,*b* l. 6).

(*e*) इन्द्रजालोपममिदम् (32*b*, l. 8).

(*f*) अग्रन्थज्ञो देवानाम्प्रियः (36*b*, l. 9).

CHAPTER II.

PSYCHOLOGY—METAPHYSICS.

BOOKS CONSULTED :—

1. Jaimini's *Sūṭras* I—i } *Bibliothica Indica.*
2. *Bhāṣya* of Shabara I—i }
3. *Shlokavārtika* of Kumārila—Text (Chaukhambha S.S. Benares) English Translation (Biblio-Ind).
4. *Nyāyaraṭnākara* of Pārṭhasāraṭhi—Commentary on (3) (Chaukh. S.S. Benares).
5. *Kashikā* of Sucharita Mishra—Commentary on (3) MS. with MM. P. Chiṭraḏhara Mishra of Darbhanga.
6. *Brihaṭī* of Prabhākara. (MS. with present writer and in the Library of the Asiatic Society of Bengal.) I—i.
7. *Ṛijuvimalā*—Commentary on (6) by Shāliknāṭha—I—i. (MS. with present writer).
8. *Prakaraṇapañchikā* by Shālikanāṭha (Chauk. S.S. Benares).
9. *Nyāyamālāvisṭara* (Ānand. S.S. Poona).
10. *Shāsṭraḏīpikā* ('Pandit' Benares), I—i.
11. Prashasṭapāḏa's *Bhaṣya* on Vaisheṣika-Sūtras (*Viz*: S.S. Benares).
12. *Nyāyamukṭāvalī* of Vishvanāṭha (Benares).

Section (1).

NATURE OF COGNITION.

1. 'Cognition' or 'Knowledge' has been divided by Prabhākara into the two broad classes of 'Valid' and 'Invalid' Cognitions. Under 'Valid Cognition' he includes all those cognitions that bear directly upon their object; and under 'Invalid Cognition' those that bear upon their object only indirectly. At the outset, this classification

corresponds to the two broad divisions of '*Anubhūṭi*' (Apprehension) and '*Smṛiṭi*' (Remembrance) put forward by the Logicians; Prabhākara regarding all Remembrance as 'invalid,'—agreeing in this with the Logician,—and all Apprehension as 'valid',—herein differing from the Logician who divides Apprehensions into *valid* and *invalid*, *pramā* and *apramā*, while Prabhākara identifies all 'Apprehension' with '*pramā*.' This view, that all Apprehensions are *valid*, appears, at first sight, to be too revolutionary; but Prabhākara and his followers have made their case strong by the reasons that they have put forward in support of it.

2. In accordance with the practice of all writers on Philosophy, the *Prābhākara* begins with an account of '*Pramāṇa*.' The starting point of the enquiry is—What is *Pramāṇa*? The word '*pramāṇa*' has been taken by Prabhākara in this connection to mean 'valid cognition,' and not the *means* of valid cognition. What then is this 'valid cognition' according to Prabhākara?" The answer is given in the following verse:—

प्रमाणमनुभूतिः, सा स्मृतेरन्या, न सा स्मृतिः ।
न प्रमाणं स्मृतिः पूर्वप्रतिपत्तिव्यपेक्षणात् ।

[*Prakaraṇapañchikā*, p. 42.*]

That is to say, '*valid cognition*' *is Apprehension*; it is something totally different from *Remembrance* which is *not valid*, inasmuch as it stands in need of a previous cognition, being, as it is, a cognition produced only by the impressions left by a previous cognition.. This definition of Remembrance does not apply to Recognition or *Praṭyabhijñā*, as this latter is not

* In this connection we find the *Pra-pañchi.* quoting a number of verses and basing its explanation upon them.—Whose verses these are, it is not clear; they appear to be by the '*Vārṭikakāra*' of the *Prābhākara* School, whom Shālikanāṭha frequently quotes.

produced *only* by impressions left by previous cognitions. Thus Remembrance cannot be regarded as *valid*, because it bears upon its object, not *directly*, but only indirectly, through the agency of previous cognitions of that object.

3. * Even though 'valid cognition' has been defined as 'Apprehension,' any wrong cognition,—*e.g.*, the cognition of silver in the shell—cannot be regarded as *valid*; not indeed because there is anything inherently *invalid* in it,—it would not be an 'apprehension' at all if it were so,—but because, as a matter of fact, the judgment or idea resulting from that cognition, 'this is silver', when referring to the shell, contains not one, but *two*, cognitions,—one pertaining to 'silver' and the other to 'this'; and of these two the idea of 'silver' is mere *Remembrance*; and as such not being 'apprehension,' it cannot be regarded as *valid*; the other factor in the idea—the idea of 'this'—is of the nature of 'apprehension,' and as such, must be regarded as *valid*. Thus we find that the *wrongness* of the judgment 'this is silver' lies in the idea of 'silver,' which is *remembrance*; and this also is regarded as *wrong*, simply because it is not found to agree with the real state of things, when the agent proceeds to act up to the judgment, and picks up the piece. Even those who regard the judgment 'this is silver' as containing a single idea, and as *wrong*, base the *wrongness* upon the fact of the judgment being one that is found to be subsequently sublated—and not upon anything in the nature of the cognition itself. But these people also cannot regard as *wrong* that factor of the judgment which pertains to 'this'; as the notion of 'this' is not found to be sublated, being retained in the sublating judgment also,—which latter is in the form '*this* is not silver, but shell.' The other typical instance of wrong cognition, 'the conch is yellow', differs

* For further discussion bearing on the nature of the so-called 'wrong' cognitions, see below, § 8.

from the judgment 'this is silver,' in that the former does not contain any element of Remembrance, both factors—*yellowness* and *conch*—being perceived by the eye; and as such it is regarded to be similar to the judgment 'water is hot,' where though the heat belongs to the fire-particles entering into the water, and not to the water itself, yet the judgment is not rejected as altogether *wrong*; inasmuch as in actual experience the judgment is found to be in agreement with the real state of things,—the water feeling really hot; in the same manner, when we have the idea 'the conch is yellow,'—if on picking up the conch it is actually found to be yellow,—it must be accepted as *valid*; even though the *yellowness* perceived belongs to the bile in our eyes, and not to the conch; just as the validity of the judgment 'the water is hot' is not denied, so also that of the judgment 'the conch is yellow' cannot be denied. Thus we find that all cognitions, *per se*, must be 'valid; this inherent validity can be denied only if the cognition is found to be not in agreement with the real state of things. This view is briefly put by Prabhākara thus*—'It is strange indeed how a cognition can be said to *apprehend* an object, and yet be *invalid*;'—

and is also supported by Kumārila who has declared† that—

'the validity of the cognition must consist in its being an *apprehension*; this validity can be set aside only by such discrepancies as the disagreement of the real state of things and so forth.'

Though this view of 'valid cognition' is supported by the above declaration of Kumārila, his followers,—Pārṭhasāraṭhi Mishra among others,—have put forward‡ the definition of 'valid cognition' as *that which, being free from*

---

* *Brihati*—MS. p. 3. *Cf. also Bhāṣya*—'*vipraṭiṣiḍḍhamiḍamuchyaṭe bravīṭi viṭaṭhañcheṭi.*'

† *Shlokavārṭika*—Sū 2, Shl. 53.

‡ *Shāsṭraḍīpikā*—p. 28.

discrepancies, apprehends things not already apprehended; and they do not accept the definition given by Prabhākara. These later writers appear to have missed the very point of the dictum of the '*svataḥ-prāmāṇya*' of cognitions; if the validity of cognitions depends, not upon its own nature, but upon such extraneous circumstances as *the absence of discrepancies* and the *previous non-apprehension of the object,*—then where would be its '*svataḥ prāmāṇya*' or self-validity'?

4. The above definition of Pramāṇa presupposes the *svataḥ-prāmāṇya* of cognitions; 'Valid cognition' can be defined as *apprehension* only if each and every *apprehension* were intrinsically valid. This '*svataḥ-prāmāṇya*' of cognitions forms the very keystone of *Mīmāmsā*: Both the *Bhātta* and the *Prābhākara* * are agreed on this point. If all cognitions were not valid, whence could we have any confidence in our own cognitions? As a matter of fact, even when the cognition may not be found to be in agreement with the real state of things, the cognition, *as cognition*, cannot but be accepted as *valid*; even though, the thing cognised may not be there, the cognition is there all right. If the character of *being in agreement with its object* or otherwise, belonged to the cognition, then the cognition would be something with a shape, each cognition having the shape of its object,—an absurdity! Nor again can there be any cause for the appearance of any such cognition as is not valid, *as cognition*; because what is regarded as the *cause* or origin of invalid cognitions is the presence of discrepancies in the cognitive agency; but upon examination we find that these discrepancies are totally devoid of creative energy, and as such, cannot produce any thing; all that they can do is merely to put obstacles in the way of the cognition of things as they are; and thus the *wrongness* would pertain to the *thing cognised*, and not to the *cognition*.

* *Prakaraṇapañchikā*, pp. 32-38; *Shlokavārtika*, Sū. 2. Shl. 33-61.

The objection generally raised against the self-evidential or self-illuminative character of the cognition is that,—inasmuch as no 'manifestation' or 'illumination' is possible, unless that which is manifested has some sort of 'form', the 'self-illumination' of cognition would presuppose some form for it; specially as unless each cognition has a distinctive form of its own, there could be no distinction among the cognitions themselves; and this 'form' cannot but be the same as that which belongs to the object of that cognition; as the only thing that differentiates one cognition from another is its object; and as no cognition is ever actually felt to be distinct from its object, there must be an absolute identity between the cognition and the thing cognised; and so the form of the *thing* must be the form of the cognition also. In answer to the above it is argued that if there were an absolute identity between the cognition and the thing it apprehends, then the latter could not be said to be *apprehended* by the former,—the one could not be called the 'cognised' and another the 'cognition.' Nor again, is it absolutely necessary to postulate a form for Cognitions, in order to serve as the basis for differentiating one cognition from another; because by the '*saṃvedana*' (cognition or knowledge) of a person we mean only *the manifestation of a special kind of his ḍharma or merit, which favours his active operation in connection with a certain object*; and even though this 'manifestation' or cognition is self-illumined, that does not render its differentiation impossible; as it is called the cognition *of that object with regard to which it favours the activity of the cogniser*; and as each cognition tends to active operation in connection with a distinct object, this would afford all the basis that is necessary for its differentiation.

Then again, we must pause to consider what is meant by saying that, if the cognition were formless there could be no illumination of it. *Formlessness* certainly cannot mean *absence of character,* as even apart from its object, the cognition is possessed of the *cognitional character.* Nor can any stress be laid on the fact that the cognition is devoid of such forms as the *blue* and the like. Because it is not necessary that it is only such things as are endowed with the *blue* and other forms that can be 'illumined.' In regard to everything, it must be admitted that it is possessed of the *form* in which it is manifested; no other criterion is possible and as all cognitions are manifested simply as 'cognition'; 'cognition' can be the only form that can belong to, them. Another argument in favour of Cognitions having the same form as their object is based upon Dreams, wherein, it is argued, even though there is no real object concerned, yet the cognition that one has is in the form of some external object. Against this it is argued that, as a matter of fact, during dreams also what the cognition renders cognisable is some object of the external world; which, even though not bodily present before the cogniser at that time, is yet one that has been cognised directly at some previous time, and presents itself to consciousness through impressions left upon the mind, which is aroused for the occasion. So during dreams also, it is the external thing that is cognised. Says Kumārila* :—

'In dream-cognition also, the basis of the external object cannot be denied; in all cognitions the ultimate basis must lie in some external object,—only in certain cases, qualified by wrong connections of time and place (when alone the cognition is regarded as wrong).'

The explanation of the fact that during dreams we do not cognise the thing as something perceived before and *remembered,*—but as something actually cognised at the time,—lies in the fact that during dreams the cognition that

* *Shlokavārṭika*—'Nirālambanavāḍa,' Shl. 107—8.

we have must be accepted as being of the nature of Remembrance, for the simple reason that it is brought about by an arousing of existing impressions; this arousing of the impression being due to the Unseen Agency conducive to the happiness or unhappiness of the agent. It is for this reason that only that much of the previously cognised thing is *remembered*, during dreams, as would cause that happiness or unhappiness to the agent for which the Unseen Agency of his *Karma* would be ripe for operation at that moment. This also explains the fact why dream-cognition is not always of the same precise kind as an ordinary waking remembrance.

5. The above explanation of Dreams serves to set aside the stock argument of the Idealist—'All cognitions must be regarded as having no counterpart reality in the external world,—because they are cognitions,—like Dream-cognitions,'—because, as Prabhākara* points out,—

'We are justified only in assuming, from a well-known effect, a cause that would make the effect possible,—and not one that would destroy it; what we find in a dream is that there is a cognition of an external object; this effect can justify us in assuming,—not indeed the absolute non-existence of the external object—but the real existence of such an object; as without this the cognition would be an impossibility; as a general law we know it to be true that that without which something else is not possible, is the *cause* of this latter; from this it follows that the cause of Dream-cognition is some object in the external world.'

The Idealistic argument is thus found to be untenable; because the corroborrative instance of 'Dream-cognition' does not support the desired conclusion; as it has been shown above that Dream-cognitions are not entirely devoid of real counterparts in the external world.

**Bṛhatī*—MS. page 5 b.

6. We have seen that Cognitions are *self-illumined*; the question now arises—what is that 'illumination' of cognitions? The explanation given by some people is that the cognition is itself cognised by another cognition, which latter is of the nature of Sensuous Perception, brought about by the agency of the organ of 'Mind', just in the same manner as the perceptions of pleasure and pain. This view of the perceptibility of Cognition has been put forward by the Idealists; and it is thus explained by the *Ṛijuvimalā* (pp. 54-55):—

'The cognition is perceptible; no perception is possible without *form* or *colour*; hence the form of *blue*, &c. that are perceived must belong to the cognition, and not to any external object.'

This view has been repulsed by Prabhākara and his followers.* Cognitions, says Prabhākara, can never be perceptible; this is what the *Bhāṣya* means by the passage—'*Arṭhaviṣayā hi praṭyakṣabuḍḍhiḥ, na buḍḍhiviṣayā*' (page 9, line 6); which means that it is the *object* that is *perceived*, and not the *cognition*;—it is not the Perception that is *perceived*, but the object. By this it is not meant that Cognition is not *cognised* or *known*; it is *cognised* certainly, but cognised only *as cognition*, not as *something cognised*—*samviṭṭayaiva hi samviṭ samveḍyā na samveḍyaṭayā*, says Prabhākara; if it were cognisable as *something cognised*, then with each individual cognition we would have to postulate Cognitions *ad infinitum*. That is to say, the Cognition, even though *cognised*, cannot itself form the *phala* (effect, object) of another act of cognition—*tasyām karmabhāvo na yukṭaḥ*; because if it were an object of another act of cognition, it would not be 'self-illumined.' We cannot regard the cognition as altogether *unknown*, as it is only when the cognition is *known*, that the cognition of *things* becomes possible. What

* *Bṛihaṭī*—MS. pp. 7 *et seq*; *Ṛijuvimalā*, pp. 54-61; *Prakaraṇapañchikā*, p. 63.

therefore, we must admit is that the Cognition is something that is *self-cognised*, and has its presence known *by means of Inference*; what we apprehend by means of Inference is not any *object*, but only the *presence* of an object,—*e. g.*, fire:—*nāpyanumānāḍ rūpagrahaṇam, sanmātragrāhyanumānambhavaṭi*, says Prabhākara. So in the case in question, all the information provided by Inference is that the Cognition *is* there, and not that it is *cognised*; the inference being thus formally stated—'the Cognition exists, because we have the apprehention of its object.' In this manner, Cognition does come within the purview of Inference, which is one of the 'means of right knowledge'; and thus it is that Cognition is held to be *prameya*; but this does not make it *samveḍya*. Prabhākara draws a subtle distinction between '*prameya*' and '*samveḍya*': the '*samveḍya*' is that where the form or shape of the object is manifested and apprehended; and this can occur only in the case of objects perceived by the senses; in the case of '*prameya*,' on the other hand, it is not necessary for a form or shape to be present in consciousness; thus as having no form or shape, Cognition cannot be '*samveḍya*' (and hence also it cannot be *perceptible*); but as having its presence apprehended by means of Inference,—which is one of the '*pramāṇas*;—it has to be regarded as '*prameya*.'

7. The above view has been accepted, to a certain extent, by Kumārila and his followers also. The *Shāsṭraḍīpikā* (p. 37) explains—(1) that the Perception of a certain thing ends not in a further cognition of that perception, but in the *āparokṣya* or *prakataṭā, direct apprehensibility*, of that thing; and (2) that every act of Perception involves a certain relationship between the *perceiver* and the *perceived*,—the former being the agent, and the latter the object of that act; this agent-and-object relationship is not possible without some activity on the part of the agent; hence

the presence of this relationship leads to the inference of its invariable concomitant,—viz., the action of the agent; and it is this *action* that, in the case of knowledge, is known as 'cognition'; and it has been shown to be *inferable* from the relationship between the cognising self and the cognised object,—'*Mānasapraṭyakṣagamyor' ṭhena sahāṭmanaḥ sambandho jñānaṅkalpayaṭīṭi ramaṇīyam,*' says the *Shāsṭradīpikā* (pp. 37-38).

8. If all Apprehensions are valid, then there arises the question—How to account for *doubtful* and *wrong* cognitions? These certainly, it is argued, are not valid; and yet they are *cognitions*. (1) In answer to the above, it is pointed out that the *object* of a cognition is that same thing which is presented to consciousness by it; and thus in the stock example of the *wrong* cognition—'this is silver'—what is presented to consciousness is the *silver*, and it is this that is the *object* of the cognition,—and not the *shell*, which does not enter into the cognition at all; for this reason the judgment in question is not found to fulfil the conditions of the *wrong cognition*, which has been defined as 'the cognition of a thing in something that is not that thing'—'*aṭasmin ṭaḍbuḍḍhiḥ*' (*Prashasṭapāḍa* p. 177), '*ṭaḍabhāvāvaṭi ṭaṭprakārakam jñānam*' (*Nyāyamukṭāvalī*); because in the case in question we find that it is not the *shell that is cognised as silver*; but as a matter of fact, the *shell* is *not cognised* at all; what is cognised is the *silver*. This sounds rather subtle; but its truth cannot be denied; to say that it is the *shell* that *is cognised* would not be true to fact. What happens in the case is that, though the object present before the eye is the shell, yet, inasmuch as the perceiver fails to notice the distinctive features peculiar to the shell, and notices only those features that are common to the shell and the silver, he fails to apprehend the difference between these two things; and this gives rise to his cognition of *silver*,—this

cognition thus being due to the non-apprehension of the difference between *silver* and the object before the eyes. The idea of silver also, comes to his mind by the force of memory, which is aroused by the perception of the properties common to the shell and silver; though the silver is *remembered*, it is not remembered as 'that'—something perceived in the past—which would have sufficed to differentiate the '*that* silver' of the past from the '*this* thing' before the eyes, —the non-perception of 'that' being due to a certain weakness of the mind; thus then the apprehension of silver in the judgment 'this is silver' cannot but be regarded as an act of memory. The *silver* not being actually before the eyes, cannot, be regarded as *perceived*; nor are there any factors available to bring about *inferential* or other kinds of cognition of it. Though the judgment in question is thus found to partake of the dual character of *remembrance* and *direct apprehension*, and as such, differs from the ordinary *valid cognition* of silver (which is wholly *apprehension*),—yet in actual experience, it is not cognised as so different; and this for the simple reason that, just as in the case of real silver, the *thing perceived* is not cognised as different from 'silver,' so in the case in question also. Thus in actual experience, there is found to be no difference between the 'right' and the 'wrong' cognition of silver; specially as both equally give rise to the same kind of activity on the part of the agent,—in both cases he stoops to pick up the thing.

The *Bhātta* view* on this point is not different :—in so far as the judgment 'this is silver' involves a cognition *per se*, it is valid,—it is quite valid for the cogniser at the time that he has the cognition; that it is sublated or rejected by subsequent experience is another matter; the subsequent experience must be regarded as destroying the validity that

* See *Shlokavārṭika*—Sutra 2. Shl. 53 *et. seq.*

belonged to the cognition *as cognised*; says the *Shāsṭraḍīpikā* (page 15, *l.* 16).—

Ṭasmāṭ svaṭaḥprāmāṇyam prāpṭam arṭhānyaṭhāṭvakāraṇa-doṣajñānābhyāmapoḍyaṭe iṭyavashyam aṅgīkarṭavyam ;—

And again on p. 31, l. 5.—

Yaṭra prayaṭnenānviṣyamāṇe kāraṇaḍoṣo bāḍhakajñānam vā nopalabhyaṭe ṭaṭ pramāṇam iṭarachchāpramāṇam.

(2) In the case of the cognition of conch as yellow, what occurs is this :—There is a real yellowness that is perceived,—that belonging to the bile affecting the eye; the whiteness of the conch fails to be noticed on account of the disease in the eye; so what is perceived is the *conch without any colour*, and also the *yellowness* without the object to which it belongs; and thus a colourless object and an objectless colour being perceived at the same time—both these perceptions being quite valid and correct so far,—what more natural than that the two perceptions should coalesce, and present to consciousness the *yellow conch*? And even when picked up the conch is found to be yellow; and thus in this cognition we find nothing that could make it a *wrong* cognition; in fact the man himself can regard the apprehension as *wrong* only when he knows of the disease in his eye (the '*kāraṇaḍoṣa*' of the *Shāsṭraḍīpikā*).

(3) In the same manner, when a person suffering from bile feels sugar to be bitter, what happens is that he fails to feel the sweetness of the sugar, which he feels to be tasteless; but he feels the bitterness of the bile in his mouth; the two coalescing present to him the *sugar as bitter*.

(4) In the case of a person seeing 'two moons,' the rays of light issue from the two eyes, at different times, and of different kinds; and so it is only natural that two images

of the moon are imprinted on the retina, and hence presented to the man's consciousness. Thus in this case also, there are two distinct perceptions; but as the interval of time between the two is subtle, the two coalesce and give the idea of 'two moons'.

(5) Where we mistake one direction for the other, the real direction is not seen; and the other quarter is *remembered*; and here also the *wrongness* lies in this *remembrance,* and not in the *apprehension*; as there is no apprehension at all.

(6) In Dream-cognition also, even though things are only *remembered,* yet they appear as if they were actually *apprehended* at the time; and what occurs is that the factor of *having been apprehended at some previous time* is lost sight of; and it is this last factor only that differentiates what is *remembered* from what is *apprehended*; then as regards the agency that excites or energises the impression,—the energising of which is needed for all Remembrance,—this is supplied by some 'Unseen Agency' which guides the percipient or dreaming souls in their earthly sojourn. If the time during which the man sleeps is one at which he is destined to experience pleasure, the unseen agency of his destiny awakens the impressions that bring to his mind pleasant memories; and so for pain also. This accounts for the fact that dreams are sometimes pleasurable, and sometimes painful; this pleasure or pain, so for as the actual *feeling* is concerned, is as real as any that is experienced during waking consciousness.

This view of Dream-cognition is thus supported by the *Shāsṭradīpikā* (p. 39, l. 10 *et seq.*) :—

'In dreams also, what is cognised is the external object perceived elsewhere, and presented to consciousness during sleep by an Unseen Agency; the cognition is quite valid, so far as the object is concerned; the *wrongness* or *invālidity* comes in only when it is regarded as something actually *apprehended* at the time, and not as only *remembered*; and the cause of this lies in such discrepancies as are due to sleep; thus the invalidity pertains only to the accessory details; and not to the cognition *per se*.'

Thus then, we find that wherever we have actual *apprehension* or *cognition*, there is nothing 'wrong,' and that the mistake comes in only when some factor of *Remembrance* creeps into the Cognition; consequently none of the so-called 'wrong' Cognitions militate against the self-validity of Cognitions.

9. As regards Doubtful Cognitions—*e. g.* 'Is this a pillar or a man?'—what is actually perceived is *some object endowed with the quality of tallness*; and this is quite valid so far; this perception of *tallness* then reminds the man of a number of tall things,—the pillar, the man, the tree, and so forth; then it is that there comes the *doubt* as to whether it is this or that particular thing; thus in all Doubtful Cognitions there are two *remembrances* involved; there is not only one act of *apprehension*; so this also leaves untouched the 'self-validity' of *Cognition*.

Section (2).

Different Kinds of Valid Cognition.

Sub-section (1)—*Perception*.

1. 'Valid Cognitions' have been divided into five classes:—(1) '*Praṭyakṣa*', Sensuous, (2) '*Anumāna*' Inferential, (2) '*Shāsṭra*,' Scriptural, (4) '*Upamāna*', Analogical, and (5) *Arṭhāpaṭṭi*,' Presumptive. Prābhākara does not accept '*Abhāva*,' Non-apprehension, as a *prāmāṇa*, as Kumārila has done. (*See* below, under *sub-section* 6).

2. Prabhākara defines '*Praṭyakṣa*' as *sākṣāṭ praṭīṭiḥ*, direct apprehension,—pertaining to the *apprehended* object, to

the *apprehending person* and to the *apprehension* itself ; that is to say, in each act of Perception the idea of each of these three enters as its constituent factor. This distinctive view of Prabhākara has been called the '*Ṭriputīpraṭyakṣavāḍa.*' We shall take up each of these three factors separately.

3. (*a*) Direct Apprehension pertaining to the *apprehended object* proceeds directly from sense-contact. Of *sense-organs*, these are *six*, according to Prabhākara,* and also according to Kumārila†. These are :—the Nose for the scenting of smell, the Eye for seeing colour and form, the Tongue for perceiving tastes, the Skin for sensing touch, the Ear for apprehending sound, and the Internal Organ or Mind, for the perceiving of such purely mental states as those of pleasure, pain, and the like.

In connection with the Sense-organs the Prābhākara raises‡ some interesting questions—How do you prove the existence of these organs? What reasons are there for postulating the number as *six* only? In course of this enquiry, we have a highly interesting and closely reasoned analytical proof of the existence and number of Sense-organs. As a matter of ordinary experience, it is found that our cognitions of things are not everlasting,—but appear at only certain times ; being ephemeral, they must have some cause ; every effect has two kinds of causes,—the *material cause* to which it owes its material composition, and the *immaterial cause*, which, in most cases, takes the form of certain circumstances or qualities, which, in proximity with, and through, the material cause, help in the bringing about of the effect ; for instance, the *material cause* of the *jar* consists of the earthenware particles that compose it ; and the *conjunction* of these particles constitutes its *immaterial* cause. The

* *Prakaraṇapañchikā*, p. 52 ;
† *Shāsṭraḍ pikā*, p. 21.
‡ *Prakaraṇapañchikā* p. 52 *et seq.*

immaterial causes of an effect may subsist either in its material cause, or in the material cause of that material cause; *e. g.*, in the case of a new form of smell being produced in a substance by fire-contact, this contact, which is the immaterial cause of the smell, subsists in that substance itself which is put in the fire, and in which the smell is produced; whereas in the case of the colouring of a white piece of cloth, the colour of the yarns, which is the cause of the colour in the cloth, subsists in the yarns which form the *material cause* of the cloth. Now then, in the case of Perceptions, we have the cognising soul as the *material* cause; and we have to find its *immaterial* cause; this latter cause cannot subsist in the cause of the soul; as the soul, being eternal has no cause; hence it must subsist in the soul itself; further, as it is only a quality that can subsist in substances, it follows that the immaterial cause of perception must be a *quality*. Then again, we know that Perception, which is a particular kind of Cognition, is a 'specific' quality of the soul, and also that, for such a quality belonging to eternal substances, the *immaterial* cause must be in the form of *contact* with some other substance, *e. g.*, the colour produced in the *earth-atom* has, for its immaterial cause, the contact with fire; from this it follows that Cognition must have for its immaterial cause, its contact with some other substance now; and inasmuch as we have nothing to show that this *other substance* is something inhering in yet another substance, we conclude that the substance whose contact would be the immaterial cause of Cognition must be one that has an existence independent of other substances. Of such independent snbstances, there are two kinds:—(1) those that are all-pervading in their character, *e. g.*, Time, Space, &c., and (2) atom. It is a well-known fact that no *contact* (which by its very nature must be ephemeral) with an all-pervading substance is possible; as these substances are in permanent contact with all things; and hence they cannot be said to *come* into contact with anything; nor can their eternal contact be the cause of anything; as being *eternal* it could bring about only *eternal effects,* which is a contradiction in terms. From all this it follows that the contact which is the immaterial cause of Cognition must be one that subsists in something atomic; the contact of atomic substances is brought about by the action—motion—of the atoms themselves; they can move up to one or more substances, thereby creating so many *contacts* for themselves, one after the other. This *atomic substance* again must reside in the body ensouled by the cognising soul, as none other could contain the substratum of the immaterial cause of the cognition of which that soul is the *material* cause. The action of this atomic substance in the body—tending to bring about the contact—is due to its coming into contact with the soul which (in every act of cognition) puts forth an effort towards the cognition. The only *atomic* substance that fulfils all these conditions is the *manas* or mind. This *manas,* alone by itself, brings about such effects as cognitions, pleasure, pain, desire, aversion, effort, and so forth; it brings about remembrance when aided by impressions left by past cognitions. Thus then we have arrived at the conclusion that the *manas,* or *mind,* is an organ whereby the Soul obtains such cognitions as those of pleasure, pain, &c. The *mind* however by, itself, is found to be devoid of any such qualities as colour, smell, &c.; and as such it cannot lead the soul to experience or cognise these qualities; hence for this it stands in need of such other organs as may be characterised by these qualities; for the cognition of colour the mind will need the aid of an organ of which colour is the distinguishing quality; for the cognition of smell, the help of an odorous organ; and so on with the cognition of touch, sound and taste. Now then we know that the organ which has colour for its distinctive quality must be one composed of *ṭejas* or *light*; as colour is a feature of light; and this proves the existence of the *luminous* organ—the Eye,—for the cognition of *colour*; similarly the organ with smell as its distinctive quality must be composed of earth; as it is to the earth that smell belongs; and this proves the existence of the *earthy* organ—the Nose—for the cognition of smell; the organ qualified by taste must be of the water, as it is to the water that taste belongs; this proves the existence of the *aqueous* organ—the Tongue—for the cognition of taste; the organ qualified by Sound must be composed of the *ākasha*, as it is to the *ākasha* that sound belongs; this proves the existence of the *ākāshic* organ—the Ear—for the cognition of sound; and lastly, the organ qualified by touch, must be of the air, to which *touch* belongs; and this proves the existence of the *airy* organ—the Skin—for the cognition of touch.

The contact of the Mind is regarded as a necessary factor in the perceptions by means of all these sense-organs; because of the fact that even when the object to be perceived is in close contact with the organ concerned, it fails to be perceived, if at the same time the organ also is not in contact with the mind,—*i.e.*, if we are absent-minded. Thus in the case of all these there are four contacts necessary—(1) that of the object with the sense-organ, (2) that of the distinctive qualities of the object with the sense-organ, (3) of the sense-organ with the mind, and (4) of the mind with the soul. In the perception of pleasure and such other purely mental states, on the other hand, only two contacts are necessary,—that of the pleasure with the mind, and that of the mind with the soul.

As regards the *object apprehended* by perception, it has been classed under three heads:—(1) *Substances*, (2) *Jāṭi* or *Class*, and (3) *Qualities*. To the first category belong only such substances as are tangible and of sufficiently large dimensions,—[substances other than these being imperceptible],—partaking of the nature of Earth, Fire, Water, and Air. To the third category of 'Qualities' belong such qualities as Colour, Taste, Smell, Touch, Number, Dimension, Separateness, Conjunction, Disjunction, Priority, Posteriority, Pleasure, Pain, Desire, Aversion and Effort,—all of which are *perceptible*. How the *Class* is perceptible we shall explain later on. (*Section* 4, para. 7.)

4. As regards the third factor entering into Perception,—that is the *Apprehension* itself,—it has been divided into two classes :—(1) *Savikalpaka*, determinate or concrete, which pertains to, and has for its object, *the thing along with its distinctive properties*; and (2) *Nirvikalpaka*, non-determinate or abstract, which pertains to, and has for its object, the *thing-in-itself*, in its pure unqualified form. As a matter of common experience, we find that when an object is first perceived,—be it a substance, a quality, or a class—it is perceived in its own pure form, free from all distinctive features that it may possess; our own experience is the sole criterion and authority for the view that whenever an object comes within the range of one of our sense-organs, and our mind is not absent, we perceive the *object itself* alone, entirely apart from all such characteristics as differentiate it from other objects. This view is supported by Kumārila also, who says*—

'The cognition that appears first is a mere *ālochana* or simple perception, called *non-determinate*—pertaining to the object itself pure and simple, and resembling the cognitions that the new-born infant has of things around himself.'

But with regard to the exact nature of the object perceived by the non-determinate Perception, Prabhākara's

* *Shlokavārṭika*, Sū. 4, Shl. 112.

view is somewhat different. He does not accept the *Bauḍḍha* view that it is the mere '*Svalakṣaṇa*' or 'specific individuality' of the thing that is apprehended by it; and his reason for rejecting this view is that, as a matter of fact, into the Non-determinate Perception there does enter the factor that pertains to the 'genus' or 'class' to which the object belongs. Herein also lies the chief difference of the *Prābhākara* from the *Bhātta* view, according to which latter,—'in this Cognition neither the *genus* nor the *differentia* is presented to consciousness; all that is present there is the Individual wherein those two subsist.'* Nor does Prabhākara accept the view that it is only the *class-character* that is apprehended; because he finds that after all, the object is apprehended *as an individual*, and not merely *as belonging to a class*. Having rejected these two extremes, Prabhākara strikes the 'golden mean' and holds that what is apprehended in the *first*, or non-determinate, stage of perception is both the *class-character* and the *specific individuality*,—but with this difference that, inasmuch as no other object has as yet entered into the apprehension, the thing is not apprehended *as actually being an individual belonging to a definite class*; because a thing can be cognised as an 'individual' only *in comparison with other things* from which it differs in certain well-defined characters; and it can be apprehended as 'belonging to a class' only when found to possess certain characteristic features *in common with some other things*; and so it follows that so long as no other thing has presented itself to consciousness, even though what is apprehended is actually *an individual belonging to a class*, yet this mixed character of the thing cannot be fully comprehended until some other things have entered into the cognition; until when the apprehension remains 'non-determinate.'

***Shlokavārṭika*, Sū. 4. Shl. 113.

As regards the other kind of Perception, the *Savikalpaka* or *Determinate,*—it follows in the wake of the above-described Non-determinate Perception, and apprehends the same object as actually being an individual possessed of certain well-defined specific features peculiar to itself, and also of certain class-characteristics in common with other things, and thus belonging to that 'Class.' The object in contact with the organ of perception is only one individual thing, and no *other things*; and as such it may be questionable how the perception can apprehend it *as an individual, &c., &c.,*—which presupposes the apprehension of things other than the one in contact with the perceptive organ; but the fact is that the real *apprehender* is neither the Perception, nor the Sense-organ, but the Soul, which, by its very nature, apprehends all that can be apprehended; and hence what happens is that, just after the Soul has had the non-determinate perception of the thing, there come to his mind those other things also—those from whom it differs and those with whom it has certain characters in common; and this accounts for the aforesaid *mixed* character of Determinate Perception. It would thus seem that according to Prabhākara, in every Determinate Perception there enters a factor of Remembrance,—as the *other things* are held to present themselves before the soul by reason of the *impression* that it has of those things. It may be due to this element of Remembrance entering into Determinate Perception that the Logician* has qualified his definition of the *valid* Perception by the word '*avyapadeshya*' which, for all intents and purposes, may be regarded as synonymous with '*Nirvikalpaka*' or 'non-determinate'; as Remembrance is not *valid cognition,* the Determinate Perception could not very well be regarded as *valid.* But this view of the *non-valid* character of Determinate Perception has not been accepted

*Nyāya-Sū. 4.

by Prabhākara ; he asserts that the Determinate Perception, even though apprehending the same thing as that apprehended by the preceding Non-determinate Perception,—is yet a *valid* cognition ; inasmuch as it also apprehends certain such factors as did not enter into the Non-determinate Perception ; as for the element of Remembrance entering into Determinate Perception, it has to be noted that that element does not pertain to the thing perceived, but to those *other things* with which it has certain characters in common, &c., &c. ; and this cannot vitiate the validity of any cognition of the thing itself.

The Bhāttas also accept both the Non-determinate and the Determinate Perception to be valid. (*Shāstradīpikā*, pp. 22—23.)

5. (*b*) The second factor entering into Perception is the 'apprehender'. (*see* § 2,)—the third being the 'apprehension' itself (already described under § 4). In all cognitions,—be they either *Direct Apprehension* or *Remembrance*,—the 'apprehender' always appears as a constituent factor; so long as the apprehending soul does not become manifest, there is no *apprehension* at all ; because all cognitions are in the form '*I know*.' It must be admitted, therefore, that whenever anything is cognised, it is cognised along with the cogniser himself ; and the cognition of the Soul is always of the nature of direct Apprehension ; even when the cognition of the object is *inferential* or *verbal*, that of the cognising Soul is in every act of cognition, purely *perceptional*, or direct, obtained through the agency and contact of the mind. The third factor—that of 'apprehension' itself—is always *self-cognised*, by direct apprehension (*see* above, sec. 1, § 6) ; even the *inferential cognition* is cognised by itself *directly*.

6. Though all these three factors enter into Perception, yet there is this difference that, so far as the *apprehender* and the *apprehended object* are concerned, these are something different from the *apprehension*; while the *apprehension* is non-different from itself. The reason for this lies in the very nature of things. The *apprehension* being of the very nature of *light, illumination* or *manifestation*, does not stand in need of any other thing to manifest it, or make it apprehended; it is therefore *self-apprehended*; the *apprehender* and the *object*, on the other hand, are not of the nature of light; hence for their manifestation, these two require something different from themselves, which is of the nature of light. That the *apprehending* soul and the *object* are not of the nature of light is proved in the following manner:—As a matter of fact we know that in the waking state both the *apprehender* and the *object* appear in the apprehension; but neither of these really appear during deep sleep (as a rule there is no apprehension); and yet it cannot be denied that they are there all the time; for if the apprehender were not there, how could we have any remembrance of dreams appearing during sleep? If then, the *apprehender* were of the nature of *light*, he would be manifested during sleep also; the mere fact therefore of his existing at the time, and yet not being manifest to consciousness proves that he is not of the nature of *light*, which is always self-manifest. The case of the *Apprehension* itself is totally different; whenever and wherever it exists, it is self-manifest and self-apprehended; and it is thus neither like the *apprehender* nor like the *object*,—both of which are never apprehended except by the *apprehension*.

7. As regards the question of the '*Pramāṇa*' and '*Phala*' as pertaining to Perception,—Prabhākara holds that if the word '*pramāṇa*' be taken to mean *that which is*

validly cognised,—that is, the valid cognition itself,—then it is the valid cognition that is the '*pramāṇa*;' and in that case, the '*phala*' would be either the *acceptance* or *rejection* by the agent of the object perceived, or his *indifference* towards it,—these three being the attitude taken up by the perceiver towards the things that he perceives. If, on the other hand, the word '*pramāṇa*' is explained as 'that *by which* something is validly cognised', *i. e.* the *means* of valid cognition,—then the name '*pramāṇa*' would apply to the contact of the soul with the mind (which is the element common to all cognitions); and in that case, the cognition itself would be the '*phala*'. So also, in the case of the name '*pramāṇa*' being applied either to the perceiving *sense organ,* or to its contact with the mind,—in all these cases, the cognition itself would be the '*phala*' or 'result'; as all these agencies operated towards the accomplishment of that alone.

Section (2)—*Sub-section* (2).

INFERENTIAL COGNITION.

1. 'When a certain fixed or permanent relation has been known to subsist between two things,—if we perceive any one of these things, we have an idea of the other thing; and this latter cognition is called *inferential*' (*Shabara-Bhāṣyu,* page 10). That is to say, the cognition of the permanent relation between two things helps in the Inferential Cognition by affording to the agent the idea of the other member when one member is cognised; when the observer perceives a certain thing, and remembers the permanent relation that it has been known to bear to another thing, the recalled idea of the relation presents to the mind the apprehension of the other member of the relation; and to this apprehension is given the name 'Inferential Cognition' (*Prakaraṇa-pañchikā,* p. 74).

2. There is a difference of opinion as to the character of the relation upon which the Inference is based. The *Prābhākara* view is that this relation must be one that is unfailing, ever true and permanent; as that which subsists between the cause and its effect, between the whole and its part, between the substance and its quality, between qualities inhering in the same substance, and so forth; for instance, between fire and smoke, between the class and the individuals forming that class, between earth and smell, between the taste and colour of a fruit. It may be noted that it is the *smoke* that bears the relation to the *fire*, and *not vice versa*; as there can be fire without smoke, though there can be no smoke without fire. This view of the relationship is also accepted by the *Bhātta* (*Shāstradīpikā*, p. 41).

3. The next question that presents itself is with regard to that means of knowledge by which we have obtained the valid cognition of the permanent or unfailing character of the relation in question:—This cannot be cognised by Perception, which is operative only with regard to things *in the present*, and in contact with the sense-organs. Nor could it be cognised by Inference or Presumption, as both of these also would, in their turn, depend upon like relationships; which would thus involve a *regressus ad infinitum*. Nor lastly could it be cognised by Perception obtained through the agency of the mind alone; as if the mind alone by itself were to bring about the cognition, then people would become omniscient, as there could be no limitations to the working of the mind, as there are in that of the other organs of perception. The question is thus met by Prabhākara:—As a matter of fact, between fire and smoke, all the relations,—of *contact* or of other kinds,—are perceived by the sense-organs; the relations being apprehended as qualifications pertaining

to the things (fire and smoke), which also are perceived by themselves; the particular time and place also are perceived as mere qualifying adjuncts of the things; thus the fire and the smoke are perceived as qualified by a certain qualifying relation and by specifications of time and place. The next step in the process is the recognition of the fact that, while in some cases, Fire is bound to be concomitant with smoke, there are instances where it is not so; this gives rise to the conviction that the relation of fire with smoke is not *constant*, but qualified by specifications of time and place; as for smoke, on the other hand, it is never found apart from fire; and this gives rise to the conviction that smoke is always (invariably) concomitant with fire,—the relation of smoke with fire being thus recognised as *constant*. After this conviction has dawned on the mind, all that is needed for the forthcoming inferential cognition of fire is the apprehension of the mere existence of smoke; for which apprehension alone there is need of the operation of a means of knowledge; as when once its existence has been apprehended, the idea of the connection and presence of fire follows naturally from the preconceived notion of the relation between the two being of a permanent character. Thus then, all that is needed for the appearance of the inferential cognition is supplied by Sensuous Perception itself. This view is open to the objection that, by the above explanation, the cognition of *smoke* would include within itself the cognition of *fire* also; and thus there would be nothing left unknown to be cognised by the resultant inferential cognition; and this last would therefore cease to be '*pramāṇa*' or 'valid' cognition. This objection would have had some force only if '*pramāṇa*' had been defined as that which affords cognition of *something not known*; as a matter of fact however, the *Prābhākara*, does not make this a necessary character in '*pramāṇa*', as we have seen above, where *pramāṇa* has been defined simply as 'apprehension'; and certainly the cognition of *fire* following upon the cognition of *smoke* is 'apprehension'. Then again, as a matter of fact, in all cases of Inferential Cognition, the *Prābhākara* argues, * the previous knowledge of the relation borne by the 'subject' to the 'probans' is absolutely necessary; and so the inferential cognition must always pertain to things already known. Then the reason why inferential cognition does not appear with regard to each and every thing that we know is that there can be no cognition of any sort unless we wish it; and as in a case where all that we wish to know of a certain thing is already known by other and more simple means of knowledge,—there is no occasion for us to recall to our minds the various relations borne by the thing; and hence, the idea of the relation not being before the mind, no inferential cognition ensues.

The *Bhāttas*, however, who accept the necessary relation between the cognitions of *fire* and *smoke*, as above explained, along with the view that the character *of being a cognition of something not already known* is a necessary factor in *pramāṇa*, regard this explanation of Prabhākara as an uncalled for ignominious retreat. They argue that even though it is true that the *smoke* is *seen*,—and the perception of smoke carries with it the vague generic idea of *fire* as related to the *smoke*, —yet the final object of the ultimate inferential cognition is not one that is *already known*, inasmuch as the perception of *smoke* does not involve the cognition of the *presence of the fire in the mountain*; and it is this *qualified fire* (and not merely fire in general) that forms the object of inferential cognition. The *Bhāttas* lay stress upon this fact,—not with a view to lend support to the *Prābhākara*, but—because they regard it as a necessary element in all *pramāṇa*, that the object should be something not already known.

---

* Prakaraṇapañchikā, p. 76.

4. The very definition of Inferential Cognition serves to indicate all the more important of the 'Defective or Fallacious Probans.' (1) For instance, the condition that 'the relation between the two factors should be one that has been previously known' precludes the '*asāḍhāraṇa*' or Too Specific Probans; that is to say, *the character that belongs specifically to the 'subject' of the inference alone* cannot form the basis of any valid inference; because such a character could not have been known anywhere else; and thus this character along with the 'subject' could never be known as related to any third object; and yet it is the relation with this third object or character that forms the essence of an inferential conclusion. *E.g.*, the Earth is related to 'Odorousness' by such a peculiar relation that that relation cannot point to the Earth in relation to anything other than 'Odorousness.' (2) Then again, the condition that 'there must be relation between the two factors' precludes the '*Bāḍhiṭa*' or Annulled Probans; *e.g.* when the eternality of word is sought to be established on the basis of its *being an effect*, we find that no positive relation is possible between the character of 'eternality' and that of 'being an effect', the two being entirely contradictory characters; for this reason the inference of 'eternality' in this case cannot be valid. (3) The mention of the condition that 'the relation should be *permanent* or *unfailing*' precludes the '*Sāḍhāraṇa* or Too Wide' Probans. *E.g.*, when the 'eternality' of the word is sought to be proved on the basis of its *being cognisable*, it is found that the relation between 'eternality' and 'cognisability' is not *permanent*, inasmuch as there are many things that are *cognisable* without being *eternal*; and thus this relation cannot lead to the valid inference of *eternality*. (4) The condition that 'one factor of the relation (which is to be the *probans*) must be *perceived* in order to give rise to the inferential cognition precludes the '*Asiḍḍha* or Impossible, or Unknown Probans. *E.g.*, when the *perceptibility* of such

things as *Ḍharma* and *Aḍharma* by the Buḍḍha is sought to be proved by his 'omniscience',—it is found that, inasmuch as this 'omniscience' has never been *perceived*, it cannot lead to any valid inference. Apart from these principal '*heṭvābhāsas*,' the *Prābhākara* does not accept any other. For instance, it has been held by the Logician and others that the Valid Inference must be one that has no counter-inference vitiating its validity; *e.g.*, when the *imperceptibility* of Air is sought to be inferred from its *colourlessness*, this is found to be opposed by an equally strong inference of the *perceptibility* of Air from its *tangibility*; and thus the validity of each of these inferences is found to be vitiated by the other; to such a fallacious inference, they give the name '*Satpraṭipakṣa*.' This view the *Prābhākara* does not accept; for the reason that, it is not possible for two mutually contradictory characters —[which are held to be the *probans* in the two contradictory inferences]—to subsist in any one 'subject'; for instance, in the case cited, it is not possible for Air to be *colourless* and at the same time *tangible*; as what is *tangible* can ever be entirely devoid of colour; hence it is only one of the two inferences that is *real* inference; the other cannot be so. Really contradictory inferences are possible only in regard to substances whose real character is not known; and in such cases of course no inference is possible; and this for the simple reason that the requisite definite knowedge of the two factors of the 'relation' is not available.

5. The object of inferential cognition is of two kinds—(1) the *ḍriṣṭasvalakṣaṇa*, that which has had its specific character perceived, and (2) the *aḍriṣṭasvalakṣaṇa*, that which has its specific character not perceived. To the former class belong all such ordinary things as *fire* and the like; and to the latter such *super-sensuous* things as the *capacity* of things and the like. In the case of the latter, though the 'specific character' may not be actually known, yet it is possible for us to cognise its permanent relation with certain factors;

and, through that relation, to get at the inferential cognition; for instance, even though we do not actually perceive the burning *capacity* of fire, yet we can infer its presence from seeing its effects, on the basis of the general relation subsisting between the effect and its cause.

6. As to what is the '*pramāṇa*' and what the 'result' of inferential cognition, we have to accept what has been said with regard to Perception. That is to say, if we regard '*pramāṇa*' as synonymous with 'valid cognition' (*pramiṭi*),—and hence '*Anumāna*' as synonymous with 'inferential cognition' (*anumiṭi*),—then what is '*anumāna*' is the *cognition of fire* proceeding from the mind-soul contact as influenced by the perception of smoke; and the 'result' in this case would be the *acceptance* or *rejection* of the cognised thing by the agent. If however we explain '*pramāṇa*' as that *by means of which* valid cognition is obtained,—and hence '*Anumāna*' as that *by means of which* the valid inferential cognition is got at,—then, in that case, the '*Anumāna*' (*pramāṇa*) would be (1) the mind-soul contact; and the apprehension of the relation between the factors of inference, as along with the perception of one of these factors, would form the 'procedure' of the *cognitive* (*inferential*) *process*; and the 'result' in this case would be the *inferential cognition* itself. If however, the 'means' or 'instrument' be regarded as that which is the *most effective* (*sāḍhakaṭama*) in the bringing about of the result, then the *perception of the probans* (smoke) would have to be regarded as the '*Anumāna*' (*pramāṇa*); as it is this that is most directly and immediately effective in bringing about the inferential cognition.

7. There are two kinds of Inference—(1) '*svārṭha*', *for one's own sake*, and (2) '*parārṭha*' *for the sake of another*; in the former, the inferential cognition is deduced for one's own benefit, from the premises recalled to the mind; and in the latter it is deduced for the benefit of another person, from premises presented to him.

8. As a rule, every inferential process consists of three factors, technically called '*avayavas*' ;—all these three are implied in the definition of Inferential Cognition given above. For instance,—(1) the condition that the cognition should be valid, 'not sublated', implies the *Pratijñā*, or 'Statement of the Conclusion'; (2) that there should be knowledge of the permanent relation implies the 'dṛiṣṭānṭa,' the *Major Premiss*, 'the statement of the corroborative instance'; and (3) that the *probans* should be perceived implies the *Minor Premiss*, or 'statement of the *probans*.' Some Logicians put forward *five* 'factors' for the inferential process,—adding to the above three two more in the shape of the reassertion of the premiss and conclusion; the *Bauḍḍhas* accept only two, discarding the 'statement of the conclusion', which, they argue, is implied in the premisses themselves. Herein appears to be the original source of the stock objection against syllogistic reasoning,—that every syllogism involves a *petitio principii*. The *Bhāttas** accept the three adopted by Prabhākara.

(1) By the 'statement of the conclusion' is meant the pointing out of what is intended to be proved; for inistance, the proposition 'Word is eternal'; it is only when this has been pointed out that we can ascertain the fact of the inferential cognition being *valid* or *not sublated*; the qualification 'not sublated' serves to reject all such propositions as are distinctly contrary to well-known facts of experience.

(2) The 'Statement of the corroborative instance' becomes necessary, as it has to be shown to the other party that there *is* a permanent relation between what is sought to be proved and that by means of which it is to be proved; and this relation must be shown to exist in a case that is well known to both parties; for instance, when it is intended to prove the presence of fire by the presence of smoke, the

* *Shāsṭradīpikā*, p. 44.

corroborative instance is cited thus—'Wherever there is smoke there is fire, *as in the kitchen*'; instances that do not apply to the case in question are regarded as *wrong*—'*ḍṛiṣṭānṭābhāsa*'; and older writers have divided the 'Wrong instance' under four heads :—(*a*) that which is not applicable to what is sought to be proved ; *e. g.*, the case of the 'Airy castle' cited to prove the fact of *word being produced by effort, i.e.*, non-eternal, where it is found that the 'Airy castle' itself is not 'something produced by effort'; (*b*) that which does not apply to the *probans* ; *e.g.*, the case of the 'jar' cited to corroborate the argument that 'word is non-eternal, *because it is incorporeal*',—where we find that the jar itself is not *incorporeal* ; (*c*) that which is applicable neither to the *probans* nor to that which is sought to be proved ; *e.g.*, the case of *ākāsha* cited in support of the argument that 'word is non-eternal, because it is an effect', where we find that the *ākāsha* is neither 'non-eternal' nor an 'effect'; (*d*) that which fails to establish the desired relation ; *e.g.*, if the instance of 'kitchen', in support of the presence of fire as proved by the presence of smoke, were cited only in the form 'like the kitchen', without recalling the relation between *fire* and *smoke*.

(3) Lastly, inasmuch as Inferential Cognition has been defined as that which follows on the perception of one of the two factors between which a permanent relation is known to subsist,—this perception of one factor becomes a necessary element in all inference ; and upon the assertion; of this 'the statement of the *probans*' becomes necessary : for instance, when seeking to prove the presence of *fire* by the presence of *smoke*, it is necessary to assert the proposition 'there is *smoke* in the mountain'; as without this the conclusion cannot be rightly deduced. The 'wrong' Minor Premiss is that where either what it asserts is not the factor bearing the permanent relation, or which fails to denote that factor.

9. There is a difference of opinion as to the exact order in which an inferential argument should state the two premises. The opinion of Prabhākara is that there need be no hard and fast rule as to this order; because the conclusion 'there is fire in the mountain' is established all the same, whether we state the argument in the form—'(a) there is smoke in the mountain', and '(b) wherever there is smoke there is fire, &c., &c.',—or in the form '(a) wherever there is smoke there is fire, &c., &c.,' and '(b) there is smoke in the mountain.' It is this freedom as to the statement of the reasoning that does away with any necessity for the *Upanaya* and the *Nigamana*, the two additional propositions that make up the 'five *avayavas*' of the Logician.

10. Some writers hold that the purposes of the 'Corroborative instance' can be also served by the *Negative instance*, or an *instance to the contrary*; for instance, in corroboration of the argnment,—'there is fire because there is smoke,'—we can put forward the statement 'wherever there is no fire there is no smoke.' This view is not accepted by the *Prābhākara*; because, he argues, as a matter of fact, the *probans* can prove the conclusion only by force of its relation to that which is sought to be proved; and this relation can be asserted only by means of a *positive* instance, and not by a *negative* one; even though in some cases, the negative instance also may serve to point out the necessary relation,—yet it can do so only indirectly, the process thereby becoming more involved than if the instance were stated in its positive form; hence in all cases, it is the *positive* instance that should be put forward. The *Bhātta** also rejects the utility of the *negative* instance.

11. The discrepancies pertaining to the 'Snbject' of the inference (*pakṣa*) are of two kinds:—(a) that it is contrary to well-known facts of experience, and (b) that it

* *Shāstraḍīpikā*, p. 48.

has a qualification that is absolutely unknown. Those pertaining to the *probans* have been explained above (§4); and so also those pertaining to the 'instance' (§6). Those pertaining to the 'Statement of the Conclusion' are—(*a*) *inexpressiveness* or indefiniteness, obscurity, and (*b*) Non-assertion. The 'renouncing of the conclusion' (*praṭijñāhāni*) does not come in here; inasmuch as one renounces his position only when he finds it assailed by insurmountable difficulties; and this is always due to some discrepancy in the main reasoning, and not only in the 'statement of the conclusion.'

SECTION (2)—*Sub-section* (3).

SHĀSṬRA—*Scriptural or Verbal Cognition.*

1. The *Shāshṭra—Scriptural*, or *Verbal* Cognition—has been defined as the cognition of something not before the eyes, produced by the knowledge of words; Verbal Cognition thus is that cognition of things imperceptible—*i. e.*, not cognised by other means of cognition,—which proceeds from the Mind-Soul contact aided by the knowledge of sounds. The 'sound' meant here is that in the form of *letters*, these alone being perceptible by the ear, and the name 'sound' being applicable to only what is perceived by the Ear. From this it would seem that, according to Prabhākara, all sounds heard are in the shape of some *letter* or the other,—there being no such thing as mere '*ḍhvani*' or indistinct sound. Nor can the 'word' be regarded as something different from the letters composing it,—as might appear from the fact that '*na-ḍī*' and '*ḍī-na*', though containing the same letters, are yet not perceived by the Ear as the same word. As a matter of fact, in the case of such words also, it is only the *letters* that are perceived by the Ear, the difference of the word lying only in the order in which the letters are pronounced and apprehended. Nor does the perception of the word '*ḍī-na*' contain a single act of perception; in fact it involves two distinct perceptions,—one of the '*ḍī*' and

another of '*na*'; so that there is a difference in the order of the perceptions of the component letters of the words also; there are as many perceptions as there are letters in the word; and the idea that the perception is one only is due to the close proximity of the two perceptions. The idea of the 'word' however must be regarded as *one* only; is it is found to admit of the denotation of a single thing.

The comprehension of this denotation or meaning of the word is not obtained through the sense-organs, because the organs perceive only the *letters*, which may be the same in more than word; and hence there can be no *sensuous* perception of *many* words; from this it follows that it is in the same letters themselves that there is a certain potency which brings about the apprehension of the thing denoted by the word composed of those letters. It is for this reason that Prabhakara* has held the *letters* to be the *means of verbal cognition*.

The perception of each letter vanishes as soon as it appears; hence it is held that every verbal cognition leaves an impression, which helps in the cognition of the next letter in the word; and so on, the impressions left by these letter-cognitions combine with that left by the cognition of the last letter in the word, and thus bring about the idea of the *whole word* which expresses the denotation. Each word has thus to be regarded as having the potency of bringing about the comprehension of a certain meaning. In a case where, even on the due hearing of all the letters of the word, no meaning is comprehended, it has to be admitted that some necessary auxilliaries are wanting. For these reasons the conclusion is that it is the *letter* that is the direct cause of verbal cognition; and neither Perception nor Inference can give us any idea of the *word* as apart from its constituent *letters*.

---

* *Prakaraṇapañchikā*, pp. 87, *et. seq.*

This view of the *word* is also accepted by the *Bhātta*, according to whom—

'The *word* is nothing apart from the letters'; and,—'just as the various subsidiary actions of an elaborate sacrifice combine to bring about the final result; so the various letters composing the word combine to accomplish the denotation of the meaning.' (*Shāshṭradīpikā*, pp. 70—71); and again—

'The order of sequence belongs, not to the *letters*, but to the *sounds*; and through these latter, it is imposed upon the *letters* that are manifested by the sounds; hence it is *letters* alone that can be held to be *expressive*.' (*Ibid*. p. 73.)

2. The next question that arises is—what is meant by the '*arṭha*', 'meaning' or 'denotation' of a word? The '*arṭha*' of the word is that which is *denoted* or *expressed* by it, and 'that which is denoted by the word' is that to which it bears a relation independent of, and not related or established by, any human agency—this relation being that of the *denoter and denoted, i. e.*, the *denotative relation*. Even though we do not comprehend the 'meaning' of the word when we hear it for the first time, yet it cannot be denied that the denotative potency of the word is something that belongs to it by its very nature. When we are listening to a conversation between two elderly persons, and fail to comprehend the 'meanings' of words used by them, there arises an uncertainty in our minds as to whether or not the words are expressive of any 'meanings' at all; we proceed to reason in our minds that if the words were entirely *inexpressive* they could not convey sense to the person to whom they are addressed; while from his behaviour it is clear that he does derive the idea of something out of the words, and yet if the words are really expressive, how is it that they do not convey any meaning to ourselves? The only explanation for this apparent anomaly must lie in the fact that in the person to whom the words

are addressed there is something, some peculiar power, which is wanting in ourselves; this power must be in the shape of the knowledge of what is denoted by the word,—it is such power alone whose presence in the man is indicated by his behaviour; we can have no idea of the man having the knowledge of any *saṅketa* or 'Convention' bearing upon the denotativeness of the word (*i. e.* some such conventional law as that 'this word denotes this meaning,' upon which some philosophers base the denotativeness of words); until we are ourselves cognisant of the meaning of the word we cannot form any idea of any such law bearing upon it; as the knowledge of the law—'this word denotes *this meaning*'—presupposes the knowledge of the meaning. From this it follows that the only power present in the person comprehending the meaning of a word consists in his knowledge of the fact that the word is expressive of such a meaning; and this proves that the expressiveness of the word is something that belongs to it by its very nature. As this is sufficient to explain the phenomena of all verbal cognition and usage, there is no reason for attributing the expressiveness of words to any 'conventional law' or '*saṅketa.*' In the case of some words—*e. g.*, *proper* names—however, the presence of such a 'convention,'—as that 'this name points to that man'— is quite patent; and is therefore admitted by Prabhākara. But in the case of such *common* words as 'cow', 'jar', 'man,' and the like, there is no justification for the postulating of any 'conventional law'; consequently the relation of all such words to their meanings must be held to be independent of all human agency.

3. The *Mīmāmsaka** lays great stress upon the denotativeness of words being independent of human agency, and belonging to the words by their very nature; because if it were not so, the *validity* of the *word* and the verbal cognition would be, not something inherent in the word itself, but

* Praka-pañch., p. 133, *et seq*.

due to the trustworthy character of the person pronouncing the word; and thus, as the *Mīmāmsaka* denies any personal agency in connection with the composition of the Veda, there would, *ipso facto*, be no validity in the Veda itself. Nor can the *Mīmāmsaka* accept the Logician's point of view, by which the denotativeness of words is created and fixed by 'conventions' among people who introduce, and make use of, the words for the first time,—according to the Logician created by God Himself. This view necessitates the postulating of a 'God' as the originator of *all* words,—and hence also of the Veda; and this militates against the *Mīmāmsā* doctrine of the *self-sufficiency* of the Veda, which must be independent of all personal agency. In fact, if the denotativeness of words depended solely upon any 'Convention', the Veda would be reduced to the position of a meaningless jumble of words; because according to the *Mīmāmsaka*, the pre-eminent function of the Veda lies in the enjoining of certain acts as accomplishing an *apūrva*,—an invisible subtle potency,—leading to a desirable result; and as this *apūrva* is something of which no 'person' could ever have any knowledge, independently of the Veda, how could the denotativeness of those words of the Veda be fixed by any 'Convention'? And as thus no 'Convention' would be found applying to these words, these would, by the *Nyāya* view, have to be regarded as absolutely meaningless. If a Creator, God, were admitted, then, as this God, being omniscient, would be possessed of the direct knowledge of the *Apūrva*, he would be in a position to lay down 'Conventions' with regard to the denotativeness of the word denoting the *apūrva*. But the *Mīmāmsaka* does not admit of such a God; hence for the sake of the Veda, his all in all, he finds it necessary to stick to the view that all words and their denotations are eternal, everlasting, independent of all 'conventions' and 'agencies.'

4. As regards the eternality of the denotativeness of words, it is argued that, in the case of *Proper* names, we can infer the fact of their denotations having been fixed by 'convention'; but no such inferential basis is available in the case of *Common* names. Those who hold 'Convention' to be the basis of all denotation infer the existence of 'Convention', in the case of each and every word, from the fact of its being found to be possessed of a certain denotation,—which, they argue, would not be possible unless there were some basic 'convention'; they formulate their inference thus:—'All words have their denotation fixed by *convention*,—because they are *denotative*,—like the proper names *Devadatta* and the like.' In controverting this, the *Mīmāmsaka* argues that in the case of Proper names, we actually find that the thing or person to whom the name is applied has had a beginning in time; and we also know that the name must have been given by some person after that thing came into existence; and thus in the case of these names we admit the 'convention' as assigned by the person giving the name; specially as in this case there is no other explanation available for the fact of the word being denotative; in the case of Common names, on the other hand, their denotativeness can be accounted for otherwise than on the basis of such a 'Convention'; and so we have no grounds for assuming this latter. It is a well-known fact that we comprehend the meaning of a word because we know its denotative potency; and thus the knowledge of this potency being the direct *perceptible* cause of our comprehension, there can be no justification for the assumption of an *imperceptible* cause in the shape of 'Convention.' Then again, this denotative potency of the word could not have had a beginning in time; it must be regarded as eternal, being cœval and co-eternal with the word itself; the word itself could not have had a beginning in time; as the thing it denotes has had no such beginning; for the simple reason that the world itself has had no beginning, according to the

Mīmāmsaka; ever since the world has existed, and man has existed, he must have talked of things by their names; and thus the words and the things denoted by them being without beginning, eternal, the relation subsisting between the two must also be eternal. That all men have, from time immemorial, applied the same names to the same things is proved by the following reasoning :—It has already been shown above that, as young men, we come to be acquainted with the meanings of words by observing the conversation and behaviour of older persons; and by analogy we infer that those older people also must have derived their knowledge from like sources; and so on and on, carrying the analogy backwards, we are led to the conclusion that the process must have gone on ever since the things spoken of have been in existence; and as these had no beginning in time, it follows that the words, their denotative potency, and the relation between the two could have had no beginning in time.

5. Having established the eternality of the denotativeness of words, we now proceed to prove the eternality of the words, or names of things. It has also been pointed out that we comprehend the meaning of words by observing their use among experienced people on various occasions. If then, at each time that the old man speaks of a thing, he were to create a new name for it for the occasion, which name would again disppear as soon as it was uttered,—necessary corrollaries of the view that the word is not eternal,—then, what basis would the younger man have for observing the use of the word and thereby ascertaining its meaning? As each time that the thing is spoken of he would be face to face with a brand-new word, never heard before; and as such the meaning of the word would remain ever uncomprehended and incomprehensible; and until the word affords some Cognition, it cannot be regarded as '*pramāṇa*.' Consequently unless the Logician be prepared to deny the character of '*pramāṇa*' to words, he must accept them to be eternal. Then there

remains the question,—'If the word is eternal, why is it not *always* present in our consciousness?' The answer to this is that, though the word is ever present, yet, in order that it may be cognised by us, it stands in need of a certain auxilliary agency that manifests it, or makes it cognisable, or presents it to our consciousness. This manifestive agency consists of the effort put forth by the man who pronounces the word. The Logician regards this effort as the *cause* of the word, bringing it into existence; but Prabhākara regards it as a force or agency that serves to manifest to our perception the word that is already in existence. And as these efforts may be many, there need be no incongruity in the same word being pronounced, and heard, by several people; wherever the manifestive agency is present, the word will be heard; if there are many men putting forth an effort for pronouncing a word, it is only natural that there should be many manifestations of the word in consciousness; that it is the same word that is cognised in each of these cases is proved by our direct cognition of all of them as one and the same; and this is another reason for regarding the word as eternal. The effort put forth by the speaker is not, in itself, sufficient to account for the cognition of the word; as in that case we could not account for the non-hearing of the word by the deaf; in fact the effort tends to manifest the word only through certain effects that it produces in the auditory organ of the person standing by. The several steps in the physiological process of speech are thus explained:—(1) The speaker puts forth an effort; (2) this effort brings the soul into contact with the air enclosed in his lungs; (3) in obedience to the impulse imparted by this effort the air rises upwards; (4) in its upward progress it comes into contact with the vocal chords lying about the various regions of the body; (5) these contacts change the character of the air to a certain extent; (6) on issuing from the mouth, the air passes onwards, and reaches the ear of the persons standing near enough to be reached by the air; the extent of whose reach depends upon the greater or less degree of the initial effort of the speaker; (7) on reaching the ear, it produces in it a certain change that is conducive to its power of making the sound audible. Thus then it is this power or faculty of the ear that is the direct agent manifesting the word to the consciousness of the person to whom the ear belongs. As the air is endowed with a certain velocity, it keeps moving onwards; and when it has passed out of the ear, the sound passes out, and the audition ceases, the person hears the sound no longer. All this process of speech and audition is acknowledged by the Logician also; the only difference lies in this that what Prabhākara regards as a mere *manifesting agency*, the Logician regards as the *Cause*. The next question that arises is—'what is the change produced in the auditory organ which makes it capable of manifesting sound?' The ear cannot be made capable of manifesting sound by the removal of any layer of air obstructing the manifestation,—for the simple reason that Air cannot obstruct sound; what occurs is that the Air-waves issuing from the mouth of the speaker, in striking the fixed layer of air enclosed in the receiving ear, produces in this latter a peculiar imperceptible change, whereby it is rendered capable of manifesting the sound. The *Mīmāmsakā* postulates the presence, in the ear-cavity, of the fixed layer of air, for the purpose of affording a screen of resistance to the sound-waves; against which screen, these waves would strike, and thereby effect the change in the auditory organ; it is a well-recognised fact that Air cannot produce any effects unless it meets with a certain degree of resistance. Another objection generally brought against the above view of the physiology of audition is that, the ear being of *ākāsha* which is one and indivisible, if there were any material change in any one ear, the change ought to affect *all* ears, and so the sound heard by one person would be heard by all persons. The answer that the *Prābhākara* has to this is this:—Even though *Ākāsha* is one, yet the ear-drum is distinct in each person,—each one being limited in its power and scope by the virtue and vice of the person to whom it belongs; then again, the change produced in the sound-waves is not in the *ākāsha* of the ear, but in the air enclosed in the ear-drum; and as this latter differs in each person, all men need not hear the sound heard by one.

As a matter of fact, we observe that when the sound-waves travel with the wind, the sound is heard at a greater distance than when it travels against the wind; this phenomenon could not be explained under the hypothesis that each sound goes on producing a fresh sound at each step of its progress towards any definite direction; as if this were so, the direction or force of the wind could not have any effect one way or the other.

6. Each time that we hear a letter or word pronounced, we at once recognise it to be the same, and not as different in each case. Even though the word may be pronounced in varying degrees of loudness, &c., yet all the difference that we are cognisant of is in the tone or pitch of the sound, and not in the word itself, which latter is always recognised to be the same. For these reasons, the conclusion is that the *word* has no cause bringing it into existence; and thus it has the same eternality that belongs to Ākāsha and such other things.

7. We have seen that, according to Prabhākara, people learn the meanings of words only by watching the usage and activity of older persons; when a set of words is addressed by one person to another, whereupon the latter person acts in a certain manner, it is clear that the meaning of the words pronounced must have been in the form of an

injunction to do what the other person has done. In the case of words where such an interpretation is not possible, the comprehension of the meaning must depend upon something indirectly connected with the injunction. This is the reason why in the definition of *Verbal Cognition* we have it that the object cognised must be one that has not been cognised by any other means of knowledge; this can be always so only in the case of injunctive words. All words ending in the Imperative or a similar termination express the injunction directly; while other words denote things related to the injunction,—such things, for instance, as the name of the *act* enjoined, the *person* enjoined and so on. This leads to the view that the whole direct denotation of the Veda must lie in the enjoining of something *to be done.* This leads to the controverting of the view held by the Veḍānṭin, that the direct denotation of all the more important Vedic texts lies, not in the enjoining of something *to be done,* but in the pointing out of certain *well-accomplished things, e.g.,* Brahman. In opposition to this Veḍānṭa view, it has been held that, though such may be the case with a few words, yet the comprehension of the denotation of those words also could not but be obtained by observing their use by older persons; and this use also must always lie in the form of an injunction addressed by one person to another for the *doing of a certain act*; thus ultimately the denotation *of all* words must lie, either directly or indirectly, with something *to be done.* Those *Veḍānṭa* texts that speak of *Brahman* must be regarded as speaking of Brahman as something on which one is *enjoined to meditate* and *know,* in order to escape from the meshes of metempsychosis.

8. Inasmuch as the meanings of words can be known only when they occur in an injunctive sentence, it follows that the words must denote things only as related to the other factors of the injunction; and no word can be comprehended as having any denotation when taken apart from such

sentence. This is the theory known as the *Anviṭābhiḍhānavāda*; and it is the main distinctive feature of the *Prābhākara* School of Thought bearing upon Verbal Cognition; and it has the tacit support of Shabara (*see* pp. 32-35 and 132). It is on this point too that it is directly opposed to the sister school of the *Bhātta*; it is here that the two schools stand out pre-eminently as the champious of two distinct theories bearing upon Verbal Cognition,—the two theories known under the names of *Anviṭābhiḍhāna* (of Prabhākara) and *Abhihiṭānvaya* (of Kumārila). According to the latter,—

'Words themselves can express their separate meanings by the function *Abhidhā or denotation*; these are subsequently (combined) into a sentence expressing one connected idea. The former, called the *Anviṭābhiḍhānavāḍinaḥ*, hold that words only express a meaning as parts of a sentence, and as grammatically connected with each other; they only express an action or something connected with an action; in *(gāmānaya)* (*bring the cow*) *gām*—does not properly mean *goṭva, but ānaynanānviṭa goṭva—i.e.*, the *bovine genus as connected with bringing*; we cannot have a case of a noun without some governing verb, and *vice versa*.' (*Sarvaḍarshana-saṅgraha*, Cowell, *Note*, p. 202).

9. According to Prabhakara, we can have a truly valid *verbal cognition* only in the case of words and sentences of the Veda; this is clear from the very name '*Shāsṭra*' that he has given to this *pramāṇa*. As a necessary corrollary to this it is held that, apart from the wordsfound in the Scriptures, no words can affordany cognition ofthings not already knowr by other means of knowledge; all words used in ordinary parlance are mostly only such that denote things that can be cognised by Perception and Inference also; and those things that can not be cognised by these latter means can be *rightly* cognised only when described in words of unquestionable authority and trustworthy character. From this it follows that cognitions provided

by *words other than these,*—and all non-Vedic words belong to this category—can have no inherent validity in themselves.

This theory becomes divested of much of its apparent absurdity when we realise the fact that, inasmuch as it is the Scriptural word alone that is inherently authoritative and trustworthy, no other words can be accepted as affording *invariably* valid cognitions; specially when it is found that in ordinary parlance, most cognitions afforded by the words of ordinary people turn out to be invalid and untrustworthy; hence, at best, cognitions derived from non-scriptural words must be regarded to be of the same kind as 'Remembrance', and hence of doubtful validity; and as cognitions of doubtful validity cannot be called Cognition, which, by its very nature, is *valid,* Non-scriptural words cannot by themselves afford any *cognition,* in the proper sense of the term; they are mere *describers* or *translators* or *refectors* of what is in the mind of the person uttering those words; the validity whereof can be ascertained only by other means of knowledge; it is in reference to such non-scriptural words that we have the saying—

'*Paḍamapyaḍhikābhāvāṭ smārakānna vishiṣyaṭe*'

('The word is not different from that which affords remembrance, as it is in no way more than this').

This cannot be said with regard to the words of the Veda; as in the case of the *non-Vedic* word, its invalidity, or doubtful validity, is based upon the generally untrustworthy character of the speaker, due to many such causes as wrong understanding, incapability of using the right words, and so on; in the case of the words of the Veda, on the other hand, as they do not emanate from a 'person', there is no source to which the *falsity* of the assertions might be due. In the case of the assertions of ordinary people, even when we find the words affording a reasonably connected meaning, we have always a lurking suspicion lest there be some defect in the source from which the speaker has derived the information that he seeks to convey by means of those words; and for this reason we can not be sure of the validity of the cognition afforded by such words, which, for this reason, cannot be regarded as 'means of right cognition.' Even in cases where the ordinary words do afford valid cognitions, it is not the *words* that bring about the valid cognition directly; as what occurs is that on hearing the words, we find that they convey a certain information; and then we proceed to *reason* that the speaker is a trustworthy person, as not one of the grounds of untrustworthiness is found present in the case; consequently what he says must be true; so the information conveyed by his words must be true. Thus in this case the words are not the *direct* cause of the valid cognition; they only indirectly indicate the presence of the cognition in the mind of the speaker; so in this case, for the hearer, the words cannot be '*pramāṇa*'; at any rate not independently of the Inference that is involved in the process whereby the word indicates to the hearer the presence of the Cognition in the speaker's mind; all such cases involve a clear inferential process; such, for instance, as—'this speaker has a particular Cognition in his mind, because he has pronounced these words.' Says the *Prakaraṇapañchikā* (pp. 15—16),—

'It is only the Veda that can be called *Shabḍapramāṇa*,; and that also only when containing an *injunction*; ordinary words cannot be so; because the cognitions afforded by them are purely *inferential*; when we hear a man saying something, our mind goes through the following reasoning—'This man speaks of such a thing,—this he must be speaking of after having known what he speaks of,—so what he says must be true;' the *speech* of the man is an effect of his *knowledge*; and hence from the *effect* we *infer* the *cause*. Thus all ordinary verbal cognition is *inferential*; that afforded by the Vedā alone is purely *verbal*. It is true that all words are endowed with an inherent denotative potency; but in the case of ordinary speakers of the world, this potency of the word is *obscured* by suspicions with regard to the trustworthy character of the persons; in the case of the words of the Veda, there being no *speaker*, and hence no grounds of suspicion, the potency remains unobscured.'

It is for this reason that Kaṇāḍa * regarding the Veda as the work of a personal author, has declared that 'Verbal Cognition' is nothing apart from *Inferential Cognition*, as all personal words afford only Inferential Cognitions, and there is no such thing as purely *verbal* coguition. From this it is clear that '*Shabḍa*' as a distiuct '*pramāṇa*' can be acknowledged only by those who regard the Veda as eternal, and not the work of a personal author.

10. That the Veda is not the work of a personal author is proved by the fact that all words aud things denoted by them being eternal (as shown above), and there being no other means (save the Veda) available for the knowledge of Ḍharma,—including, as it does, such super-sensuous things as the *Apūrva* and the like,—the Veda itself, being only a collection of words speaking of such things, must be eternal, and as such independent of all authorship.

11. The above theory of *Verbal Cognition*, which restricts it to the cognition afforded by Vedic injunctions only, is not accepted by the *Bhāṭṭa*, † who, at the very outset divides the '*Shabḍa Pramāṇa*' into *paurūṣeya*' or *human* and '*apauruṣeya*' or *super-human*, the latter includiug Vedic sentences, and the former all utterances by such human beings as are trustworthy; both of these cognitions—*human* as well as *superhuman*—are regarded by him as *valid*; because the only ground of invalidity in a word lies in the fact of its emanating from an untrustworthy source; and this

---

* *Vaisheṣika Sūṭra*, I-i-3; II. 2-32; VI-i-1; IX-2-3; X-2-9.

† See *Shāstradīpika*, p. 51.

ground is as absent in the case of the utterances of trustworthy persons as in that of Vedic declarations.

12. Just as in the case of the other *pramaṇas,* so here also, if we regard the word '*Shāstra*' as an Accusative Abstract Noun, *shiṣyaṭe yaṭ ṭaṭ*—equivalent be '*Shiṣti*'—then it is synonymous with '*Verbal or Scriptural cognition*'; if however it be taken as an Instrumental Abstract Noun,—'*shiṣyāṭe anena,*'—then it is synonymous with the *word affording verbal cognition.*

13. 'Words,'—or what is the same, according to Prabhākara, 'Scriptural texts',—are divided into two classes,—(*a*) one that is actually found in the Veda, and (*b*) that the presence whereof in the Veda has to be inferred. To the latter class belong all those texts that are inferred as supplying the basis for the injunctions of actions found in the *Smṛiṭis,* whose sole claim to authority rests on the fact that they contain no injunctions save what are vouched for by Vedic texts. It may be observed here, as the *Prakaraṇa-pañchikā* (p. 101) remarks, that the '*Shāsṭra*' or Vedic injunction often stands in need of some factors being supplied from without; *e. g.*, the text, that speaks of a certain action merely as accomplishing certain desirable results, stands in need of some such injunctive words as that 'this action should be performed,' which have to be supplied. Similarly it also stands in need of certain well-ascertained facts of ordinary experience; *e. g.*, for ascertaining the true signification of the injunction '*uḍbhiḍā yajeṭa,*' it is necessary to have recourse to ordinary experience; the word '*uḍbhiḍ*' primarily means a tree; so the sentence might well be taken to mean that 'one should sacrifice *with the tree;*' but here our ordinary experience steps in and shows that such sacrifice would be an impossibility; and it is only on account of this impossibility that we are led to take the word '*uḍbhiḍ*' here as the name of a sacrifice,—which is the correct interpretation.*

* Vide *Mimāmsā Sūtra*, I-IV-2.

Then as regards the question as to how a number of words can be regarded as a *single* '*Shāsṭra*' or *text*,—the answer is that just as we regard a number of letters as *one word* on the ground of their denoting one definite thing,—so in the same manner, we regard a number of words as a *single sentence or text* on the ground of their expressing one definite complete idea*; or properly speaking, we have to regard as a single sentence those words which together go to speak of any one *action*; as it is the *action* that forms the main factor in the denotation of all Injunction.

SECTION (2)—SUB-SECTION (4).

Upamāna—ANALOGY.

1. *Upamāna* or Analogical Cognition is the cognition of *similarity* as subsisting in an object not in contact with the sense-organs, brought about by the perception of similarity in some other object which is perceived by the senses. For instance, when a man who has seen a monkey happens to see the ourang-outang, he *sees* the latter as being *similar* to the former, and then comes to cognise the similarity of the *monkey* to the *ourang-outang*; the similarity of the ourang-outang is *seen*; and from that follows the cognition of the similarity of the monkey; and it is this latter cognition that is 'analogical.'

The *Bhāttas*† are in agreement with Prabhākara on this point. According to them also,—

'When we see a certain object, and remember another object, the cognition that we have of the *remembered* object as being similar to the *seen* object is *analogical*; for instance, the notion—*the cow that I had seen in the city is similar to this gavaya that I see now*—is analogical.'

But unlike the *Prābhākara*, the *Bhātta* does not regard 'similarity' as a distinct category; as according to them

---

* *Ibid*, II-1-16.

† *Shāsṭradīpikā*, p. 52.

it is only a *quality* consisting in the fact of more than one object having the same set of qualities.

2. Analogical Cognition is distinct from *Perception*; as it is the cognition of something not in contact with the senses; for instance, the monkey is not actually seen at the time that we have the cognition of its similarity to the ourang-outang. Nor is it mere *Remembrance*; as at the time that the monkey was *seen*, the ourang-outang had not been seen, and hence at that time the *Similarity* could not have been *seen*; and what has not been *seen* cannot be *remembered*. Nor lastly, can it be regarded as *Inference*; as none of the factors essential for Inference are found to be present in the case cited.

3. Some philosphers have defined *Upamāna* as pertaining to the similarity of something unknown with what is known. This definition cannot be accepted; because according to this definition, the resultant analogical cognition would be in the form 'this animal is the ourang-outang';—this cognition coming to the man who, going to the forest, sees the ourang-outang, and remembers the words of a forester to the effect that 'the ourang-outang is like the monkey;' such a cognition could not be valid; (1) because the words 'the ourang-outang is like the monkey,' as emanating from a human source, could not be absolutely trustworthy; and as such could not form the basis of any valid cognition;—(2) the cognition of the ourang-outang, and that of the similarity of that animal to the monkey, can not be regarded as 'analogical;' as this is Perception pure and simple;—(3) the cognition that 'this animal that I see is what is denoted by the word *ourang-outang*' is also merely *inferential*; as the word is not pronounced at that time, having been told to the man at some previous time. Thus then, by this definition, there would be nothing left that could form the subject of any such cognition as 'analogical.'

SECTION (2)—SUB-SECTION (5).

Arṭhapaṭṭi—PRESUMPTION.

1. In a case where the well-ascertained perception of a thing or things (*arṭha*) cannot be explained or reconciled without the presumption of another thing or things, then it is this *presumption* that constitutes *Arṭhāpaṭṭi*. For instance, when we know that Ḍevaḍaṭṭa is alive, and perceive that he is not in the house, these two 'things'—*being alive* and *non-existence* in the house cannot be reconciled unless we *presume* his existence somewhere outside the house; and the presumption of this external existence is what is called '*Arṭhāpaṭṭi*.'

The principal point on which this differs from Inference is that, in the case of the latter, no kind of *doubt* enters as a necessary factor; while in Presumption it is necessary that there should be a doubt as to the validity of the two irreconcilable facts of perception. Thus the source of Presumption lies in the *perceived thing*, which, in the absence of something else, remains *inconsistent*, and hence *doubtful*; and for the sake of removing this element of doubt with regard to itself, it leads to the *presumption* of that other thing;—in the case of Inference, on the other hand, the *probans*,—which forms the real source,—is not beset with any doubt; in fact no inference from it would be possible if its validity were at all uncertain. Thus in the case of Presumption, the source or origin is doubtful; while in that of Inference, it must be absolutely free from all invalidating circumstances. For instance, it is only when the smoke is perceived to exist, beyond the shadow of a doubt, that it leads to the inference of fire; while in the case of Presumption, the perceived non-existence in the house leads to the presumption of external existence, only when it has thrown itself, and also the other known fact of the man's being alive, into uncertainty.

This view of Presumption is not accepted by the *Bhātta*, who argues that in the case of the example cited, if the fact of the man being alive were at all *doubtful*, it could not afford a sound basis for the requisite Presumption; it is only when the fact of his being alive is *known for certain*, that it can warrant the presumption of the man having gone out. Then again, this doubt, if there were any, as to whether the man is alive or not, would be set aside, not by the cognition of his *being outside*, but only by the *certainty* of his *being alive*.* According to the *Bhātta*, the basis of Presumption lies, not in a Doubt, but in the mutual *irreconcilability* or *inconsistency* between two *well-ascertained* things; which inconsistency is removed by the presumption of a third thing, which presumption constitutes '*Arṭhāpaṭṭi*'.† There is no such inconsistency between well-ascertained things in the case of Inference; and it is in this, according to the *Bhāṭṭa*, that lies the difference between Presumption and Inference.

2. In the other well-known instance of Presumption,—where the fact of Ḍevaḍaṭṭa eating at night is presumed on the ground of his being fat and yet not eating during the day,—some people have held that what is *presumed* in this case is the assertion 'he eats at night'; but this is not right; as what effects a reconciliation between the two facts of the man being fat and that of his not eating in the day, is only the *fact* of his eating at night, and not the mere *assertion* of his doing so.

SECTION (2)—*Sub-section* (6).

Other So-called Pramāṇas.

1. The above five are the only *pramāṇas* accepted by Prabhākara. Over and above these five some philosophers have postulated three more,—(*a*) *Abhāva* or Non-apprehension (*b*)

* *Shāsṭradīpikā*, pp. 53—54.

† *Ibid.* p. 55.

Sambhava or Probability, and (*c*) *Aiṭihya* or Rumour. These Prabhākara rejects, on the following grounds :—

2. (*a*) The *Bhāttas** posit Non-apprehension as a distinct *pramāṇa*, and they argue as follows ;—In the case of the conception 'there is no jar in this place,' what is cognised is the *absence of the jar* ; this absence cannot be cognised by Perception, which stands in need of positive sense-contact, which is not possible in the case ; nor can it be cognised by Inference or any other of the above-mentioned *pramāṇas* ; what then affords the cognition of the *absence* is only the non-operation of any of the aforesaid *pramāṇas* ; and thus this *Non-operation* would be the *means* whereby we obtain the valid cognition of absence ; this means of right cognition is thus quite independent of the five described before ; and it is to this that the name 'Non-apprehension' is given.

In controverting the above, the *Prābhākara* advances the following arguments :—All cognitions of things are of two kinds,—in one kind we cognise the thing as along with something else, and in another we cognise the thing alone by itself ; and in this case this latter cognition is apprehended in terms of things that are not there, and which, if present, would have been cognised. In all cases where *absence* is cognised, what we have is only the non-perception of some thing that would have been perceived, if present; hence the *negative* cognition can be nothing more than the cognition of the one thing in terms of those other things which are not perceived, and which, if present, would have been perceived. Thus in the case of the conception 'the jar is not in this place', all that this means is that—'even though the jar would have been quite perceptible, if it were present, what we perceive is the *place* only' ; and this is an ordinary *positive* cognition, pure Perception in this case. In this manner it can be shown that there is nothing that could be

* *Shlokavārṭika*—'Abhāva,' Shl. 18 *et seq* ; and also *Shāsṭradīpikā*, pp. 60-65.

cognised by means of *Non-apprehension*, which, therefore, cannot be regarded as a '*pramāṇa*.'

3. (*b*) As regards *Probability*, people who accept it as a distinct *pramāṇa* cite as an example the cognition that we have of the lesser number (*f. i., ten*) in the larger number (*twenty*). According to Prabhākara, and also according to the *Bhātta*,* this is only a case of *Inference*; the larger number bears an invariable relation to the lesser number, and hence the presence of the former implies that of the latter.

4. (*c*) Lastly, as regards *Rumour*, this can never be accepted as a *means of valid cognition*, because the source of information not being known, it could not be ascertained whether or not it is trustworthy; hence there can be no certainty as to the validity of the resultant cognition. The *Bhātta*† agrees with Prabhākara in rejecting *Rumour* as a *pramāṇa*.

SECTION (3)—*Sub-section* (1).

Āṭman—SELF.

1. It becomes necessary for the *Mīmāmsaka* to prove the existence of the Self or Soul as apart from the body; as without some such permanent entity ensouling the body, there would be no sense in those Vedic texts that speak of the performer of a certain action going to heaven, and so forth. With regard to the real character of this entity however there are various differences of opinion among philosophers:—(*a*) It has been variously regarded as identical with the body, the sense-organs, and Buḍḍhi;—(*b*) some have held it to be *perceptible* by the mind; others as cognisable by Inference only; and others as self-illumined; while others regard it as being the element of *chiṭ* or consciousness appearing in all cognitions;—(*c*) it has been regarded as transient by some, and by others as eternal; (*d*) some people have held it to be atomic in size; others as of the size of the body; others

* *Shāstraḍ pīkā*, p. 65.

† *Shāstradīpikā*, p. 65.

again as all-pervading, omnipresent ; – (*e*) according to some it is one only, in all things ; while according to others it is many, one with each body.

2. According to Prabhākara,—(*a*) the Soul is something entirely distinct from the body, the sense-organs and Buḍḍhi; (*b*) it becomes manifest in all cognitions ; (*c*) it is eternal, (*d*) omnipresent, and (*e*) many, one in each body.

(*a*) That the *cogniser* is something entirely different from *Buḍḍhi* is proved by the fact, among others, that Buḍḍhi is absent during sleep ; and yet during sleep there are cognitions. Then again, the mere fact of Buḍḍhi being always concomitant with the Soul—even if true—could not establish the absolute identity of the two. The sense-organs cannot be regarded as the Soul ; because we often perceive a single object by more than one organ ;—'I am touching with the hand the same thing that I am seeing with the eye ;' and this fact shows that the factor of 'I' which is present in both perceptions cannot be either the hand or the eye, each of which is present in one cognition only. Then again, we find that the blind man remembers the things that he had seen before he became blind ; which shows that visual memory persists after the visual organ is gone ; it the organ were the 'seer', then, with the eye, the *perceivsr* haying gone, the remembrance of what it had seen would not be possible. Lastly, as regards the Body we find by its very nature, that it can never be the *cogniser*. Because, in the first place the Body is of the earth ; and Cognition is a 'specific' quality ; [as is proved by the facts that, (1) while subsisting in substances, it does not, by itself, bring about the conjunction or disjunction of substances, which fact proves that it is a quality ;—and (2) that it is never found apart from bodied or corporeal beings] ; and it is a rule with ali 'specific' qualities that, in order to be present in any product, it should abide in the constituents of that product; but in the case of the Body, we find, as a matter of fact, that Cognition or Consciousness is not present in earth-particles,—as we learn from the fact that there is no cognition in such earthy substances as the jar and the like; and from this it follows that it cannot be present in any thing made up of earth-particles; and this leads to the conclusion that that in which cognition abides is something distinct from all such things as are made up of material particles. Apart from this, in all cognitions, we are actually conscious of the *cogniser* as apart from the Body; *e. g.*, when we see the jar, we have the notion 'I see the jar'; in this notion we do not find any idea of the *body*, which is only the collective name given to the hands, legs, head, &c., and none of these limbs, either severally or collectively, enter into our consciousness at the time; while in all individual cognitions, it is necessary that there should be a manifestation of the *cogniser*; as, otherwise there would be no difference between the cognition of one person and that of another; and as in the notion 'I see the jar' the factor of 'cogniser' is found to be manifested, not in the form of the body or the sense-organs,—it follows that the cogniser must be something apart from these. In cases where the word 'I' is found to be used in connection with the body, the use of the word must be regarded as figurative or poetical. Then again, the word 'Soul' can be applied to that only which is endowed with intelligence; and as the body is not found to be so endowed, it cannot be spoken of as the 'Soul'; the sole proof of anything being endowed with intelligence lies in the testimony borne by our own Consciousness; and inasmuch as we have the consciousness of things of the past and the future also, intelligence cannot be regarded as belonging to any material objects perceived by the senses; as in the case of our cognition of past and future objects, the objects are *not present* at the time.

3. If *all* cognitions were due solely to the Soul, then inasmuch as the Soul is everlasting, we would never have a

cessation in our cognitions. In view of this difficulty, it has been held that even though the Soul may be regarded as the material or constituent cause of cognitions, it must stand in need of the aid of other auxilliary agencies, in the bringing about of cognitions. As this auxilliary agency, some philosophers postulate the *operation of the mind.* This view however is not accepted by Prabhākara; because, he argues, by its very nature, this *operation of the mind* would itself stand in need of further auxilliaries. He, therefore, puts forward, as the required auxilliary of the Soul, the *contact of the Mind with the Soul*;—this contact being brought about by a certain action of the Mind, due either to the effort of the Soul or to the 'Unseen Agency' set going by the previous '*karman*' of that Soul; these *Efforts and Unseen Agencies* also, in their turn, are the effects of previous *Mind-Soul contacts*; and so the infinite circle goes on.

4. The existence of the Mind is proved by the manifestation of the qualities of the Soul itself, which would not be possible without the operation of the mind. These qualities of the Soul are—Buḍḍhi or Intellection, Pleasure, Pain, Desire, Aversion, Effort, Desṭiny (Unseen Force) and Faculty. The existence of *Buḍḍhi* is self-manifest, in the form of Valid Cognitions and Remembrances; Pleasure, Pain, Desire Aversion and Effort are apprehended by mental perception. By 'Faculty' or '*Samskāra*' is meant a certain force or power or capability imparted to the Soul by its cognitions; its existence is proved by the fact that, unless we have some such force intervening between the cognition of an object and its remembrance, we cannot account for this latter. As for Destiny, this always takes the form of Virtue and Vice—whose real character can be known only from Scriptures, which alone can be the safe guide as to what is *virtue* and what is *vice*.

5. All our cognitions are not due to Mind-Soul contact only; *e. g.*, in the perception of colour, if that contact

were the sole cause, then the blind man would also be able to perceive colour; it is in view of this fact that we have to admit the agency of the external sense-organs, the Eye, &c.; and as all perceptible external objects fall within five classes, we postulate five organs of perception; these five, along with the Perceptive Mind which may be regarded as the Universal Organ, form the six organs of which the Body is the abode.

6. Thus the Body may be defined as *the abode of the six sense-organs.* Of Bodies there are three kinds—(1), born of the womb, (2) born of eggs, and (3) born of sweat. Prabhākara does not accept the Vegetable body, on the ground that we have no proofs for the view that vegetable organisms are endowed with the six organs of perception. Nor does he admit any such body as is not made of the Earth. Two of the six organs—the Mind and the organ of Touch—are present in all bodies. That the Mind is a substance is proved by the fact of its having contacts with the Soul and with the objects of cognition. It cannot be made of many constituent particles, as that would involve an unnecessary multiplication of assumptions. Then again, as the Soul is omnipresent, and without parts, if the Mind also were of the same character, no contact between the two would be possible; as between two omnipresent things either there can be no contact, or the two must be one and inseparable. Hence it follows that the Mind is atomic in its dimension. And as it exists, and yet has no cause, it is eternal; it is extremely mobile, as is proved by the very swift contacts formed by it, at the time that we have one perception following another in quick succession, which must be due to the Mind coming into contact with one perceptive organ after the other. Unless aided by the Mind, no organ can apprehend its object; as is found in the case of the absent-minded man who fails to see things even before his eyes. The contact of the Mind with the conscious

Soul is due to the endless series of virtues and vices—effects of the past deeds of that Soul.

7. Thus then, the Soul is *the experiencer* or enjoyer, the Body *the abode of experiences*, the Sense-organs *the instruments of experience*; and the *Objects of experience* are of two kinds—*Internal*, in the shape of pleasure, pain, &c., and *External*, in the shape of the Earth and the rest; and *Experience* consists in cognition or consciousness. It is in these five that all truth is centred; there is nothing that exists that does not fall within one or other of these.

8. The Soul as *Cogniser* is never cognised apart from the cognised object; nor is the Object ever cognised without the *Cogniser* entering into the Cognition as a necessary factor. It is what has already been explained above as 'Triune Cognition' under 'Perception.' From this it follows that the Soul is cognised by the same means of Valid Cognition as the objects themselves. Even though in this manner, the Soul would be that upon which the operation of cognising would come to bear, it is not the *objective* but the *nominative* agent of that operation; just as even though the person who walks has the operation of walking bearing upon him, he is regarded as the Nominative agent of the walking, and not its objective; specially as a true *objective* is that upon which bears the operation of something other then itself; which is not the case with the Soul, upon which its own action of cognising bears. Thus then, according to Prabhākara, the Soul is not *self-illumined*; he could not regard it so, as he draws a distinction between Cognition and the Soul, both of which are regarded as identical, by the Vedāntin, who alone regards the Soul as self-illumined; according to Prabhākara it is Cognition alone that is so; and as the Soul is something different from cognition, it cannot be so. This is plainly stated in the *Prakaraṇapañchikā* (p. 51). The Soul then is that which is the substratum of the self-illumined cognition, in which it

also enters as the cognitive element of 'I', which is inseparable from all cognitions. The cognition of the Soul being obtainable only along with the cognition of some other things, it is only natural that during sleep, when no things are actually cognised, there should be no cognition of the Self. During the 'fourth' or highest stage of consciousness, however, the Soul is present, merely as *something existing*, a pure *esse* subsisting as the substratum of the collective cognition of all things taken together.

9. While putting forward the above view with regard to the Cognition of the Soul, the *Prābhākara* rejects the other two theories,—(1) the hypothesis of the Logician that the Soul is *perceived by the mind*; this view is rejected on the ground that under this hypothesis the Soul would become the *perceiver* as well as the *perceived*, which is absurd; this absurdity the *Prābhākara* has tried to explain away in his own case, as shown in the preceding paragraph; but the real ground for rejecting the Logician's view appears to lie in the fact that, so long as the Cognition of the Soul can be explained either by self-luminosity, or by making it a part and parcel of the cognition of all things, there can be no justification for postulating an independent mental perception for the Soul; (2) the second hypothesis rejected is that of the Vedāntin, according to whom the Soul is self-illumined; this view may be thus briefly stated :—

" *Illumination* is the purpose served by all means of knowledge; as such, these are necessary only in the case of the cognition of such things as are by themselves devoid of inherent luminosity; the Soul however is by its very nature illumined; and as such does not stand in need of any other means of knowledge; the ordinary object of cognition cannot be regarded as self-luminous, because in that case every object would be always cognised and cognisable; hence we could not account for sleep and such other apparently unconscious states of the Soul; during which states the cognition is not manifested, because it does not exist at the time; during final Release also, the self-luminosity of the Soul does not cease; as if it did, then, there being nothing present in consciousness during final release, this would not be something desirable."

This Vedānṭa view is rejected by Prabhākara on the following grounds:—If the Soul were self-illumined, it would be present in consciousness during the state of Deep Sleep also, just as during the waking, dreaming and fourth states; as that which belongs to a thing by its very nature can never be set aside from it; and as self-luminousness would belong to the Soul by its very nature (according to the Vedānṭin), it could never cease, in whatever state the Soul might be. And further, so long as we can explain all our consciousness under the hypothesis of the self-luminosity of *cognitions*, there is no reason why anything else should be regarded as self-luminous. That the Soul is not the same as the Cognition has already been shown above.

10. According to Kumārila also, the Soul is different from the body, and eternal (*Shlokavārṭika*, Āṭmavāḍa, 7 and 147); and omnipresent (Ibid. 20, and also *Ṭanṭravārṭika*, Translation, p. 516). But he holds the Soul to be either the *substratum* (*Shlokavārṭika*, Āṭmavāḍa, 110) or the *object* (Ibid. 126) of the notion of 'I' (*Shāsṭradīpikā*, p. 100), which enters into all acts of cognition; while according to Prabhākara, the Soul is that *notion of 'I'* itself (*see* above, § 8). Kumārila holds that the Soul is not self-luminous, but known by mental perception (*Shāsṭradīpikā*, p. 101), which latter fact Prabhākara denies. Kumārila again, with the Vedān, in regards the Soul to be of the nature of pure Consciousness (*Shlokāvarṭika*, Āṭmavāḍa 73, and *Ṭanṭrāvārṭika*, Translation, p. 516), while according to Prabhākara, consciousness is only a quality of the Soul. Unlike the Vedānṭin however, Kumārila holds the Soul to be many, but indivisible, being eternal and

omnipresent (*Ṭanṭravārṭika*, Translation, p. 521 and *Shāsṭraḍīpikā* p. 102).

11. According to Prabhākara, the Soul, in its liberated state, continues to exist as a mere *esse*, '*saṭ*'. What proof is there, it is asked, for the assertion that the Soul continues to exist as an *esse*, free from, and beyond, all perceptible things? The answer to this is that it is an universally recognised fact that anything that exists, without having been brought into existence by a cause, is imperishable; as is the case with *Ākāsha* for instance; it is also admitted that the Soul exists, as also that it is not brought into existence by any cause; hence it must follow that the Soul is imperishable.

The Soul again is omnipresent, like the *Ākāsha*; but its properties—pleasure, pain, &c.—cannot manifest themselves anywhere except in a body; as the manifestation of the properties of the Soul can be brought about only by the contact of the Soul with the Mind, and the Mind cannot subsist apart from the body. This omnipresence of the Soul obviates the necessity of postulating *movement* for it. Nor is the Soul perceptible anywhere else except in a body; as by itself, it is beyond the reach of the senses; hence its imperceptibility is not incompatible with the fact that the dimension of the Soul is the *largest*,—which is only another name for omnipresence; and Prabhākara, on this account, denies that the Soul is of the size of the atom ,or of that of the body it ensouls. Even though the Soul is omnipresent, it cannot experience what is going on in another body; because all *experiencing* needs certain bodies and organs, the nature of which depends upon the past *karma* of the experiencer; hence a particular Soul can experience only that which goes on in the body equipped with the organs brought about by the past *karma* of that Soul.

12. This leads to the question as to whether the Soul is one and the same in all beings as held by the Veḍānṭin, or

one distinct in each body, as held by the Logician and the Sāṅkhya. Prabhākara, as also Kumārila, favours the latter view; and that for the following reasons:—

(*a*) In the case of other bodies, we infer the presence therein of the Soul, only from certain activities manifesting therein, not accountable without the presence of the Soul; howsoever deeply we ponder over it, we feel it to be not the same soul as our own, but something that is always known as the *not-my-soul*, for the person who has inferred its presence in the other body; in fact it is always known as *another* Soul; what we feel is that, just as the activities of my body are due to the effort *of my* Soul, which ensouls *my* body, so the activities of that other body are due to the effort of *another* soul, which ensouls that body; we never look upon the activities of another person as due to our own effort.

(*b*) We always find a distinct difference between the *Ḍharma-Aḍharma* and the consequent Pleasure-Pain of different persons. All these are qualities of the Soul; consequently if the Soul were one only, the same in all persons, its qualities also would be the same in all bodies ensouled by it; and thus the *Ḍharma*, *&c.*, of one person would be the same as those of another person; and the resultant experiences of the two would also be the same; that is, when one person would be happy, the other also would be happy, and so on. Nor would it be right to bring forward against this reasoning the fact of the localisation of pain, wherein, even though pain is felt by the Soul ensouling the *whole* body, it is actually felt as localised in only a particular part of the body—*e. g.*, the leg, the arm, and so forth. Because as a matter of fact, in all cases the *pain* is felt by the Soul only; and it subsists also as a quality in the Soul only; and is is only what causes the pain,—*e. g.*, heat or cold—that is present in the part of the body, where the pain is localised. As regards the *Veḍānṭin's* conception that—'just as the sun, though one only, yet, when reflected in different substances, becomes endowed with distinct properties, so the Soul also, though one only, yet as ensouling different bodies, becomes endowed with diverse qualities',—it has to be observed that the analogy in this case is not quite correct; as in the case of the Sun, the qualities that appear different are only those that belong to the reflecting medium and not to the Sun which is reflected; and so if the analogy were true, the diverse qualities appearing in connection with the Souls would also belong to the bodies ensouled, and not to the Soul; while as a matter of fact, it cannot be denied that pleasure, pain, &c., are qualities of the Soul, and not of the body, or of any other accidental adjuncts of the Soul.

SECTION (3)—SUB-SECTION (2).

Mokṣa—LIBERATION

1. The *Liberation* of the Soul, according to Prabhākara, consists in the disappearance of all *ḍharma* and *aḍhārma*. It is on account of the *ḍharma* and *aḍharma* accruing to the Soul that it is born in various bodies; consequently when there is an entire disappearance of all *ḍharma* and *aḍharma*, there remains nothing that could lead the Soul to be born again into any body; and when the Soul ceases to have any connection with bodies,—and also with the organs, &c.,—all his metempsychic troubles are ended, and he is *free*. As to how all this comes about, the following explanation is given:—(1) First of all, the man becomes disgusted with the troubles that he has to undergo during mundane existence;—(2) finding the pleasures of the world also to be invariably accompanied by some sort of pain, he comes to lose all interest in, and longing for, pleasures also;—(3) he turns his attention towards Liberation;—(4) he ceases to perform such deeds as are prohibited and which lead to trouble, as also from those that are prescribed only as leading to some sort of happiness here or hereafter;—(5) he attenuates all

previously accrued *ḍharma* and *aḍharma* by undergoing the experiences resulting from them;—(6) he destroys the sole receptacle or abode of his experiences by the *knowledge of the Soul*, along with such auxilliaries as contentment, self-control, and so forth,—all of which are laid down in the Scriptures as tending to put a stop to the further return of that Soul into the world;—and it is only when all this has come about that the Soul is *free*. The Vedic texts speaking of the 'non-return to this world' cannot be regarded as mere *Arṭhavāḍa*; because the *knowledge of the Soul* not being laid down as subservient to anything else, the result spoken of must be regarded as a qualification for the man entitled to that knowledge.

2. There does not appear to be much difference on this important point between Kumārila and Prabhākara; The *Bhātta* view of Liberation we find stated in the *Shloka-vārṭika*, chapter on *Sambanḍhākṣepaparihāra*, *Shlokas* 108-110, in the following words—

'For those that have realised the real character of the Soul, all their past *Karma* having been exhausted by experience, and there being no further Karmic residua to wipe off,—there is no further body; as the Soul is burdened with a body only for the experiencing of the results of *Karma*;—therefore, one desiring Liberation should not engage in such actions as are either prohibited, or are enjoined with a view to material results; but he should continue to perform those that are prescribed as *necessary duties*, in order to avoid the sin of the neglect of such duties.'

The *Nyāyaraṭnākara* and the *Kāshikā* on Shl. 106, go on to add that—'Liberation must consist in the destruction of the present body, and the non-production of any further body.' And in the *Prakaraṇapañchikā* we find the *Prābhākara* view briefly stated that—'Liberation is the absolute cessation of the body, caused by the disappearance of all *ḍharma* and *aḍharma*,'—and 'not by Knowledge'

ledge' (adds Kumārila, *Shlo. Vā.*, *Sambandhākṣepaparihāra*, Shl. 103). Both are also agreed as to the negative character of Liberation, as otherwise it could not be eternal (*Shlo. Vā*, 105-107) They are also agreed as to Liberation not being a mere *cessation of pain* (as there being no body, the Soul is free, not only from pain, but from pleasure also); or a mere blissful state (as without the body, the Soul can have no experience, and *bliss* is only a kind of experience). [See *Pra-pañ.* p. 153, and *Shlo-Vār. Sambandhākṣepaparihāra* 105].

SECTION (3)—SUB-SECTION (3).

God.

1. The *Prābhākara* denies a creator for the Universe. Even though he admits that the Universe is made of constituent parts, and as such it must have a beginning and an end in time,—yet he finds no reason for believing that the Universe, as a whole, had a beginning at any one point of time, or that it would all come to an end at any one point; hence if the constituent factors of the Universe have a beginning, they must have beginnings one after the other, and they must also cease one after the other; in fact this is what is actually found to be the case in every-day experience. Thus then, if it were true that certain factors of the Universe are brought into existence by an ultra-mundane Supervisor of *Ḍharma-Aḍharma*, this could not be true for the entire Universe, as a whole. For instance, the bodies of all men and animals are found to be produced by the functioning of the parents, and not by a supervening agency; and this fact will enable us to infer the same with regard to the bodies of all animals, past and future also. *

Nor is there any force in the Logician's argument that our *Ḍharma-Aḍharma* must have for a supervisor a being

* The Prābhākara view is set forth in great detail in the *Prak-Pañ.* p. 137, &c.

possessed of intelligence higher than our own. Because the *Ḍharma-Aḍharma* of the body that is the product of these must always belong to the same intelligent being to whom the body belongs; any being, howsoever intelligent, can never have any knowledge of the *Ḍharma-Aḍharma* of any other being; hence the ultra-mundane 'God' can have no knowledge of the *Ḍharma* or *Aḍharma* of the beings born as men, animals, &c.; and without such knowledge he could not exercise any intelligent control over them; 'God' could not perceive *Ḍharma* by his senses, as *Ḍharma* is absolutely imperceptible; nor could he perceive it by his mind alone, as the mind by itself can not perceive things outside the body, and the *Ḍharma* of all beings born in the world would always be outside the body occupied by the mind of he perceiving person, 'God.'

Then again, it becomes necessary to examine the character of the 'supervision' that 'God' is said to exercise over *Ḍharma* and *Aḍharma*. (*a*) This 'supervision' cannot be of the nature of *contact* or *conjunction*; because *Ḍharma* and *Aḍharma* being *qualities* are not capable of conjunction, which is possible for *substances* only. (*b*) Nor could it be in the form of *Samavāga* or *inherence*; as the *Ḍharma-Aḍharma* inhering in other Souls could not inhere in the 'God.' And as these two are the only possible alternative forms of relation, no other kind of 'supervision' is possible. In the case of ordinary agents,—the carpenter, for instance,—the 'supervision' consists in their contact with the tools and implements; and this is not found to be possible in the case of 'God.' Nor is it possible for the operations of 'God' to have any effect upon *Ḍharma-Aḍharma*; because, being qualities, they could not have any actions bearing upon them. Nor can the action bringing about the creation be held to lie in the atoms, which operate under the Will of 'God; because in all our experience, we never come across any such 'supervision' or 'guidance'; as all 'supervision' or 'guidance' is found to be done by the Soul over that body which it ensouls by virtue of its *Ḍharma* and *Aḍharma*; and the atoms can not be said to be such a body of 'God'; hence he could not guide the activity of these. Even if we grant such a 'body' for 'God,' the activity of the body could not be due to mere *wish*; it must be due to an *effort* put forth by him. Nor could the *wish* be eternal, as, in that case, the activity of the atoms also would be eternal, which would lead to the absurdity of an *unceasing* creation.

2. The argument that the Logician puts forward in proof of his 'God' is that, "The body must have a supervisor, because it is non-intelligent." To this his opponent opposes the counter-argument that God cannot be the Supervisor, because he cannot have any motive in doing so; we cannot deny the truth of the proposition that there is intelligent supervision only in cases where some purpose of the supervisor is served by it. Then again, the same argument that would prove the existence of the intelligent supervisor wonld also prove that supervisor to be a bodied or corporeal being; as the Logician bases his argument upon the analogy of the carpenter supervising and guiding the making of wooden articles; and as this carpenter is a *bodied* being, the analogy, extended a little farther would prove this supervising 'God' also to be a bodied being; but at the same time we know that no bodied being can exercise any intelligent control over such subtle things as the *atoms*, *Ḍharma* and *Aḍharma*. Even if he did, he would himself, as a bodied being, have to be the creation of another Creator or Supervisor, and so on, *ad infinitum*. Thus then no supervision of the creation of the Universe being possible it has to be regarded as a never-ending process of things coming into existence and passing out of it, under the influence of the *Ḍharma* and *Aḍharma* of the Souls ensouling

the bodies coming into touch with those things; and there is thus no room for the assumption of an ultra-cosmic 'God.'

3. Kumarila's views in regard to 'God' are found in the *Shlokavāṭrtika*, 'Sambanḍhākṣepaparihāra'. He also denies the *creation* (*shloka* 47) and *dissolution* (68) of the Universe as a whole (113); he bases his denial of the creator on the same grounds as that of the 'omniscient person.' (47-59; 114-16).

SECTION (4).

Paḍārṭhas—THINGS OF THE WORLD.

1. According to Prahākara the external world is real; the stock argument of the Idealist—'Cognitions have no real counterpart in the external world,—because they are cognitions,—like dreams'—being rejected; (1) on the ground of its being contrary to all experience; and (2) by showing that dreams also are not absolutely devoid of real counterparts in the external world (*see* above, Sec. 1).

2. As regards the constituents of the Universe—called '*paḍārṭhas*' or '*categories*'—we have not been able to find in any Prābhākara work, a systematic statement of what these are, according to Prabhākara. We believe such a isystematic statement is contained in the '*Prameyapārāyaṇa*' mentioned in the *Prakaraṇapañchikā*, on pp. 110-11; from its name it appears to be a chapter of this latter work, following closely upon the chapter on '*pramāṇas*' called the '*Pramāṇapārāyaṇa*.' In the printed edition of the work however we do not find any such chapter; nor is it found in the portion wanting in the printed text,—manuscripts of which have just come to hand from Travancore. So our information on this point depends upon stray declarations in the *Prakaraṇapañchikā*, and upon a comparatively recent work, called the '*Sarvasiḍḍhānṭarahasya*' From this latter work we glean the following:—The '*paḍārṭhas*,' according to *Prabhākara*, are—(1) *Ḍravya* or Substance, (2) *Guṇa* or Quality, (3) *Karman* or Action, (4) *Sāmānya* or Generality, (5) *Paraṭanṭraṭā* (Subsistence or

Inherence), (6) *Shakṭi* or Force, (7) *Sādṛishya* or Similarity, and (8) *Saṇkhyā* or Number. 'Action' is inferred from the separation of a thing from one point in space and its conjunction with another point. 'Subsistence' or 'Inherence' is not *niṭya* or *eternal* (like the '*Samavāya*' of the Logician); because it subsists in perishable things also, being a relation whereof it cannot be eternal; it is both *produced* and *not-produced*, and also *perceptible* and *imperceptible*, in accordance with the nature of things to which it belongs. Nor is it *one* (like the Logician's '*Samavāya*); it is as many as there are things. '*Shakṭi*' or 'Force' is the common name given to that by virtue of which, Substances, Qualities, Actions, and Generalities come to be regarded as the 'Cause' of things; it is to be inferred from the effects; it is eternal in eternal things, and non-eternal in perishable things. 'Similarity' [and 'Number' also], like Force, cannot come under any other category and so have to be regarded as distinct categories. The '*Vishesa*' of the Logician cannot be a 'category', because the *differentiation* among eternal things like the *ākāsha* and the various kinds of atom—for the purposes of which the Logician posits the *Vishesa*—can always be done on the basis of the ordinary qualities of such things. '*Abhāva*' also is nothing apart from the point in space where it is supposed to exist. The mention of 'number' in this connection appears to be wrong; as on p. 54, the Prak-Pañ. speaks of 'number' as a 'quality.'

We shall now see what we can gatner direct from the '*Prābhākara*' books. The *Prakaraṇapañchīkā*, on page 110, prefaces the proving of 'Similarity' as a distinct category, with the statement that it cannot come under any of the six categories of 'Substance,' 'Quality,' 'Action,' 'Generality,' 'Inherence' and '*Vishesa*'; but with regard to the last—'*Vishesa*', it says (on the same page) that '*Vishesākhyaniu padārṭham pramāṇavāḍino nānumanyanṭe*' ('People learned in the science of reasoning do not accept any such category as *vishesa'*). So herein we have the authority of a *Prābhākara* work as regards the first five of the eight categories mentioned above. On the same page, the *Prakaraṇa-pañchikā* proceeds to give the following account of 'Similarity,—

'What is *similarity*? It is neither Substance, nor Quality, nor Generality, nor Inherence; it is something entirely different from these; as is proved by the fact that it enters into our consciousness exactly in the same manner as any other category; and our consciousness is the sole criterion as to the existence of categories,—that of which we are conscious as a *category* we regard as such. It cannot be Substance, because it subsists in Qualities and Acticn also (which no Substance can do); as we speak of *similar colours, similar motions*, and so forth. It cannot be Generality, as it does not form the basis of any comprehensive conception [says the *Brihatī* p. 8 *b*]. Inherence is a kind of relation, and as such cannot include *Similarity*. Lastly, as regards the *Vishesa* of the Logician, it is not a distinct category, being nothing more or less than the quality of *Separateness*; just as anordinary quality *separates* or differentiates between ordinary things, so the *Vishesa* of the Logician differentiates atoms; virtually the two are precisely the same; in any case, this *Vishesa* is something quite contrary to *Similarity*. For these reasons, *Similarity* must be regarded as a distinct category by itself; and as subsisting in perceptible objects it is apprehended by the apprehension of the qualities, actions and constituent parts as common to two or more things.'

The *Bhātta** does not accept *Similarity* as a distinct category; his chief objection being that, if it were a category, we could not account for the varying degrees of similarity that we are cognisaut of, in our ordinary experience.

As regards *Shakti* or *Force* we learn from the *Prakāraṇapañchikā* (pp. 81-82) that, as a matter of fact, all things in the

* *Shāstradīpikā*, p. 52.

world are found to be possessed of some sort of *shakṭi*; we cannot *perceive* it, but it can be inferred: For instance, we see the fire producing a certain effect, in the shape of burning; but the same fire, when under the influence of certain *manṭras*, fails to produce that effect; there is nothing in the visible form of the fire itself that can account for this phenomenon, the form of the fire remaining exactly the same in both cases. This leads us to the conclusion that there must be something in the fire by virtue of which it can burn, and in the absence whereof it cannot burn; from this it follows that in all things there is something which enables them to bring about their effects, and being deprived of which they are not able to do so. To this imperceptible something, *Prabhākara* gives the name of '*Shakṭi*' or Force.' In eternal things, it is eternal, and in transient things it is brought into existence along with them. It differs from '*Samskāra*' in that this latter is transient in eternal things also.

'*Karman*' or 'Action is also one of the *imperceptible* categories. When a thing moves, what we actually see is not the *moving* of the thing, but only the various conjunctions and disjunctions of the things with certain points in space; the expression 'the thing moves' also refers to these conjunctions and disjunctions, which latter cannot be regarded as the 'Action' of *moving*; because the action of moving subsists in the moving thing, while the conjunctions and disjunctions subsist in outside space; and as it is only these latter that we actually perceive, Action cannot be held to be *perceptible*, as maintained by Kaṇāḍa; it is always to be *inferred* says the *Prakaraṇapañchikā* (pp. 78-79). The above view is not in agreement with the *Bhātta* view; says the *Shāsṭradīpikā* (p. 50):—

"Action can never be inferred; as it could be inferred only as the immaterial cause of the conjunctions and disjunctions of the thing with points in space; and as such it would have to be ognised as subsisting in the thing as well as in space; this is not the case; as it is cognised in the *thing* only. Action must be regarded as being *perceived*; we see the thing undergoing certain conjunctions and disjunctions with points in space; but the cognition that we have is that what brings about these conjunctions and disjunctions is in the thing, and not in space; and that which forms the basis of this cognition is called the 'action' of the thing."

Inberence, says the *Prakaraṇapañchikā* (pp. 26-27) cannct be regarded as everlasting; because as a matter of fact we find that the inherence of the class and character in an individual belonging to that class is produced, and also perishes, along with that individual. The *Bhātta* view of '*Samavāya*' is that, as subsisting between inseparable things, it cannot be anything distinct from these things themselves; it must be regarded as a particular phase of the things themselves, among whom it is believed by the Logician to subsist. (See *Shlokavārṭika*, Sū. 4, Shl. 146-50).

3. As regards 'Substance' we find the *four*—(1) Earth, (2) Water, (3) Air, (4) Fire—mentioned in the *Prakaraṇapañchikā* (p. 24); where also we find the '*gaganādayaḥ*' mentioned; so (5) '*gagana*' or '*ākāshā* would be the *fifth* substance; (6) '*Āṭman*' is admitted as a substance in the section dealing with '*Āṭman*' (the chapter of *Prakaraṇapañchikā* called '*Ṭaṭṭvālokā*), where we also find '*Manas*' (7) mentioned (p. 149), as something whose contact with the *Āṭman* brings about *Buḍḍhi, Sukha, Ḍuḥkha,* and such other specific qualities of the *Āṭman*; then again, on page 84, we find the eternal substances enumerated, wherein, apart from the *atoms*, the *Ākāsha* and the *Āṭman*, we also find—(8) *Kāla* or Time, and (9) *Ḍik* or Space. *Ṭamas* is not a quality: nor is it a substance; it is nothing apart from *absence of light* (*Prakaraṇapañchikā* pp. 143-45). Earth, Water, Air, and Fire are

perceptible by the Eye and also by Touch. *Ākāsha* and the rest cannot be regarded as *perceptible*, because they can not be seen or touched. (*Pra-pañ*. p. 24); *Ākāsha* cannot be seen by the eye, because it is devoid of colour; if it had colour it would also be tangible; as colour and tangibility always go together; the whiteness that appears in the *Ākāsha* belongs to the particles of fire hanging in the atmosphere; and the darkness noticed at night is not the quality of anything, it is mere absence of light; if it were a positive quality it would be perceptible during the day also. (*Pra-pañ*. pp. 143-44). In this connection it may be noted that, inasmuch as *Ākāsha* is imperceptible, Prabhākara does not accept the view that it is one of the five constituent factors of the *body*. Though *Ākāsha* cannot be *perceived*, it can be *inferred* as the substratum of sound: Sound cannot belong to the source from which it proceeds; as the organ of hearing can appreheud only where it can reach, and as a matter of fact, it can never reach or approach the source of sounds. (*Pra-Pañ*. p. 145).

The touch of Air is *neither-hot-nor-cold*; its apparent *coolness* being due to the water-particles hanging in the Air and the *hotness* to the fire-particles floating with it. (*Pra.-pañ*. pp. 77-78).

4. Among Qualities, Colour, Taste, Smell, Touch, Number, Dimension, Separateness, Conjunction, Disjunction, Priority, Posteriority, Pleasure, Pain, Desire, Aversion and Effort are *perceptible*.

Conjunction is of three kinds:—(1) Due to both the things concerned, (2) due to the action of one of the two, and (3) due to another conjunction. (*Pra-pañ*. p. 26 and 151).

5. The *Sarvasiḍḍhānṭarahasya* has the following with regard to the *Bhātta* view of the Categories:—All categories are divided into (1) *Bhāva* or Positive and (2) *Abhāva* or Negative; the latter is of four kinds—(*a*) Prior Negation, (*b*) Utter Destruction, (*c*) Absolute Negation, and (*d*) Mutual

Negation. Of *Bhāvas* there are four—(*a*) Substance, (*b*) Quality, Action and Generality. Of substances there are eleven,—Earth, Water, Light, or Fire, Air, *Ākāsha*, Space, Time, *Ātman* Mind, Darkness and Sound (some people adding *Gold* as the twelfth). Of qualities there are thirteen,—Colour, Taste, Smell, Touch, Dimension, Separateness, Conjunction, Disjunction, Priority, Posteriority, Gravity, Fluidity and Viscidity. There are five actions—*Throwing upwards* and the rest ; two 'generalities'—Higher and Lower. *Shakṭi* and *Sādṛishya* are all included under 'Substance ;' of *Shakṭi* there are two kinds —*sahaja* or inborn, and *ādheya* or *produced* and *borrowed*.

6. The word '*Svārga*' or 'Heaven' is applied to that happiness which is totally free from all touch of pain, and which, as such, is desired by all men (*Pra-pañ*, pp. 102-3). *Sukha* or Pleasure is not mere absence of pain. In the absence of pain what we experience is that there is no pain, the feeling being a negative one ; and hence, from the very nature of the Cognition of Negation (as shown above) it follows that what we are conscious of in this case is only the *Soul* by itself, *as without pain*,—and not as with some positive quality ; on the other hand, when we feel pleasure, we are conscious of something positive, a positive quality as belonging to the Self,—or, more properly, the Self as endowed with a positive quality. (*Pra-pañ*. p. 149).

7. We have reserved the consideration of '*Jāṭi*' or 'Generality' for this last section, because on this matter we have a very full explanation available in the *Prakaraṇapañchikā* (pp. 17-32).

There is a difference of opinion among philosophers, as regards the exact character of *Jāṭi* :—(1) According to some the notion of the '*Jāṭi*' is purely imaginary ; (2) according to others, it has a real existence, but not apart from the individuals in which it subsists, and as such is cognised along with these ; (3) others again hold that it has a real existence, apart from the individuals comprising it, and its existence can be apprehended only by inference; (4) lastly, according to some it is different, as well as non-different, from the individuals comprising it.

According to Prabhākara, the '*Jāṭi*' is something real, distinct from the individuals which are its substrates, and is perceptible by the senses. Says the *Kārikā* —'*Jāṭirāshrayaṭo bhinnā, praṭyakṣajñānagocharā*'. When we properly analyse the notion of '*Jāṭi,*' we find that the only basis that we have for accepting any such thing lies in our conception of some form of *non-difference* among a number of things which, hitherto, have been known as different. Says the *Prakaraṇapañchikā*—'*Bheḍagrahaṇapurassaramabheḍajñānam bhinneṣu jāṭyabhyupagame sharaṇam.*'

3. According to Kumārila, the *Jāṭi* is not something different from the component individuals (*Shlokavārṭika*, 'Ākriṭi' 52-62, and also 'Vanavāḍa,' 75-76); and the distinct ideas of the 'individual' and the 'class' that we come across in ordinary experience, are thus explained :—

'In perceiving an object, when we cognise the '*Jāṭi*' as identical with the individual, what presents itself to consciousness is the individual only,—the '*jāṭi*' or class-character lying latent in it, and helping its existence; when, on the other hand, we cognise the individual as identical with the *jāṭi*, it is the class-character that is present in consciousness, and the individual character continues to lie latent.' (Ibid. '*Ākriṭi*,' 59-62).

Kumārila agrees with Prabhākara in regarding '*Jāṭi* as something perceived by the senses—'*Jāṭirindriyagocharā*' (*Vanavāḍa*, 24).

4. All the main objections against *Jāṭi* are based upon the denial of the possibility of any aggregation of constituent parts; the '*Jāṭi*' is only an aggregate of the individua composing it; hence those individuals bear to the *Jāṭi* the same relation that is borne by the constituent particles of a

substance to the substance itself; consequently if one admits of the fact that substances are made up of constituent particles, the whole ground is cut off from under the theory that denies all '*Jāṭi*'; if you accept aggregation in one case, you can have no reason for denying it in the other.

We shall review, in brief, the objections that are brought —chiefly by the Idealist—against all 'aggregates' in general. With a view to make his position unassailable, the Idealist begins with the denial of any such thing as 'Substance'; and it is the substance that is regarded as the substrate of the '*jāṭi*.' Such a generic 'substance' could be either in the form of the subtile 'atom', or in that of the gross product of atoms; as regards the former alternative, no such '*jāṭi*' as 'atom' is possible; because such a *generic* entity is made to rest upon the comprehensive conception that we form of a number of things as 'one'; and as a matter of fact, we find that we have no all-comprehensive conception with regard to the four primitive atoms of the Earth, the Water, the Air and the Fire; and under the circumstances, how could there be any such generic name as 'Atom'? Then as regards the conception of 'atom' that we find persisting in regard to all atoms,—this can be explained on the basis of the *atomic* dimension possessed in common by all atoms. In the same manner the generic conception of 'Earth' is based upon the common property of *smell*; and so on with 'Water' and the rest.—Nor in the second place can there be any gross substance as the substrate of '*jāṭi*'; for the simple reason that there is no proof for the existence of any such substance; all such substances are held to be the products of the conglomeration of atoms; but as a matter of fact, no such conglomeration is possible; as there can be no *Conjunction* amoug atoms, which are, *ex hypothesi*, devoid of extension, and hence of parts. Nor can it be ascertained whether the gross *whole* resides in its entirety in each of its component parts, or only in all of these latter collectively; as the former alternative is, on the very face of it, absurd ; in the latter alternative also, no perception of the *whole* would be possible until *all* its parts had been perceived (which latter contingency is seldom possible). Then as regards the conception of the 'gross' object common among all men, it may be explained in the following manner :—Certain atoms continuing to appear one after the other, become, after a certain number have appeared, perceptible by the senses ; and we, who were unable to perceive them before, on coming to perceive them, are led to attribute this phenomenon to the fact of the atoms having formed themselves into a conglomerate *whole* ; this notion of the *whole* however is a pure fancy ; as what is actually before us is only a number of atoms, each one imperceptible by itself, but perceptible when appearing in the company of one another. Thus then, inasmuch as the 'atom' cannot be the substrate of the '*jāṭi*', and there is no *gross* subtance apart from the *atom*, we are led to the conclusion that there can be no such thing as '*Jāṭi*.' Then again, the '*Jāṭi*' cannot be perceived by the senses, as it is held to be by Prabhākara ; because being eternal, it could not be perceptible, as otherwise it would be liable to unceasing perception, which is an absurdity. Then again,—does the '*Jāṭi*' come into existence, and cease to exist, along with the individuals comprising it ? If so, then it would be something totally distinct from each of these individuals, and would therefore lose its essential character Then, if it is eternal, it must exist before the individual is brought into existence ; and yet if it is held to come into existence along with the individual, it cannot subsist before this latter. The '*Jāṭi*' again cannot be either different or non-different from the individuals. It cannot be non-different as in that case, it would have to appear and disappear with the Individuals, which involves the aforesaid absurdity. If then, it were different from them, it would be cognisable independently, and apart from them—another absurdity. The question put in conuection with the *gross* object is put in connection with the '*jāṭi*' also. Does the '*jāṭi*' subsist in its entirety in each individual, or in all individuals collectively? If the former, then there are as many '*jāṭis*' as there are individuals. If the latter, the '*jāṭi*' cannot be cognised until *all* the individuals composing it have been cognised; as this is never possible, no cognition of the '*jāṭi*' would be possible. For the above reasons it is concluded that any such thing as '*jāṭi*' has no real existence; nor are there any 'substances' which could be the substrate of '*jāṭi.*'

5. In answer to the above, the *Prābhākara* argues that the proof for the existence of anything must ultimately rest in our own consciousness; and it cannot be denied that there are present, in our consciousness, distinct coguitions of the *gross* forms of things; and what is thus distinctly cognised cannot reasonably have its existence denied. As regards the constitution of the *gross* substance,—the gross object exists as we actually perceive it; that it is made up of subtler constituent particles is implied by its very nature, in fact without this, our very conception of it would be impossible. Such being the indisputable fact, it becomes necessary for us to find out an explanation for the fact of a number of subtler particles combining to make up a *gross* object. The only explanation possible is that a number of particles, on acquiring a conjunction among themselves, tend towards the bringing into existence of a single object, which being perceptible, (while the particles are imperceptible) is called '*gross*,'—a single Conjunction subsisting over all the particles, and that same Conjunction tending to combine the particles into one conglomerate *whole*. Thus then, in the bringing about of the *whole*, the particles are the *material* cause, and their conjunction the *immaterial* cause.

This *whole* subsists over all the particles collectively, and not in each part individually; in this it differs from the '*Jāṭi*' which resides in its entirety in each individual.

constituting that *Jāṭi.* It is not necessary for all the particles to be perceived before the *whole* is perceived; because the *whole* is something different from the parts; and as in every case the 'cause' that we are justified in assuming is only that which is sufficient to account for a certain given effect, for the perception of the *whole* we must regard as the necessary cause the perception of only those parts without which the perception of the whole would not be possible; and as a matter of fact, if only a few of the parts are perceived, this brings about the perception of the *whole.* Then again, the fact of the *whole* being always found together with the *parts* is due to one being the cause of the other; that the *whole* is different from the parts is shown by the fact that the two give rise to entirely different effects in our consciousness; for instance, the *whole* gives rise to the notion of something that is *one* and *large* or *extensive*; while the *parts* produce the notion of things *many* in number and *small.* Thus then, inasmuch as the *whole* is different from the parts, it can be perceived, even when all its parts are not perceived.

These *wholes* are of four kinds—Earth, Water, Fire and Air; the first three being *large* and having colour, are perceptible by the organ of touch, and also by that of vision; Air being devoid of colour is perceptible by touch alone. The atoms of these are by their very nature imperceptible; so also is the compound of *two* atoms; as the *large dimension,* which is a necessary condition in all perceptibility, is present in only such substances as have *many—i. e.,* not less than three—constituent particles. Akāsha, Time and Space, even though *large,* are not perceptible, as they are devoid of touch and colour.

The existence of the *whole* substance having been proved, the existence of '*Jāṭi*' cannot be denied merely on the ground that there can be no *wholes* made up of parts.

6. Though the *Jāṭi* or 'class-character' is eternal, yet when a new individual belonging to that class—*i. e.*, possessing that class-character—comes into existence, what is brought into existence by this appearance of a fresh individual is not the 'class-character,' which is ever present, but only the relation (inherence) of the individual with that class-character. There is nothing objectionablei n the 'production' of 'inherence,' because 'inherence,' according to Prabhākara, is not eternal (as held by the Logician) [*see above*, §2] nor is there anything incongruous in the inherence of the individual being produced before, or along with, the individual itself; because 'Inherence' is not, like 'Conjunction,' dependent upon the previous existence or action of the members between whom it subsists. Similarly when a particular individual ceases to exist, the 'class-character' does not go away elsewhere (because it has no *motion*);—nor does it subsist in that individual (as this has ceased to exist);—nor does it itself cease to exist (as it is found present in other individuals);—but what ceases is the inherence of the 'class-character' with that particular individual; it is only natural that when one member of the relation has ceased to exist, the relation itself should cease with it.

The 'class-character' resides in its entirety in each individual; as is proved by the fact that we recognise the same 'class-character' in every individual. Nor is the 'class character' ever percieved apart from the individual. It is perceptible by the senses; as is shown by the fact that its cognition is brought about by its coming into contact with the organs of perception, through the individual in which it resides, and which is in direct contact with the organs. We cannot deny that when we perceive a thing quite distinctly, we perceive it as having a certain 'class-character.'

While admitting such '*jāṭis*' as *Substance*, *Quality*, &c., Prabhākara does not accept any such *summum genus* as '*Saṭṭā*' or 'Being', as including all that exists; and this for the simple reason that we have to accept such a *jāṭi* as *Substance* because we perceive a number of individual things as having certain characters in common; and on the basis of this conception we postulate the '*jāṭi*' *Substance.* We have, as a matter of fact, no such cognition of a number of things as merely 'existing'; and in the absence of such a conception we can have no basis for the postulating of such a class as 'Being.' Though we have such a word as '*saṭṭā*' (Being), yet that cannot warrant our regarding it as the name of a 'class-character;' as all that the word denotes is the mere *individuality* of things—*Svarūpasaṭṭā*; when we speak of a thing as '*saṭ*', we do not mean that it is possessed of any such 'class-character' as '*saṭṭā*'; what we mean is that it has an individual existence of its own.

Nor does Prabhākara admit of such '*jāṭis*' as *Brāhmaṇaṭva*', '*Kṣaṭṭriyaṭva*' and the like, all of which cannot be perceived by the senses. What is meant by calling a man 'Brāhmaṇa' is not that he belongs to any such *jāṭi*, but only that he is descended from a particular line of ancestors. So says Kumārila also—'*Brāhmaṇaṭvāḍi yoniṭaḥ*' (*Shlokavārṭika*, 'Vanavāḍa', 29); The purity of descent has to be accepted until there is sufficient proof to the contrary (Vide, *Ṭanṭravārṭika*, under I—ii—2).

CHAPTER III.

An Analytical Account of the Mīmāṁsā Shāsṭra.

[*Books consulted* :—

1. The *Mīmāmsā-sūṭras* of Jaimini (Bibliothica Indica).
2. The *Bhāṣya* of Shabara (do.)
3. The *Shlokavārṭika* of Kumārila (Chaukhambha Sanskrit Series, Benares).
4. The *Nyāyaraṭnākara* of Pārṭhasaraṭhi Mishra—a Commentary on (3). (Chaukhambha Sanskrit Series, Benares).
5. The *Kāshikā* of Suchaṛiṭa Mishra—a Commentary on (3). (*Manuscript* with Mahāmahopāḍhyāya P. Chiṭraḍhara Mishra, Darbhanga).
6. The *Ṭanṭravārṭika* of Kumārila (Benares Sanskrit Series).
7. The *Tupṭīkā* do (do).
8. The *Nyayāsuḍhā* by Someshvara—Commentary on (6) (Chaukhambha Sanskrit Series).
9. The *Vārṭikābharaṇa* by Someshvara, Commentary on (7) (*Manuscript* with Mr. Govinḍaḍasa, Benares).
10. The *Shāsṭraḍīpikā* by Pārṭhasāraṭhi Mishra—a Commentary on (1) (' Pandit, ' Benares).
11. The *Ṭanṭraraṭna* by Pārṭhasāraṭhi Mishra—a running Commentary on the last nine chapters of (2). (*Manuscript* with Mr. Govinḍaḍāsa, Benares).
12. The *Mayūkhamālikā* by Somanāṭha—Commentary on (10). *Manuscript* with Mahāmahopāḍhyāya Pandit Chiṭraḍhara Mishra, Darbhanga).
13. The *Nyāyamālā* and *Visṭara* of Māḍhavāchārya (Ānandasram Series).
14. The *Subodhini* Commentary on the Sūṭras (' Pandit,' Benares).

15. The *Mīmāmsānayaviveka* by Bhavanāṭha Mishra—a Commentary on (2), *Manuscript* with Mr. Govinḍaḍāsa, Benares).
16. The *Mīmāmsānukramaṇī* by Maṇdana Mishra—an abstract of (2)—(*Manuscript* with the writer).
17. The English Translations of (3) and (6) by the writer (Bibliothica Indica).
18. The *Mīmāṁsābālaprakāsha* of Shaṅkara Bhatta (Chaukhambhā Sanskrit Series).
19. The *Bṛihaṭī* of Prabhākara Mishra (*Manuscript* with the writer, and also in the Library of the Asiatic Society of Bengal). Adhyāyas I to V, and Adh. VI (pādas 1 and 2).
20. The *Ṛijuvimalā* of Shālikanāṭha Mishra—(*Manuscript* with Writer, at the India Office Library, and at the Travancore Palace Library). Adhyāyas I (incomplete), and III to V.
21. The *Prakaraṇapañchikā* of Shālikanāṭha Mishra (Chaukhambhā Sanskrit Series).
22. The *Bhāṭṭabhāskara* of Jīvadeva (*Manuscript* with Writer).
23. The *Viḍhiviveka* of Maṇdana Mishra ('Pandit').
24. The *Nyāyakaṇikā* of Vachaspaṭi Mishra—Commentary on (23) (' Pandit').
25. The *Nyayaraṭnamālā* of Pārṭhasāraṭhi Mishra (Chaukhambha Sanskrit Series).
26. *Rāmānuja's* Commentary on (25) (*Manuscript*, first half, with Mr. Govinḍa-ḍasa, Benares, and second half at the Bodleian Library, Oxford).
27. The *Mīmāṁsāparibhāṣā* of Kṛiṣṇayajvan (' Pandit ').
28. The *Mīmāmsānyāyaprakāsha* by Ananṭadeva (' Pandit').
29. The *Bhāttālaṅkāra*—Commentary on (28) (MS. with writer).

30. The *Viḍhirasāyana* of Appayya Ḍikṣiṭa (Chau-khambha Sanskrit Series).
31. *Mīmamsāviḍhibhūṣana*—by Gopala Bhatta (MS. with Mr. Govinḍa-ḍasa).
32. The *Arṭhasangraha* of Laugākṣi Bhāskara (Benares Sanskrit Series).
33. The English Translation of (30) by Dr. G. Thibaut (Benares Sanskrit Series).
34. The *Shaṭapaṭha Brāhmaṇa* (Berlin Edition).
35. The *Shrauṭapaḍārṭhanirvachana* ('Pandit').
36. The *Trikāṇḍamaṇḍana* (Bibliothica Indica).

*SECTION I—SUB-SECTION (1).

Veda—its bearing and authority in regard to Ḍharma.

1. The understanding of the true nature of Ḍharma being the avowed aim of the *Mimāmsaka,* he takes care to justify it, at the very outset, by proving that an earnest enquiry into the nature of *Ḍharma* was something that in itself was absolutely necessary for every responsible agent; unless he knows what his Ḍharma or Duty is, how can he regulate his actions? The next question that arises is—why should this enquiry be carried on in the manner in which it has been done by Jaimini and his followers? In this connection, the Mīmāmsaka holds that the Veda is the sole authority for *Ḍharma* (Sū. 2),—the only source from which a right knowledge of *Ḍharma* can be obtained; for this reason the proper study of the Veda becomes necessary. But as this study of the Veda itself would be a *Ḍharma,* this also must have its basis in the Veda; consequently the Mīmāṁsaka makes it his business to show that the proper study of the Veda—for the special purpose of obtaining the knowledge of *Ḍharma*—is something that is laid down in the Veda itself. This forms the subject-matter of the first '*adhikaraṇa*' or 'Topic of Consideration.'

* The 'section' corresponds roughly to the '*Aḍhyāyav*' and 'sub-section' to the 'pāḍa' of the *Mīmāmsā-sūṭras.*

2. Kumārila and his followers take as their basic text, in this connection, the sentence '*svāḍhyāyo' ḍhyēṭavyaḥ*,' 'the Veda should be studied,' and proceed to explain that the '*study of the Veda*' herein laid down cannot be the getting up of the mere *words* of the Veda; but this, and also the due understanding of the *meaning* of the sentences; the getting up of the mere word would serve no useful purpose for the student. And as the meaning of the Vedic directions cannot be comprehended without due investigation and enquiry, an investigation, such as the one initiated by Jaimini becomes necessary.

3. To the above view, Prabhākara and his followers demur. Their objections are briefly these:—By the above reasoning, all persons desiring to understand *Ḍharma*—no matter whether he be a *Ḍvija* or not—would be entitled to the study of the Veda; and this would be against the express injunctions of the Veda. Here, as elsewhere, the 'Prābhākara' view is more orthodox than the 'Bhātta' theory. In order to avoid the said difficulty, the Prābhākara takes for his text the sentence from the Smṛiṭis—'*upanīya ṭu yaḥ shiṣyam veḍamaḍhyāpayeḍ ḍvijaḥ sakalpam sarahasyañcha ṭamāchāryam prachakṣaṭe*,' 'that Brāhmaṇa who, having initiated the pupil, teaches him the Veda along with the ritualistic rules and esoteric explanations,—him they call the *teacher*',—as taken along with the Vedic text '*aṣṭavarṣam brāhmaṇamupanayīṭu*,' 'the Brahmaṇa should be initiated when he is eight years old.' The motive desire towards the enquiry into Ḍharma, in this case, is on the part of the Teacher, and not on that of the pupil (as in the case of the text quoted by Kumārila). The teacher wishes to obtain for himself the title and honours of the true *āchārya* or *teacher*; and as there can be no *teacher* without some one who is taught, he has to *take* (*upa-nī*) a pupil (*shiṣya*); but as the latter cannot be a 'pupil' unless he is made to 'study,' this *studying* by the pupil is implied in the

above texts; and as the 'study' cannot be carried on without the aid of a 'teacher,' the one is implied by the other. This explanation is free from the objection to which the *Bhātta* view is open; as the learned 'Teacher,' who, in his turn, cannot but be a *Ḍvija*, cannot take a *non-dvija* pupil. The injunction of *Vedic study* being thus implied in the injunction of taking a pupil for the purpose of obtaining the title and honours of the 'Teacher,'—it becomes necessary to find out a purpose for this study,—at any rate, so far as the pupil is concerned, for whose action the purpose of the teacher cannot supply the requisite motive. This purpose lies in the due comprehension of the meaning of the Vedic texts studied; and as this is not possible without due reflection and pondering of the texts, the investigation carried on in the *Mimāmsā-shāsṭra* becomes fully justified.*

4. The necessity of the enquiry for the purpose of obtaining knowledge of *Ḍharma* having been established, the question naturally arises—What is the '*Ḍharma*' for the knowing of which we have to carry on all this difficult investigation? This forms the subject of the second *aḍhikaraṇa* comprising the *sūṭrā* I—i-2. The word 'ḍharma' here is not used in the ordinary sense of the *merit* acquired by the perfamance of some good deed; it is used in the much wider sense of such act or acts as are laid down in the Veda as conducive to the happiness of the agent.

5. According to the *Bhātta* view this *aḍhikaraṇa* meets the position that *Ḍharma* is something that cannot be defined; and hence for a knowledge of it there is no valid means available. The answer to this is that we have a good definition of *Ḍharma* in that *it is that which, while being conducive to happiness, is mentioned in the Veda*; and this same also shows that in the Veda we have the valid means of knowing *Ḍharma*. Thus then *Sūṭra* 2 contains three statements;—*viz*: (1) that *Ḍharma* is that which is laid

* See *Prakaraṇapañchikā*, pp. 5-12.

down in the Veda as conducive to happiness; (2) that the Veda is the means of acquiring the right knowledge of *Ḍharma*; and (3) that the Veda is a trustworthy means of knowledge. The *Prābhākara* view on the other hand is that the first *Sūṭra* having declared that, (1) the enquiry into *Ḍharma* is to follow the study of the whole Veda, that (2) the whole Veda is intended to be expressive, and that (3) hence the word '*Ḍharma*' applies to all that is mentioned in the Veda,——the question natually arises—'What do you mean here by *all that is mentioned in the Veda?*' Does it include *all* that we find there,—for instance, also those parts that contain mere *descriptions* of things as they are,—or only those parts that contain *injunctions* of what is to be done? And in regard to this question, the conclusion is that the 'Veda' meant here as to have its meaning studied as providing Knowledge of *Ḍharma* is only that part of it which speaks of *something to be done*; and the reason for this is that, according to the *Anviṭābhiḍhāna* theory (chapter II, §8), we can construe a sentence and find out its meaning only when it contains some sort of an injunction for something to be done. For instance, when we find certain effects in the shape of joy and so forth, produced by a mere statement of facts,—*e. g.* 'a son has been born to you,'——as the effect is one that can be due to a number of causes, we cannot necessarily know that it was due to the news of the birth; but when we see that the boy brings the jar on being ordered to 'bring the jar,'—we at once conclude that the sentence *means* the bringing of the jar. Thus then, we find that the chief point at issue between the '*Bhāṭṭa*' and the '*Prābhākara*' Schools lay in Prabhākara's theory of verbal construction, called the '*Anviṭābhiḍhānavāḍa*' as distinguished from the '*Abhihiṭānvayavāḍa*' of Kumārila and his followers; and though Prabhākara could not have any serious objections against the *Bhāṭṭa* view of the *aḍhīkaraṇa*, yet he has put forward his own interpretation with a view to emphasise, at the very ontset, what forms the keystone of his School of Thought. According to *Bhatta* the word '*Choḍanā*' of Sū. 2 stands for the *Veda*, while according to Prabhākara it stands for *Vedic Injunctions*.*

6. That the Veda affords the means of knowing *Ḍharma* having been proved in *sūṭra* 2, the qnestion arises as to whether or not it is necessary to examine the character of the Veda. The answer as given in *sūṭrā* 3 is that snch an examination is essential, specially for the *Mimāmsā-shāsṭra* which makes it its bnsiness to enquire into all matters relating to *Ḍharma*. According to Prabhākara, the qnestion dealt with in *sūṭrā* 3 is whether it would not be the right order of procednre,—after baving proved the fact of the Veda affording the means of knowing *Ḍharma*,—to ascertain what is contained in the Veda (which is dealt with in *Aḍhyāyas* II, *et. seq.*), rather than proceed with an enquiry as to the validity or the trustworthy character of the Veda. The conclnsion is that, though when it comes to *action*, then certainly what is contained in the Veda, as *to be done*, becomes of prime importance; but when we are carrying on an enquiry into the character of *Ḍharma* and the means of knowing it, our first business is to ascertain how far our avowed sonrce of knowledge is valid and can be relied npon; as it is only then that we can be sure as to what is actually mentioned in the Veda as *to be done*. Another reason for taking np this point first lies in the fact that the validity of a means of knowledge is something inherent in itself, and as such independent of everything else; whereas, whether a certain act is, or is not, laid down by a certain authoritative text depends npon the trustworthy character of that text itself.†

7. Before proceeding to explain the valid means of the knowledge of *Ḍharma*, our authors prove by various arguments that the ordinary means of knowledge—Perception,

* *Bṛihaṭī*, Ms. pp. 3—5; and *Ṛijuvimalā* Ms. pp. 10 and 14.

† *Ṛijuvimalā*, Ms. p. 27.

Inference, Words (in the ordinary sense), Analogy and Presumption—are by their very nature unable to afford a knowledge of *Dharma*. We have already given above (Chapter II) a detailed account of these 'means of knowledge'. The author of the *Sūṭra* takes up in Sū. 4, only Perception, and shows that it pertains only to such things as are in the present, and are in contact with the organs of perception; and from this the natural conclusion is that it cannot afford any knowledge of *Ḍharma*, which is neither a thing of the present, nor one that can ever be in contact with any organ of perception. Inference, Presumption and Analogy are all based, directly or indirectly, upon Perception; and hence these also cannot apply to *Ḍharma*, which is entirely beyond the range of Perception.

8. Having thus, in Sūṭra I—i-4, which also forms the fourth *Aḍhikaraṇa*, shown what is *not* the means of knowing *Ḍharma*, the Mīmāṁsaka proceeds to show, in Sūṭra I-i-5, which also forms the fifth *aḍhikaraṇa*, what *is* such means. Herein it is pointed out that 'Word' is the only means of obtaining valid information on the subject of *Ḍharma*. What is meant by this 'word' and how it brings about the cognition of what it denotes we have already explained (under Chapter II). It would suffice here to state briefly that in regard to all matters not within reach of the organs of perception, 'word' is the infallible source of knowledge, independently of all other agencies. In proving the eternality of the word and what is denoted by it, the Mīmāṁsaka meets the opposition of the Idealist and the Nihilist; for this reason, Shabara, and Prabhākara and Kumārila with him, devote a section to each of these systems, and herein it is proved that the things of the external world have an independent reality of their own. In order to establish the validity of such Vedic texts as speak of agents going to heaven, it also becomes necessary to establish the existence

of the Āṭman or Self, as something apart from the perishing body.

9. In *Aḍhikaraṇa* 6 (*Sūṭras* 6-23), the eternality of 'words' is proved in greater detail; and all objections to the contrary are met. In *Aḍhikaraṇa* 7 (*Sūṭras* 24-26) we have the proof of the capacity of the Veda to afford valid knowledge of *Ḍharma*. *Aḍhikaraṇa* 8 (*Sūṭras* 27-32) proves the fact that the Veda is not the composition of an author, either human or divine. This is a necessary corollary to the eternality of the Veda. Thus the whole of the First Aḍhyāya is taken up in the establishing of the two main propositions propounded in *Sūṭra* 2,—that the Veda is authoritative and trustworthy, and that in the matter of *Ḍharma*, it is the only source of valid knowledge available. On these two points there is a general agreement among all Mīmāmsakas.*

10. The Veda has been defined as 'The collection of Manṭras and Brāhmaṇas'. Of 'Manṭra' no formal definition has been attempted by the earlier writers. Later Sūṭra-writers have however defined it as 'the karaṇa or instrument of offering'; but this definition is too wide; as the substances offered, the various implements used, and such other accessories of the sacrifice, are all as much 'instruments of offering' as the *manṭras*. It is for this reason that the more logical writers on Mīmāṁsā have contented themselves with explaining '*manṭra*' as a name including all those Vedic passages to which the learned men apply that name. (*Mīmāmsā-sūṭra* II—i-38). Says the *Bṛihaṭī* *MS*. p. 50 b.—

'In the Veda some passages are *Manrṭas* and others *Brāhmaṇas*; those to which the learned apply the name 'manṭra' are *manṭras*; while all the rest, to which they also apply the name '*viḍhi*', are *Brāhmaṇas*;—the *Arṭhavāḍas* and the *Nāmaḍheyas* are also included under these latter,—'*Brāhmaṇa*' proper being the name applied to

* *See* Mīmāmsābalāprakāsha, pp. 1-8.

the Injunction, and the *Arṭhavāḍa* and *Nāmaḍheya* passages being included under that name, by reason of their always, in some way or the other, subserving the Injunctions along with which they are construed.

11. The *Brāhmaṇas* or Injunctive Sentences have been divided into five classes:—(1) The *Karmoṭpaṭṭi-vākya*, which enjoins a certain act,—*e. g.* 'one should perform the *Agnihoṭra*,'; (2) the *Guṇavākya* which enjoins certain necessary details connected with a prescribed act, *e.g.* 'one should perform the *homa* with curds'; (3) the *Phalavākya*, which mentions the result following from the performance of a certain act, *e.g.* 'one desirous of attaining heaven should perform the *Agnihoṭra*'; (4) the *Phalāyaguṇavākya*, which lays down a certain accessory detail as conducive to a particular result,—*e.g.* 'one desirous of having efficient sense-organs should perform the *homa* with curds'; and (5) the *Saguṇakarmoṭpaṭṭivākya*, which enjoins an action along with an accessory detail,—*e.g.* 'one should perform the sacrifice with *soma*.'

Another classification of Injunctions is under the following three heads:—(1) the *Apūrvaviḍhi* or *Original Injunction*, which enjoins something not otherwise known, as possible—*e.g.* 'the grains should be washed'; (2) the *Niyamaviḍhi* or *Restrictive Injunction*, which fixes upon a certain method as the one to be adopted in all cases, while in the natural course it would be adopted in a few cases only;—, *e g.* 'the thumping of the corn' insisted upon as the only one method to be adopted for removing the chaff from the grains; and (3) the *Parisaṅkyāviḍhi* or *Preclusive Injunction*, which precludes some from among a number of possible alternatives, —*e.g.* the preclusion of the use of the *Manṭra* '*Imāmagṛibhṇan rashanām*, &c.' in the holding of the reins of the ass. In the *Niyamaviḍhi* that which is enjoined is already *known* as possible, but only as an alternative, and as such it is possible in one case only, and *not possible* in other cases; in the *Apūrva-*

viḍhi what is enjoined is entirely unknown as possible: this is what is meant by the saying – *Viḍhiraṭyanṭamaprapṭe niyamaḥ pākṣike saṭi*;—in the *Parisaṅkhyāviḍhi* on the other hand, all that is enjoined is already known; but not necessarily as possible alternatives; they may be known as all simultaneously possible; there nothing is *unknown*; all are known; and out of these a few are chosen and enjoined.

12. *Manṭras* are classed under three heads—(1) Ṛik, Sāman and Yajuṣ; on these three names the *Bṛihaṭī* (Ms. p. 50 *b*) remarks as follows:—

'The words *Ṛik*, *Sāman* and *Yajuṣ* are found to be used in connection with the Vedas; hence it becomes necessary to ascertain what part of the Veda is to be called *Ṛik*, what part *Yajuṣ* aud what part *Sāman*. On this point, our conclusion is that the name *Ṛik* is applied to those sentences that are divided into *feet,—i.e.*, into certain well-defined parts, each consisting of a definite number of syllables—and are called, on that account, by such prosodial names as *Gāyaṭrī Ṭriṣtup*, &c.' (Mīm. Sū. II—1-35).

The word 'pṛiṣtha" is sometimes used to imply the Rigveda (Mīm. Sū. VII—iii—35-36). The word *Sāman*' does not strictly apply to the *manṭras* themselves; it is applied to the *music* to which certain *manṭras* are set, and not to the *words* (Mīm. Sū. II—1—36), and hence a *manṭra* can be called '*Sāman*' only when it is set to music and *sung* as such (Mīm. Sū. VII—ii—1 to 21). Thus one and the same *manṭra* set to different kinds of music, becomes known under different names—such as 'Raṭhanṭara,' 'Bṛihaṭ', and the like. This setting to music is regarded as a *samskāra* or purification of the *manṭras* (Mīm. Sū. IX—ii—3 to 13), and as such owes its origin to the singer; and in so far it cannot be regarded as *Veda* proper, which is independent of all sources, human or divine. For instance, the syllables *ā hau*, &c., that are added to the *manṭras* by the exigencies of music, are by no means fixed, they depend upon the singer, who may or may not use a certain syllable, or sets of syllables. (Mīm. Sū. IX—ii—29). In the case of all *manṭras*, wherever they are used as *praise*, they must be used in their *Sāman* form—that is, set to music and sung; as the praise pleases more when it is sung than when it is merely recited. (IX—ii—30-31).

Sāmans are divided into several kinds, the division being based upon the different methods of singing; for instance, the *Brihaṭ* Sāman is to be sung with force and very loudly, while the *Raṭhanṭara* is to be sung not loudly, and not with force (Mīm. Sū IX—ii—46). The name '*Yajuṣ*' is given to all those *manṭrās* that are neither arranged in metrical feet, nor set to music (Mīm. Sū. II—i—37). There are some *manṭras* that have been called '*nigaḍas*'; this is a name given to those *manṭras* that are addressed to others. These also are included in the '*Yajuṣ*'; because like these latter, they also have neither metre nor music; hence they have been defined as such *Yajuṣ* manṭras as are addressed to others, and are recited *loudly*, and not in the low voice prescribed for the *Yajuṣ* in general. The *Ṛik* and the *Sāman Manṭras* also are to be recited loudly.

13. What we have explained above is the main threefold classification of *Manṭras*. There is also another classification based upon the difference in the character of the signification of accentuation and so forth. This classification pertains only to the *Ṛik* and the *Yajuṣ Manṭras*. Of the former there are 273 kinds, and of the latter, 50. These have been described and exemplified in detail by Shaṅkara Bhatta in his *Mīmāmsābālaprakāsha* (pp. 58-70). We shall note here only those that have been mentioned by Upavarṣa in his *Vriṭṭi* mentioned in the *Bhāṣya* of Shabara (page 126):—(1) *asyanṭa*—those ending in the word '*asi*'—e. g. '*meḍhā 'si &c.*' (2) '*Ṭvānta*'—those ending in the word '*ṭvā,*' *e. g.* '*Īkhē ṭvā*' (*Vājasaneyasamhiṭā* I-1). (3) *Benedictory—e. g.*

'*Āyurḍā asi, &c.*' (*Vājas. sam.* 3-17). (4) *Eulogistic—e. g.* '*Agnirmūrḍhā, &c.*' (*Ṛigveḍa* 8-14-16). (5) *Incoherent—e. g*, '*akṣī ṭe Inḍra piṅgale ḍuleriva.*' (6) *Plaintive—e.g*, '*Ambe ambike &c.*' (Vājas. Sam. 23-18). (7) *Injunctive—e.g.*, '*Agnīḍagrīn vīharā*' (Ṭaiṭṭi. Sam. 6-3-1-2). (8) Inquisitive—*e. g.*, '*Ko-si kaṭamo-si*' (Vajas. Sam. 7-29). (9) *Interrogatory—e. g.*, '*Ṗrichchhāmi ṭvā, &c.*' (Ṛigveḍa 1-164-34). (10) *Descriptive—e.g.*, '*Iyam Veḍiḥ, &c.*' (Ṛigveda 1-164-35) (11). *Elliptical—e.g.* when the words '*achchhiḍreṇa paviṭreṇa*' are added to the *manṭra* '*Chiṭpaṭisṭvā punūṭu*' (Ṭaiṭṭi. Sam. 1-2-1-2). (12) *Prayoga-manṭras—i. e., Manṭras* with three-fold and four-fold accent—*e. g.*, '*Ikhe ṭvā &c.*' (Vāj. Sam. 1-1) and '*Agnimīle, &c.*' (Ṛigveda 1-1-1) respectively. (13) *Indicative—e. g.*, the *manṭra* '*Ḍevasya ṭvā—nirvapāmi*' is indicative of *nirvāpa* (*i.e.*, the putting in of a handful of corn into the winnowing basket).

14. Manṭras have also been classfied according to their metres. This classification pertains to the *Ṛik Manṭras* only. The following are the principal metres :

(1) *Gāyatrī*—having 24 syllables, with its 9 sub-divisions.

(2) *Uṣṇik*—having 28 syllables, with its 8 sub-divisions.

(3) *Anuṣṭup*—having 32 syllables, with its 7 sub-divisions.

(4) *Bṛihaṭī*—having 36 syllables, with its 9 sub-divisions.

(5) *Prakṛiṭi*—having 40 syllables, with its 8 sub-divisions.

(6) *Ṭriṣṭup*—having 44 syllables, with its 10 sub-divisions.

(7) *Jagaṭī*—having 8 syllables, with its 3 sub-divisions.

(8) *Aṭijagaṭī*—having 52 syllables.

(9) *Shakvarī*—having 56 syllables.

(10) *Aṭishakvarī*—having 60 syllables.

(11) *Aṣṭi*—having 64 syllables.

(12) *Atyaṣṭi*—having 68 syllables.

(13) *Dhṛiṭi*—having 72 syllables.

(14) *Aṭiḍhṛiṭi*—having 76 syllables.

Of these, the Gāyaṭrī, the Ṭriṣṭnp and the Jagaṭī are found mentioned in the *Shaṭapaṭha Brāhmaṇa* in 1.2.2.6; 3.4.1.22; 3.4.4.8.; and 4,1,1,8; some others are mentioned in 8.2.2.6 also.

15. From the very definition of the *Ṛik* it would follow that there can be no metre in the *Yajuṣ manṭras*. But Piṅgala in his *Chhandaḥsūṭra* says that there are metres in these also. That this is a later innovation is proved by the fact that true 'Vedic authority' is not accepted by many old writers (Karka for instance) to belong to those *Yajuṣ-manṭras* that are differentiated by metres; and that even those who accept their authority (for instance Devayājñika) assert that there is no metre in many *Yajuṣ manṭras* on account of the number of syllables in them not being fixed. Herein may be found an orthodox authority for the view propounded by Western Orientalists, that the metrical portions of the Yajurveda are comparatively modern.

16. Having described the *Brāhmaṇa* and the *Manṭra*, we proceed to describe the *Arṭhavāḍa*. *Arṭhavāḍa* passages are of three kinds:—(1) Descriptive by indirect implication; (2) Descriptive by direct intention; and (3) Descriptive of au accomplished fact. This is the main classification; there is another classification, whereby we have 38 kinds of *Arṭhavāḍa*. These are described and exemplified in detail in the *Mīmāmsā-bālaprakāsha* (pp. 48-58). We shall note here a few of the more important kinds:—

(1) *Benedictory*—'*so-kāmayaṭa prajaḥ sṛijema;*' (2) *Anecdoṭal*—'*Puruṣam vai ḍēvāḥ pashumālabhanṭa;*' (3) *Ratiocinative*—'*Shūrpeṇa juhoṭi, tena hyannaṅkriyaṭe;*' (4) *Deprecatory*—'*so-roḍīṭ*' (5) *Eulogistic*—'*vāyurvai kṣepiṣṭhā ḍevaṭā*' (6) *Descriptive of deeds done*—'*Iṭi hasmāha, &c.*' (7) *Indicative of deity*—'*Annādam vā ya eṭamāṭmano janayaṭe yaḍagnin.*' (8) *Indicative of material*—'*eṭaḍvai sarvaḍevaṭyam vāso yaṭ kṣaumam.*' (9) *Indicative of action*—'*upari hi ḍevebhyo ḍhārayaṭi*'.

(10) *Indicative of the agent*—'*eṣā vā-nāhiṭāgne*'. (11) *Indicative of time*—'*upamshupaurṇamāsyam yajan.*' (12) *Indicative of place*—'*Ṭāṇdake sarasvatyā vinashanē, &c.*' (13) *Figurative*—indicative of similarity—'*yaṭhā vai shyeno niṭpayāḍaṭṭe evan ḍviṣanṭam bhrāṭrivyam nipaṭyāḍaṭṭe.*'

17. When dealing with *Manṭras*, Jaimini lays down three principles governing the construing of sentences. Among the three kinds of *manṭrās*, with regard to those that are in the metrical form, and those that are set to music,—*i. e.*, the *Ṛik* and *Sāman manṭras*,—there is not much difficulty in ascertaining how far the *manṭra* extends. When however we come to the prose *manṭras*—the *Yajuṣ* and the *Nigaḍas*—it is sometimes difficult to ascertain how far a certain *manṭra* may be regarded as extending. It is in connection with this question that the 'principles of interpretation' are discussed and laid down. These principles are known by the names of—(1) The *Ekavākyaṭāḍhikaraṇa* or the Principle of 'Syntactical Connection' (Mīm. Sū. II—i—56),—(2) the *Vākyabheḍāḍhikaraṇa* or the Principle of 'Syntactical Split' (II—i—47),—and (3) the *Anuṣangāḍhikarāṇa*, or the Principle of 'Elliptical Extension' (II—i—48). We shall explain each of these Principles in some detail; as they play an important part in the whole science of *Mīmāmsā*, and serve a directly useful purpose in all textual interpretations.

I.—The *Principle of Syntactical Connection.** The principle may be thus stated :—*When a number of words are found to be such that when construed collectively, they are expressive of a single idea,—and when taken severally they are not expressive of any idea, being short of some necessary syntactical factor,—these words must be regarded as forming a single sentence.* (II

* See *Bṛihaṭī*, M.S. p. 51; and *Ṭanṭravārṭika*, pp. 423—31.

Both Prabhākara and Bhatta take this principle, as here laid down, to apply to the Yajuṣ Manṭras only; as the extent of the Ṛik is fixed by the metre, and that of the Sāman by the music.

—i—46). As an example we have the following:—In connection with the *Ḍarsha-Pūrṇamasā* sacrifices, we read the sentence '*Ḍevasya ṭvā saviṭaḥ prasave—ashvinorbāhubhyām—pusṇo hasṭābhyām agnayē jusṭam nirvapāmi*' (Shaṭapaṭha Br. I. 1-2-17). Here we find four distinct parts, each of which might be taken as an independent sentence and *manṭra*, unless we had something to show that the whole must be taken and used as a single sentence and *manṭra*. This something we have in the form of the principle in consideration. If we take the first part—'*ḍevasyā ṭva saviṭaḥ*'—we find that it does not express any idea, being wanting in the verb; similarly with each of the other parts we find that it is wanting in some integral syntactical factor; the last part also—'*agnayē jusṭam nirvapāmi*'—though otherwise complete, is found to be in need of an instrumental nominative in connection with the passive past-participle '*jusṭam*'; we further observe that if we take the whole together, it expresses the single idea of the *nirvāpa or preparation of something resorted to or accepted by the arms of the Ashvins and the hands of Pūṣan.*

There is a difference of opinion among the followers of Kumārila as to the exact meaning of the word '*arṭha*' (translated above as *idea*) in the *suṭra* enunciating the principle. Pārṭhasāraṭhi Mīshra takes it to mean *purpose*; and thus according to him, all the words, phrases and clauses *that serve a single purpose* are to be regarded as 'one sentence.' Someshvara Bhatta, on the other hand, in his *Nyāyasuḍhā* takes it in the sense of *idea*. According to Prābhākara, '*arṭha*' here means 'the reminding or indicating of what is to be done'; and he distinctly favours the 'Mishra' view; specially as being an *Anviṭābhiḍhānavāḍin*, he could not very well accept the words to have any meaning apart from the other words; hence he says that the word 'arṭha' must mean *prayojana*, 'purpose'; as this is the most important factor, and all words must be related to the most important factor (See *Brihaṭī* p. 51.)

II.—The *principle of Syntactical Split.** This principle, an antithesis of the foregoing, may be thus stated :—*When a number of words are found to be such that when each word, or set of words, taken severally, independently of others, is equally capable of expressing one complete idea,—each of these should be regarded as a distinct sentence.* For instance, in the passage,—'*Āyuryajñena kalpaṭām—prāṇo yajñena kalpaṭām* &c.' (Vājas. Sam. 9-21), each part is a distinct sentence complete in itself; because it expresses a complete idea, independently of the other. That this construction is the correct one is also proved by the Vedic junction '*klṛipṭīrvāchayaṭi*' where the passage in question in spoken of by the name '*klṛipṭīḥ*' in the plural, which shows that the passage contains as many distinct sentences as there are '*kalpṭāms*' in it. This principle applies, not only to cases where the words of the *manṭra* are found to be so construable, but also to those cases where, even though the words actually present in the *manṭra* are such as not allowing of separate construction, yet such construction becomes possible by virtue of certain words added to the *manṭra*, under proper authority. For instance, in the *manṭra*— *Ikhe ṭvorjē*, &c. (*Vājas. Sam.* I-1), we find that the *manṭra*, as it stands, is not capable of being broken up into many sentences; but in connection with the several parts of this passage we meet with such Vedic injunctions as—'with the words *ūrjē* he washes it' and so forth (Vide *Shaṭapaṭha Br.* 1, 1, 6, 6; 1, 7, 1, 2; 4, 3, 1, 1, 7); on the authority of these injunctions then, it becomes necessary to supply to the *manṭras* such words as '*chhinaḍmi*' and '*anumārjmi* and the like; and with these words supplied, each of the several parts of the passage becomes a complete sentence, expressing a complete idea,—such as—(1) *O palāsha* branch, I am cutting thee for the obtaining of desirable food,' and (2) 'I am washing thee for the obtaining of strength,' and so forth. In

* *Bṛihaṭī* MS. p. 51 b. and *Ṭanṭravārṭika* p. 431.

connection with this however, it may be noted that a single *Yajuṣ* cannot be broken up into many sentences without sufficient authority. We had such authority in both the cases cited above. This 'syntactical split' as it has been called, is permissible only in very rare cases; in fact, not until it is shown that no other construction is possible,—either in view of the structure of the sentence itself, or in virtue of some direct injunction necessitating such split; and the reason for this is that in a case where the nature of the sentence is such that it admits of being taken as a single sentence, if we do have recourse to 'syntactical split,' we incur the responsibility of abandoning the natural, syntactical construction without any authority; and further, where the sentence, taken as a single *manṭra*, would lead to a single transcendental result, we—by forcing the syntactical split—make it necessary to assume a number of such results preceding from each of the defferent *manṭras* into which the original passage may be split up. And in a case where we have no direct injunction necessitating the syntactical split,—and where the split necessitates the addition of more words,—these words, being supplied by ourselves without the authority of the Vedic injunction, cannot be regarded as 'Vedic'; and hence the *manṭra* containing those non-Vedic words would no longer remain '*manṭra*' in the proper sense of the term.

To this Principle we have a corollary to the effect that, *when different parts of a manṭra are found by their implication to be meant for serviug distinct purposes, each such parts should be regarded as a distinct sentence.* For instance, in the manṭra—*Syonanṭe saḍanankriṇomi......ṭasmin sīḍa*' (*Ṭaiṭṭi. Brāhmaṇa*, 3, 7, 5, 2; and *Mānava Shrauṭasūṭra* 1-2-6-19),—we find that the first part, by its meaning, is intended to be employed in the act of preparing the 'seat' for the cake, while the last part, in the same manner, for that of actually keeping the cake upon that 'seat'; hence the passage is regarded as containing two distinct *manṭras*. This has been called 'Syntactical Split due to difference in Use.' (See *Bṛihaṭī* Ms. p. 79 b).

*III. The Principle of Elliptical Extension.**

In many *Yajuṣ* passages it is found that there are several sentences that stand in need of a certain word or phrase or clause, while the whole *yajuṣ* contains only one such word phrase or clause; in such cases it would appear that this word, phrase or clause is to be construed and used along with only that one of the several sentences which happens to be nearest to it; and it is the possibility of this construction that the present principle precludes. By this principle the word, phrase or clause is to be used along with every one of the sentences,—provided that every one of these is of the same type and form; and the reason for this is that the intervention of a similar sentence does not become an obstacle to syntactical connection. As an example we have the passage—'*yā ṭe agne' yaḥshayā ṭanūrvarṣiṣṭhā gahvareṣṭhā ugram vacho apāvaḍhīṭṭveṣamapāvaḍhīṭsvāhā—yā ṭe agne rajāshayā—yā ṭe agne harāshayā* (Vājas. Sam. 5-8; and Shaṭapaṭha Br. 3-4-4-23). Here by the principle above stated, the clause '*ṭanūh........svāhā*' has to be repeated along with '*yā ṭe agne rajāshayā*', as also with *yā ṭe agne harāshayā*; and its connection does not cease only with '*yā ṭe ayaḥshayā*.' In this example, the clause to be connected with different sentences, forms the principal clause in each sentence; but it does not make any difference even if the clause in question be a subordinate one. For instance, in the passage—*Chīṭpaṭisṭvā punāṭu—Vākpaṭisṭvā punāṭu—ḍevasṭvā saviṭā punāṭu—achchhiḍreṇa paviṭreṇa vasoḥ sūryasya rashmibhiḥ*'—(Ṭaiṭṭi. Sam. 1-2-1-2) the subordinate clause '*achchhiḍreṇa......rashmibhiḥ*' has to be taken with each of the sentences ending in *punāṭu*.'

* *Bṛihaṭī*. Ms. pp. 51 b—52, and *Ṭanṭravārṭika* pp. 434 *et. seq.*

SECTION I—*Sub-section* (2).

Authoritative character of the *Mantra*, the *Arthavāda* and the *Nāmadheya*.

1. Iu the last sub-section we have seen how the whole Veda is regarded as authoritative; and we have also seen that 'Veda' is the name given to a collection of sentences, which have beeu roughly classed under the three heads of the *Brāhmaṇa* or *Vidhi*, the *Mantra* and the *Arthavāda*. And the question that we shall consider under the present sub-section bears upon the degree of authority attachiug to these three kinds of senteuces.

2. As regards the *Vidhi* or Injunctive passages, they lay down directly what coustitutes *Dharma*; and as such they constitute the 'Veda' *par excellence*; aud as such there can be no questiou as to their trustworthy character. This has been shown, iu the very definition of *Dharma*, that *Dharma* is that act which is laid down by the injunctive passages of the Veda, as conducive to happiuess. We shall proceed now to consider the case of the *Arthavāda* and the *mantra* passages.

3. * Though as we have seen above, *Arthavādas* are of many kinds, yet for our present purposes we shall take only the two classes uuder which most of them fall,—*viz*. the *Eulogistic* and the *Deprecatory*. Those belonging to the former class are found to praise something—material, action or deity—related, directly or indirectly, to some act laid down by an iujunctive passage; while those of the latter class are found to deprecate something related to an act that has been prohibited. Both these sets of passages have their use, in persuading men towards the speedier fulfilment of the injunction, or the quicker avoidance of what is prohibited by the prohibition, with which they may

* Mim. Sū. I—ii-7.

be respectively connected. And so far as the *Arṭhavāḍa* is found to be capable of being construed along with injunctions,—it is regarded as authoritative; specially as it serves the distinctly useful purpose of helping the injunction in its persuasive or prohibitive function.

4. As regards the Prābhākara view of the authority of the *Arṭhavāḍa*, Gaḍāḍhara (from what he says in his *Shakṭivāḍa*) would have us believe that *Arṭhavāḍas*, according to Prābhākara, are not *untrustworthy*, but they are simply *inexpressive*; as, in accordance with the *Anviṭābhiḍhāna* theory, only that sentence is really *expressive* which lays down something *to be done*; and hence it is only the injunction that can be really *expressive*; as meanings of word can be comprehended only through injunctions addressed by the old to the young. Though this may be true with regard to the *Arṭhavāḍa* passage taken by itself; yet this cannot be accepted as the final conclusion accepted by Prābhākara; as on referring to Prābhākara's own work, the *Bṛihaṭī*, we find that the view expressed above represents only the '*Pūrvapakṣa*'; and is demolished by the final '*Siḍḍhānṭa*.' The *Bhātta* '*pūrvapakṣa*' is that *Arṭhavāḍas* are *apramāṇa* or untrustworthy. While the *Prābhākara* represents the '*pūrvapakṣa*' as that they are *avāchaka* or inexpressive,—the opponent finding this a more suitable view to be propounded in face of the *Prābhākara*, who holds tenaciously to the *Anviṭābhiḍhāna* theory of word-denotation. The *Siḍḍhānṭa* or final conclusion as adopted by Prābhākara is that 'the *Arṭhavāḍa* is as much *Veda* as the *Viḍhi* itself, as it also, like the *Viḍhi*, expresses the *Kāryaṭā* or *performability* of certain acts.'* Though it is quite true that, according to the Prābhākara view of syntactical connection, the *Arṭhavāḍa* by itself cannot be *expressive* in the correct sense of the term,—yet this can be urged against only such *Arṭhavāḍas* as are absolutely incapable of being construed with any injunction.

* *Bṛihaṭī*. MS. p. 30.

Most of the *arṭhavāḍas,* however, are actually found capable of being syntactically connected with injunctions; and as such helping by the *praise* the persuasive power of the injunctive word, they serve a most useful purpose by expressing the fitness of the act to be performed; and hence they are fully entitled to the name '*Veda.*' Says the *Bṛihaṭi* (*MS.* pp. 29-30):—'*viḍhyuḍḍeshāḍeva kāryāvagaṭiḥ ......yaṭo hi karṭavyaṭa-vagamyate sa veḍaḥ; asmāchcha karṭyavaṭā-vagamyaṭe.*' It may be that Gaḍāḍhara's interpretation of the *Prābhākara* view is based upon some later work of the School; and it would be interesting to investigate the matter. But it cannot be done here; as the only later work known to us at present is the *Ṛijuvimala* of Shālikanaṭha Mishra, of which the only manuscript available is found to be wanting in this part.

5. The next question that arises is thus explained in the *Bṛihaṭi* (MS. page 30):—

'Thus then, the trustworthy character of such descriptions as are contained in the *Arṭhavāḍas* having been proved, the question arises as to how to regard those few passages which are found to be capable of being taken as independent injunctions, as also as mere descriptive *Arṭhavāḍas* related to, and subserving, other injunctive passages. For example, the passage—'the post is of *Uḍumbara* wood......the *Uḍumbara* is powerful; one obtains powerful cattle by using that wood,'—the first sentence, 'the post is of Uḍumbara wood' indicates one action, *the making of the post with a particular wood*; and the other sentence, 'one obtains powerful cattle, &c.', indicates another action, *the obtaining of cattle.* This latter sentence again is also capable of being taken as merely a *praise* related to, and subserving the injunction of, the action indicated by the former sentence,—the meaning of the whole passage being that, "*inasmuch as* the Uḍumbara wood brings powerful cattle, the post should be made of that wood."

Thus this latter sentence has all the appearance of an injunction; while as containing no injunctive word, it is liable to be taken as mere *arṭhavāḍa*.

Now the question arises as to which of the two significations of the latter sentence should be accepted; both cannot be accepted, as that would make the exact meaning of the Veda doubtful, and thereby lead to its absolute authority being doubted. The conclusion is that the meaning is not at all doubtful; the sentence must be taken as an *arṭhavāḍa*. So long as we can construe the sentences occurring together as constituting a single complex senteuce, it is not permissible to find in them many injunctions; as uunecessary multiplication of injunctions is to be avoided. In fact, even if we regard the two as independent injunctions, the latter sentence would lay down an action that would follow only from the action enjoyed by the preceding sentence. For instance, it would lay down the 'obtaining of cattle' *by* the 'making of the post with *uḍumbara* wood,' which 'making' is enjoined by the preceding seutence. In this manner also, the two sentences are shown to be related, as pointing virtually to the same action—the 'making of the post with *uḍumbara* wood.' Says the *Bṛihāṭī* (MS. page 30 b):—

'*Sāḍhyaḍvayāvagame-pi pramāṇaṭaḥ siḍḍhasāḍhyaṭayaiva hyekārṭhāvagaṭiḥ.*'

In explaining this passage, the *Ṛijuvimalā* (MS. p. 332) remarks—

'*Yaḍyekārṭhāvagaṭiḥ ṭaḍānukūlannimiṭṭaṅkalpaṉiyam; ekorṭhaḥ siḍḍharūpo—bhyūpagamyaṭām, aparashcha sāḍhyarūpaḥ, yena parasparasambanḍhe saṭyekārṭhāvagaṭiḥ upapaḍyaṭe.*'

That is to say, 'if the whole passage is taken as pointing to one signification, then sufficient reason should be found for such interpretation; and this reason consists in the fact that one of the acts (*i. e.*, the obtaining of cattle) mentioned must be regarded as something *accomplished*, and the others (the making of the *yūpa* with uḍumbara wood) as *to be accomplished*; it is only thus that the two sentences could be construed to afford a single meaning.'

The *Bhātta* presentment of the Pūrvapakṣa on the point is somewhat different; by which the sentence in question is taken as pointing out the result that *actually* follows from the action prescribed in the preceding sentence; the final conclusion is that it does not describe the *real* result, it is a mere ***arṭhavaḍa.***

6. * This leads us on to another class of *Arṭhavāḍa* passages,—those that appear to be laying down reasons in favour of a certain course of action prescribed by an injunction. For instance, the sentence 'the libation should be poured with the ladle, as it is with this that food is got ready'—lays down, in the latter part, a reason for the action prescribed in the former part. In regard to this it is argued that, the ratiocinative section of the passage must be taken as expressing the mere *praise* of the ladle; as for what is directly enjoined in a Vedic sentence, there is no need for the support of any reasoning or argument, which, therefore, even if present, would be wholly irrelevant; and in the Veda there can be no irrelevancy or superfluity.

7. †Having considered the authoritativeness of *Arṭhavāḍas*, we now proceed to consider the case of *manṭras*. From the very nature of *manṭras* it is clear that they cannot be taken as injunctions;—being as they are entirely devoid of any kind of injunctive word; also because all *manṭras* are found, either syntactically, or by direct declaration, or by indirect implication, construed along with other passages which are injunctions; so if the *manṭras* themselves were to enjoin another action, there would be two actions enjoined

---

* *Mīm. Sū.* I—ii—27.

† *Mīm. Sū.* I—ii—31 to 53.

by what is practically only one 'sentence.'* Nor are the *mantras* found to contain any *praise* or *deprecation*; so they cannot be taken as *Arthavāda.* With all this however, the *mantras* cannot be regarded as absolutely meaningless or useless; forming an integral part of the Veda, they must serve some purpose, must have some meaning, expressing something that is needful in the actions prescribed by the injunctive passages. This is thus explained by the *Brihati* (p. 31):—

Nāvivakṣitārthā mantrāḥ, svādhyāyaniyogasambandhitāyā; Svādhyāyasyārthavattoktā, kārye prāmāṇyābhidhānāt......Anuṣthīyamānārthaupayikatayā vivakṣitārthatvameva gamyamānan. na shakyate......hantum.'—

This usefulness of the *mantras* cannot be in their mere recitation bringing about transcendental results. There can be no justification for such an assumption in face of the fact that the *mantras* convey a distinct meaning,—that indicating something, in most cases the deity, in connection with sacrifices enjoined elsewhere. The *mantras* are generally found to be in the form of address to a certain power or being;—which shows that the power or being to whom the *mantra* is addressed is the 'deity' to whom one should offer the sacrifice enjoined by some sentence in the same context. There are some *mantras* however which are not found to be indicative of anything related to the sacrifice; such *mantras* are relegated to the category of '*Arthavāda*.'

8.† There is one portion of the 'Veda' left to be considered:—It is that comparatively smaller portion which has been called '*Nāmadheya*'; that is to say, those words that have the appearance of a name of action, and are yet

* *Brihati.* Ms. p. 50.

† Mim Sū. I. iv.—*Brihati* MS. pp. 38—38b. This forms the subject matter of the fourth *pāda*, and as such, by our arrangement, should have formed our sub-section 4.' But the subject-matter is closely allied to this section; and hence we have included it here.

capable of another interpretation. For instance, the sentence '*uḍbhīḍā yajēṭa pashukūmaḥ*'; 'one desirous of acquiring cattle should sacrifice with the *Uḍbhiḍ*'; it would appear that what is laid down here is a certain substance to be offered at some worldly act of sacrifice not prescribed by a Vedic injunction, but performed by men in their ordinary life. But as a matter of fact, it is found that there is no sacrifice prescribed by any Vedic passage where an offering could be made of the '*uḍbhiḍ*'—which can only mean *that with which something is dug*, a spade for instance; and under the circumstances the injunction of such a substance would be absolutely meaningless, and this would vitiate the trustworthy character of the Veda. In order to avoid this, the word '*uḍbhiḍ*' has to be taken as the *name of a sacrifice*,—the sentence in that the case being taken as enjoining the particular sacrifice *named* '*uḍbhiḍ*' as to be performed by people desirous of acquiring cattle.

9. The *Bhātta* statement of the *Pūrvapakṣa* is somewhat different; accordiug to which the *Uḍbhiḍ* is regarded as the 'spade' to be offered at one of the well-known sacrifices—the *Jyoṭiṣtoma* for instance (and not at a special sacrifice prescribed by some unknown sentence).

10.* The word 'Āgneya' is another example cited. In regard to this word as occurring in the sentence '*yaḍāgneyo—ṣtakapālo—māvāsyāyām*, &c.,' it is argued that this word also must be regarded as the name of a sacrifice (in accordance with the *Pūrvapakṣa* as stated by Kumārila), or the whole sentence must be rejected as devoid of any signification helpful to sacrificial performance, the word '*āgneyā*' being a mere *name* of action, and not laying down anything to be used at sacrifices (according to the *Pūrvapakṣa* as stated by Prabhākara). But the conclusion, according to Kumārila as well as Prabhākara, is that the sentence serves the useful purpose of indicating, by means of the word

* *Bṛihati* MS. pp. 41b—42.

'*Āgneyaḥ*,' Agni as the deity to whom 'the cake baked upon eight pans' is to be offered. As on this point, so in regard to the discussions over some other words also, the final conclusion is the same according to Kumārila and Prabhākara; but as regards the statement of the *pūrvapakṣa*, there is a difference, in almost every case; Kumārila in every case stating it in a specific form, and Prabhākara always making a it bear upon the general significance of the passage. For instance, in regard to the word '*varhi*,' the *Bhūtta pūrvapakṣa* is that is denotes, not '*varhi*' in general, but that particular *varhi* which has been consecrated; whereas the *Prābhākara pūrvapakṣa* is that the sentence in question is incapable of affording any meaning likely to help a prescribed action, and as such, must be rejected as altogether devoid of 'Vedic' authority.

SECTION (1)—*Sub-section* (3).

The authoritative character of Smṛiṭis, Puraṇas and Iṭihāsās.

1. Though like an orthodox *Mīmāmsaka*, Jaimini has declared in Sū. I—i—2, that "Veda" is the sole authority on matters relating to *Ḍharma*, aud is the only source from which right knowledge of *Ḍharma* can be derived, yet, in actual practice he found that, by the time that he systematised in his *sūṭras* the Vedic exigetics, the Vedas had become so remotely ancient that they were not found sufficient for all religious purposes; and the knowledge derived from them had to be supplemented by that derived from other sources,—notably the collection of works known under the comprehensive name of '*Smṛiṭi*,' and the 'usage' of respectable men. It was in view of this indubitable fact that Manu and other writers laid down at the very beginning of the *Ḍharmashāsṭra* compilations, that the source of the knowledge of *Ḍharma* lies (in the order of precedence) in the Veda, the Smṛiṭi, the usage of good men, and also self-satisfaction. It was in view of this again that

Jaimini found it necessary to devote a special section of his *Sūṭras* to the consideration of the authoritative character of the *Smṛiti*. Says the *Bṛihaṭī* (MS. p. 31):—

'The *Smṛiṭi* also has been accepted by people learned in the Vedas as *authoritative* and *trustworthy*; hence it is necessary to enquire into this matter also.'—

And in this section Jaimini shows that whenever they do not flatly contradict the Veda, the *Smṛiṭis* are to be regarded as authoritative,—but (in order to be consistent with what he had said with regard to the Veda being the *sole* authority) only in so far as they are based upon, and derive their authority from, the Veda. In considering this question, Kumārila has cited a Smṛiṭi text which lays down the *Aṣṭakā* performance which is not prescribed by the Veda; but Prabhākara, consistently with his determination to connect all discussions with the question of the authority of the Veda, cites the *manṭra*, '*Yāñjanāḥ praṭinandanṭi* &c.' which is not found to be used at any Vedic sacrifice, and should therefore (according to the *Pūrvapakṣa*) be rejected as useless; and hence the authority of the Veda to that extent becomes vitiated;—and the final conclusion is that the *Smṛiṭi* has its source in the Veda, hence what is laid down in the Smṛiṭi should also be regarded as Vedic; hence the *Aṣṭakā* at which the *manṭra* in question is used, being *Vedic*, the *manṭra* is not useless.

2. It is interesting to note what reasons the orthodox *Mīmāmsaka* puts forward for justifying his doubts with regard to the authority of the Smṛiṭis. Kumārila in his *Ṭanṭravārṭika* (translation, p. 105) sums up these reasons in the following words:—

'Inasmuch as these *Smṛiṭis* emanated from human authors (and are not eternal, like the Veda) their authority cannot be self-sufficient. Nor can they be rejected as altogether untrustworthy; because of the firmness of popular trust in them......The *Smṛiṭis* of Manu and others are dependent upon the memory of the authors, and memory depends for its authority upon the truthfulness of its source ; consequently the authority of not a single *Smṛiṭi* can be held to be self-sufficient, like that of the Veda ; and inasmuch as we find them accepted as authoritative, by an unbroken line of respectable people learned in the Vedas, we cannot regard them to be absolutely false either. And hence it is only natural that there should be a doubt on the point."—

Prabhākara however, in his *Bṛihaṭī* (Ms. pp. 31-31 b) makes the whole discussion turn upon the main subject of the authority of the Veda. In his introductory remarks on the *aḍhikaraṇa*, he justifies the enquiry into the character of the *Smṛiṭis* on the ground that the enquiry is directly connected with the question of the authority of the Veda; as many actions that are laid down in the *Smṛiṭis*, and not in the Veda,—for instance, the *Aṣṭakāshrāḍḍhas*—are found to be referred to and indicated in the Veda; for instance, those *shrāḍḍhas* are enlogised in the seutence '*Yāñjanāḥ-praṭinanḍanṭi*, &c.' (Pāraskara Gṛihyasūṭra 3. 2.2). And thus the enquiry into the *Smṛiṭis* is only au off-shoot of the enquiry into the Veda. Consequently, when the *Pūrvapakṣin* puts forward the view that the *Smṛiṭis* are not trustworthy, he tries to vitiate by this contention the trustworthy character of the Veda itself. It may be noted that in thus making all *aḍhikaraṇas* of the first *aḍhyāya* turn upon the main subject of the *aḍhyāya*,—the Authority of the Veda,—Prabhakara has shown himself more consistent than Kumārila, who leaves the connection to be inferred; while Prabhākara emphasises it at each step.

3. In later classical literature, the word '*Smṛiṭi*' *is found* to include the *Iṭihāsas*, *Purāṇas* the *Sūṭrās*—*shrauṭa* and *smārṭa*—and also the so-called *Smṛiṭis* proper, such as those of Manu, Yājñavalkya, Aṭri, Vashiṣtha and others.

In the present context, however, the word has been accepted (by Kumārila* and his followers) to include only those *Smṛṭis* which are applicable throughout Āryāvarṭa and to all men. In this category, Kumārila classes—(1) the *Purāṇas*, (2) the *Iṭihāsas* and (3) the *Smriṭi of Manu*. The other '*Smṛiṭis*'—those of Aṭri, Gauṭama, Vashiṣṭha, &c.,—he relegates to another category; and considers them later on, under *sūṭrās* 15—16 *et. seq.* With regard to the *Iṭihāsas* and *Purāṇas*, Kumārila † takes a liberal view. Direct injunctions are found embedded in a mass of matter of a purely descriptive character. These latter passages are relegated to the category of '*Arṭhavāḍa*,' being descriptive of acts done by good and bad men of ancient and modern days. These are regarded as '*arṭhavāḍa*', because, if the stories found therein were taken as literally true, then, with reference to these at least, the injunction to recite would be useless, as no purpose could be served by mere descriptions or stories; hence these have to be taken as indirectly implying the *praise* or *deprecation* of certain courses of action; and as these stories have been inserted with the sole purpose of such praise or deprecation, they need not be regarded as absolutely correct with regard to facts. In justification of this method of instruction adopted by the writer of *Iṭihāsas* and *Purāṇas*, Kumārila makes the following remarks :—

'Guided as they were by the study of the Veda, Vālmiki, Vyāsa, and others, composed their works on the same lines as the Veda; hence it is that we find in the works of these men, as in the Veda, many apparently useless stories &c. and as those for whom these works were intended, were persons of varying degrees of intelligence, and of diverse tastes, it was only proper for them to insert every kind

---

**Ṭanṭrṭivārṭika*—Translation, p. 244. The *Bṛihaṭi*, like the *Bhaṣya*, says nothing as to what works are intended to be included; under the term '*smṛiṭi*.

†*Ṭanṭravārṭika*. Translation, pp. 25-26.

of matter in their works, so that they might be of use to all men. Hence it is that in certain parts we find pure injunctions; while in others, the injunctions are mixed up with *Arṭhavāḍas*,—the sole motive for this diverse procedure lying in the making of the works attractive to all men.'

4. As regards the authority attaching to these works, it is held that some of the injunctions contained in them are found to be based directly upon the Veda, while others are based upon considerations of pleasure and pain as experienced in the world; among the *Arṭhavāḍas* also, some are those that appear in the Veda, some are based upon ordinary experience, and some are purely imaginary, like ordinary poetry; but all these have an anthority based upon the fact of their praising enjoined actions, or deprecating probibited ones. As for those portions that are not capable of being taken along with any injunctions or prohibitions, some of these are such as give pleasure in their mere recitation,—to this class belong such descriptions as those of the '*Ganḍhamāḍana*' and the like; and some, for instance, the descriptions of wars, serve to encourage the brave as well as the coward, and thereby serve a distinctly useful purpose for the kings of men. In those cases however, where none of these explanations is possible—for instance, in the case of hymns to deities, which are not found capable of serving any useful purpose,—we assume an 'unseen' or transcendental result. Then again, the Purāṇic descriptions of the parts of the earth serves the purpose of distingushing places fit for the due performance of religious acts. The histories of families recounted serve to differentiate the people of diverse castes, and are based upon memory and direct perception. The details as to measures of time and space are intended to regulate the ordinary practices of men, and also the science of astronomy and astrology; these are based upon direct perception and mathematical calculation. The descriptions of future states of things serve to point out the character of the varions

periods of evolving time, and also the results of righteous and unrighteous conduct; these are based upon the Veda directly. *

5. Thus far we have dealt with the *Iṭihāsas* and the *Purāṇas*; now as regards the *Smṛiṭis* proper,—those that constitute the '*Ḍharmashāsṭra*',—only five assumptions are possible :—(1) That the authors of the *Smṛiṭis* were totally mistaken in what they said;—this is rejected, on the ground that it is not compatible with the fact that all these works are excellent compilations containing useful teachings, and also on the ground that this assumption would necessitate further assumptions as to the foolish character of the people who have accepted these teachings. (2) The second hypothesis is that the assertions are based upon the personal observations of the compilers;—this view is rejected, as it assumes, in the first place, the observation and, in the second place, the possession by those authors of extraordinary powers of observation by means of which they could make correct observations in connection with *Ḍharma*, which has been shown to be beyond the reach of the ordinary means of knowledge. (3) By the third hypothesis, the authors learnt what they have written from other persons,—their authority thus being based upon tradition; —this also is not accepted; as in matters relating to *Ḍharma*, no trust can be reposed upon mere tradition, which, in this case, has been likened to an information relating to colour handed down by a tradition handed along a race of blind men. (4) The fourth hypothesis is that the authors have purposely put forward wrong teachings for the purpose of leading people astray;—this involves a number of baseless assumptions,—such for instance, as a motive sufficiently strong to make them adopt this deceptive course, and also that people have allowed themselves to fall into the trap laid for them, and so forth. (5) All the above

* *Ṭanṭravārṭika*—Translation, p. 119.

hypotheses being found inacceptable, the othodox Mimāmsaka puts forward the view that the assertions contained in the *Smṛiṭis* are all based upon Vedic texts. This view necessitates only one assumption,—that of the existence, and the subsequent disappearance, of such Vedic texts as are not to be found in the Vedic texts as we have them at the present day. For most of the injunctions contained in the *Smṛiṭs,* corroborative Vedic texts are easily found; but there are some for whom we seek in vain for corroboration in the Vedic texts; and with regard to these it is held that Vedic texts corroborative of these also were known at the time of the *Smṛiṭi*-compilers, and have since become lost among the numerous Vedic recensions no longer current. *

Instead of compiling a collection of these Vedic texts themselves, the authors had recourse to another method, because the order in which the injunctions were found in the Veda, was found, in the later degenerate times, to confuse the ordinary man; and so the writers set about arranging and classifying the various duties; and putting them forward in a language more intelligible to the ordinary householder. As in the case of the Iṭihāsas and Purāṇas, so here also, those portions that pertain directly to *Ḍharma* or to *Mokṣa* have their source directly in the Veda; while those that have in view pleasure, &c., are based upon the ordinary experience of the world; and lastly, as for the stories met with here and there, they serve the purposes of the *Arṭhavāḍa.*

6. The *Prābhākara* view of the trustworthy character of *Smṛiṭis* does not differ materially from the above, except on the point of such Smṛiṭis as are neither injunctive nor prohibitive of actions. We append here what the *Prakaraṇa-pañchikā* (pp. 100-101) says on the point :—

---

* See *Ṭanṭravārṭika*—Translation, pp. 112—114.

'The *Smṛiṭi* texts for which direct corroboration is found in the Vedic texts are undoubtedly authoritative. Those for whom such corroboration is not available, are *inferred* to have such corroboration,—the inference being based upon the long traditional lines of *Smṛiṭi* writers, each of whom drew his information from a predecessor, and so on and on to time immemorial, from eternity. This eternal corroboration of *Smṛiṭis* is proved in the same manner as the eternality of the relationship between words and their denotations.'

But on page 150—

'Those *Smṛiṭis* however that do not prescribe or prohibit any actions need not be taken as authoritative. For instance, such passages as speak of souls being born in vegetable bodies. In all these cases also, the texts may be regarded as having meanings other than those that they directly express.'

7. As regards the *Aṅgas*, or Subsidiary Sciences, of the Veda, Kumārila (*Ṭanṭravārṭika*—Translation pp. 119-22) says—

'Among the auxilliary sciences, there are certain portions that treat of things useful in sacrificial performances; and all these have their source in the Veda; while other parts are useful, only in the serving of some visible worldly purpose; and these have their basis in ordinary experience.'

(1) In the *Shikṣā*, we find the differentiation of the organs of pronunciation, accents and such other subjects. These have their perceptible use in the recitation of Vedic hymns; while it is upon the Veda that are based such declarations as that, if the *manṭra* is recited with a wrong accent, it does harm to the reciter. (2) In the *Kalpasūṭras* we find explanations of the real purport of the injunctions deducible from the rules found scattered in the Veda. These have their source in these same Vedic texts. The rules of

conduct herein laid down for the priests are based upon considerations of general convenience. (3) As regards the *Vyākaraṇa*, the knowledge afforded by it of the correct and incorrect forms of words serves a perceptible purpose, and is based upon direct perception. (4) The case of the *Niruķṭa* is similar to that of Grammar; as it serves to regulate the sense in which a word can be correctly used. As regards the science of Prosody, the correct differentiation of the metres of *manṭras* serves a useful purpose in the Veda as well as in ordinary experience. (6) Lastly, the science of *Jyauṭiṣ* provides the knowledge of dates and asterisms, which is based upon mathematical calculations. These serve useful purposes in fixing the times for sacrificial performances. Astrology, which represents another phase is based upon the Veda itself, dealing as it does, with things 'unseen', and also the future. The case of ṭhe Science of Architecture is similar to that of Jyauṭiṣ. (8) *Mīmamsā* is based partly upon the Veda, partly upon ordinary experience, and partly upon perception, inference and the other means of knowledge; and like the other main '*Aṅgas*,' this also has been worked upon by a long unbroken line of teachers. The Science of Reasoning has its use in saving men from unrighteous paths. Based upon the Veda,—in its three parts, Injunctions, Arṭhavāḍa and Upaniṣads,—it points out the trend of the ordinary misconceptions from which unrighteous conduct proceeds, not dogmatically, but in a manner calculated to bring conviction home to the sceptic; it begins with laying out the strong reasonings available for the two opposite views on a particular issue; and then after duly weighing the arguments for and against each view, it leads on to the correct final conclusion. If such standard typical reasonings were not available in a collected form, ordinary men would be at the mercy of any and every stray person that might turn up; and there would be no standard by which to judge of the soundness or otherwise of the reasonings propounded. As regards the philosophical hypotheses relating to the origin of the world and such other matters,—these have their origin in ideas arising from certain *manṭras* and *arṭhavāḍas* ; and they only serve to point out the general truth that the *gross* has its source in the *subtle* ; and the use of all this lies in the due comprehending of the relation of cause and effect, without which the relation between the Sacrifice and its results could not be grasped. The theories of Idealism, of the momentary character of things, and so forth have all been propounded for the sole purpose of dissuading people from cultivating an undue attachment to things of the world. Thus then, all the *Smṛiṭis* as well as the Auxilliary Sciences are authoritative,—deriving their authority directly from the Veda. In the case of all these, we find two classes of results depicted—those to appear in the very distant future, and those appearing immediately in the present ; and the texts pertaining to the former class are based upon the Veda, and those relating to the latter have their basis in ordinary experience.

8. The authority *of Smṛiṭis* in general having been established, the question arises as to how we should regard those *Smṛiṭi* texts which are found to contradict well-known Vedic texts. In connection with these also, as indeed throughout *Aḍhyaya* I, Prabhakara turns the *Pūrvapakṣa* on to the authority of the Veda. * The *Pūrvapakṣa* propounded by him is that, as there is contradiction between the Veda and the *Smṛiṭi*, and through this, the Veda upon which the Smṛiṭi is, *ex hypothesi*, based,—they nullify each other ; and thus no Veda can be regarded as absolutely authoritative. The conclusion is that, inasmuch as the *Smṛiṭi* is not self-sufficient in its authority, being dependent as it is upon the corroboration of Vedic texts, inferred from certain reasons —whenever a *smṛiti* text is found to contradict the Vedic text that is well known, and has not got to be *inferred*, there

* Bṛihaṭī, Ms. p. 32.

can be no justification for the assumption of a Vedic text contrary to one that is already known,—which would lead to the nullification of both the Vedic texts. Hence when it comes to a choice between the Vedic text, on the one hand, and the *Smriṭi* text—not based upon any Vedic text—on the other, there can be no hesitation in rejecting the latter in favour of the former. The opposite courses of action laid down in the two texts cannot be regarded as optional alternatives; as such option is permissible only in cases where the two texts are possessed of equal authority. This is not so in the case in question,—the authority of the Veda being direct and self-sufficient, and that of the *Smriṭi* dependent upon Vedic texts that might, at best, be assumed (which too, under the special case in question, is not posible). Hence the conclusion is that no authority can attach to such *Smriṭi* texts as contradict the direct assertions of the Veda.

9. The above facts have been deduced from *Mīm. Sū.* I—iii—3. The Sūṭra that follows has been doubly interpreted by the *Bhāṣya*. By the first interpretation, it is made to supply a further argument in support of the conclusion arrived at in the preceding *Sūṭra*,—the argument being that the *Smriṭi* texts contradicting the Veda can have no authority, as they are found to have their source in the ignorance or avarice of the sacrificial priests. The other interpretation makes the *Sūṭrā* an *aḍhikaraṇa* by itself,—dealing with such *Smriṭi* texts as do not contradict any Vedic texts, but are found to be apparently due to the ignorance or covetousness of the priests. Such texts for instance as the one speaking of the giving away, to the priest, of the cloth with which the sacrificial post is covered. The conclusion with regard to these is that they can have no authority. The *Brihaṭī* (Ms. Page 32 *b*) adds that what is denied here is, not the trustworthy character of all that may be found to have its source in the world of visible effects, but the authority of only those passages that claim to pertain to the world of

invisible effects, and are yet found to have their source in visible facts; that is to say, the sentence laying down the giving of the cloth to the priest has nothing inherently untrusworthy in itself, so far as the mere *giving* is concerned; bnt if the giving be regarded as bringing abont an invisible result in the shape of 'merit' for the giver,—then its anthority becomes vitiated by the fact that it has its source in the covetonsness of the priests.

10. The above interpretation of the last two *aḍhikaraṇas* by which many *Smṛiṭi* texts become deprived of trustworthy character, is not accepted by Knmārila, who with his orthodox instincts, wonld not reject the authority of any *Smṛiṭi* texts. In the *Ṭanṭravārṭika* (translation, pp. 154—63), he has shown that there is no real contradiction in the instances cited in the *Bhāṣya*; and so long as there is no contradiction, there is every justification for the assuming of Vedic texts in corroboration of the *Smṛiṭi* texts concerned; and thus the two courses of action—one laid down directly in the Veda, and the other in the *Smṛiṭi*,—can be reasonably regarded as optional alternatives. Consequently Sū. 3 must be interpreted to mean that—'in a case where we find the Vedic text laying down one action, and the *Smṛiṭi* laying down another,—thns there being an apparent contradiction between the two on that point,—it is desirable that in practice, we should adopt the course laid down in the Veda.'* This does not imply the *rejection* of the *Smṛiṭi*; it lays down only a *preference* for the Veda; and that on the ground of the latter being independent of extraneous snpport.

11. † There is yet another interpretation of the *aḍhikaraṇa* suggested by Kumārila:—The *Smṛiṭis* spoken of here as to be disregarded are, not indeed the *orthodox Smṛiṭis* compiled by Manu and others, but those so-called '*Smṛiṭis*' that have been compiled by the later secessionists from the

* *Ṭanṭravarṭika* Translation, p. 164. † *Ibid.* p. 165.

orthodox fold. It is interesting to note that the *Smṛiṭis* relegated by Kumārila to this category are :—

'(1) The compilation of certain texts bearing on *Ḍharma* and *Aḍharma* by Shākya, and by the propounders of the systems known as the *Sāṅkhya*, the *Yoga*, the *Pañcharāṭra*, the *Pāshupaṭa* and the like,—all of which have in them a certain support of the Veda......based upon the strength of certain visible results quite unconnected with the Veda, and upou arguments seemingly based upon perception, inference, analogy and presumption. (2) Those that lay down certain instructions with regard to the gaining of a living...... treating also of certain incantations and recipes for the treatment of diseases, hypnotism and the like,......the efficiency whereof is based upon success in a few stray cases. (3) The compilations treating of the most repugnant practices, and yet classed as *Smṛiṭi.*'

12. With regard to *Sūṭras* 5-7, there is a difference of opinion between Shabara (and in his wake, Prabhākara) and Kumārila : The former takes them as embodying an independent *aḍhikaraṇa*, dealing with one further instance of the contradiction of *Veda* by *Smṛiṭi*. But as Kumārila would not admit of any such real contradiction between his '*Smṛiṭis*' and 'Veda,' he suggests that *sūṭrās* 5 and 6 be taken as parts of the preceding *aḍhikaraṇa*, to which they raise certain objections and answer them. In course of his explanation of *sūṭra* 6, Kumārila makes the following declaration with regard to the trustworthy character of the works of human compilers*:—

'In matters relating to Ḍharma, we accept as authoritative the declarations of only such persons as are mentioned in Vedic *manṭras* and *Arṭhavāḍas* as the authors of the *sciences*.'—

And again—

'We conclude that Ḍharma brings about its due results only when it is understood with the help of those scriptures that are recognised to be not incapable of having their basis in the Veda......Just as we do not admit that knowledge of Ḍharma to be true which is obtained by an improper study of the Veda, so also in the case of the works of such authors as are known to have conduct against the teachings of the Veda,......we do not accept these as valid means of knowing Ḍharma.'

The seventh *Sūṭra* has been taken by Kumārila as embodying an independent, and rather important, *aḍhikaraṇa*, dealing with the authority attaching to the practices of good men.* The opponent having cited many instances of men universally recognised as 'good' and 'righteous' having deviated from the right path,—the author has tried to explain away those cases, and has finally come to the conclusion that—

'When we find that certain actions are performed by good men, and we cannot attribute these actions to any such perceptible motives as greed and the like, they should be accepted as *Ḍharma*; and the reason for this is that when good men regard a certain act as *Ḍharma*, the very fact of their being good men and learned, coupled with the fact that the act in no way proceeds from greed or any such motive, is proof of the fact that the act must have some basis in the Veda; as all good men know that no action not countenanced by the Veda can be regarded as 'Ḍharma'; specially as only those people are universally recognised as 'good' who are found to be always acting in accordance with Vedic injunctions.'

From this it is clear that it is not *all* that good men *do* that is to be regarded as 'Ḍharma'; it is only what they *do* and *regard as* '*Ḍharma*' that has to be so regarded.

Kumārila proposes also a third interpretation of *Sūṭras* 6 and 7, whereby these embody an independent *aḍhikaraṇa*,—

* *Ṭanṭravārṭika*—Translation, pp. 182-83.

Sūṭra 6 containing the *Pūrvapakṣa* that, "inasmuch as the scriptures are limited in their scope, the practices of good men, devoid of Vedic support, cannot have any authority relating to Ḍharma";—in answer to which *Sūṭra* 7 provides the *Siḍḍhānṭa* as explained above.

It is interesting to note that Prabhākara does not take any notice of these important interpretations propounded by Kumārila.

13. Sūṭras 11-14 consider the authoritative character of the *Kalpasūṭras.* A distinction has been drawn between the *Smriṭis* and the *Kalpasūṭras* on the ground that while ṭhe latter lay down the rules of sacrificial procedure exactly as laid down in the Vedic texts still available, the former are mere compilations based *presumably* upon many such Vedic texts as are now lost, and can have their existence only *inferred*; and for this reason, the authority of the *Kalpasūṭras* cannot be made to depenḍ entirely upon the arguments that have been brought forward in support of the authority of the *Smriṭis.* The *Pūrvapakṣa* view with regard to the *Kalpasūṭras* is that they are as self-sufficient in their authority as the Veda; and hence the *Ḍarsha* sacrifices should be performed on *all days* as laid down by them, and not only on the *New-moon day* as prescribed in the Veda.* The *final conclusion,* on the other hand, is that, in view of the fact that the *Kalpasūṭras* only repeat in more intelligible language what is found to be already mentioned in the Vedic texts still available, there can certainly be no doubt as to their trustworthy character; but that at the same time, they can have no self-sufficient authority; as such authority can belong only to those scriptures that are independent of human authorship; which the Vedas alone are. Says the *Brihaṭī* (MS. P. 33b)—

'*Naiṭaḍupapaḍyaṭe pauruṣeyaṭvam anapekṣaṭvam cheṭi, siḍḍhañchāsya pauruṣeyaṭvam*'—('It is not possible that what

* *Shaṭapaṭha Brahmaṇa* X. 1-5.

proceeds from a human source should be self-sufficient in its authority; and it is well-known that the *Kalpasūṭra* is the work of human authors').

The above is the interpretation of the *Aḍhikaraṇa* propounded by Shabara, and also adopted by Prabhākara and Kumārila. The latter however proposes three more likely interpretations :—(a) It refers to the trustworthy character of the *Smṛiṭis* along with the *Kalpasūṭras*; with regard to both of which, it having been established that they are authoritative, it is now proved that neither the one nor the other is *self-sufficient* in its authority, independently of the Veda. (*b*) It refers to the authority of the *Aṅgaviḍyās* or Subsidiary Sciences—*Shikṣā, Kalpa, Vyākaraṇa, Nirukṭa, Chhanḍas* and *Jyauṭiṣ*,—with regard to which the conclusion is that they derive all their authority from the Veda, and have no authority apart from it. (*c*) It refers to the so-called *Smṛiṭis* of the *Bauḍḍha*, and proves that these can never be regarded as 'eternal scriptures,' and as such are of no consequence in matters relating to Ḍharma.

14. We shall take up here the case of the *Smṛiṭis* of Gauṭama, Vashiṣṭha, Hāriṭa, Shaṅkha, Āpasṭamba, Bauḍhāyana and others, which have only limited scope, and pertain to certain specialised areas and classes of men. These, according to Kumārila, are included in the subject-matter of the *Holakāḍhikaraṇa*—the *aḍhikaraṇa* dealing with local customs (*sūṭrās* 15-23). Prabhākara's Pūrvapakṣa is that, inasmuch as the *smṛiṭi* passages laying down these customs themselves contain such limiting words as 'pertaining to the East' and so forth, they and the Vedic passages on which they are based, must be regarded as limited in their scope; and thus the Veda, to this extent, cannot be accepted as *universally* and absolutely authoritative. The final conclusion arrived at in regard to these *smṛiṭis* is that, on account of the universal character of the

Injunctions and Prohibitions contained in them, they must be accepted as applying to *all men*. Nor is this view incompatible with the fact that the *smṛiṭis* themselves speak of certain acts as to be done by certain persons only; because such injunctions with limitations are found in the Veda also, —which, for instance, speaks of the *Rājasūya* as to be done by the Kṣaṭṭriya only (*Shaṭapaṭha, Brā.* 5-1-1-12).

15. The *fifth aḍhikarana—sūṭras* 8, 9—is another important point where Kumārila is entirely at variance with the *Bhāṣya* and Prabhākara. From the consideration of the Practices of Good Men in regard to *action*, the next step is to their practice in regard to the *usage of words*. In different parts of the country, and in different communities, different meanings are found to be attached to the same word; and the question arises as to which of these significations is to be accepted as the most authoritative. The conclusion is that—'the sense in which the word is used by those persons that take their stand upon the *Shāsṭras* is to be accepted as the most authoritative' (*Sūṭra* 9).

This is the interpretation of the *aḍhikaraṇa* by the *Bhāṣya*, accepted by Prabhākara; who says—'*Shiṣṭaprayoga eva balavān iṭyuchyaṭe*' (*Brihaṭī* MS. p. 33). Kumārila, however, takes the *aḍhikaraṇa* as pertaining to the usage of words current,—not indeed among two sets of good men in the *Ārya* country, but—among the *Āryas* on the one hand, and the *Mlechchhas* or Foreigners on the other;—the conclusion being in favour of the former.

Kumārila also proposes a third interpretation:—The comparison instituted is between the sense attached to words in ordinary parlance of the present day, and that in which they are found to be used in Vedic passages; and the conclusion is in favour of the latter.

Apart from the above three interpretation, Kumārila proposes* what appears to be the most cogent interpretation

*Ṭanṭravārṭika, Trans. pp. 209-12.

of the *aḍhikaraṇa* :—He institutes a comparison between the authority of the *smṛiṭis* and that of the *Practices of Good Men*, and this appears to be the most natural point to follow after the last *aḍhikaraṇa* ; after the establishing of the authority of the *Veda*, we have established the authority of the *Smṛiṭis* ; this naturally gave rise to the question as to which of these two possesses the greater authority, when they are found to differ ; after this we established the authority of the *Practices of Good Men* ; and the question naturally presenting itself is as to which of these two—*Smṛiṭi* and *Practice*—should be regarded as possessing superior authority. What gives rise to this question is the fact (proved above) that both of these ultimately derive their authority from the Veda, upon which they are both based. On this question, the final conclusion is in favour of greater authority attaching to the *Smṛiṭi* ; and the reason for this is that it is based directly upon the Veda, while the Practice of Good Men gets at its authority in the Veda only though the intervention of the *Smṛiṭi* ; that is to say, it is the authors of the Smṛiṭis alone who are believed to have derived their ideas of Ḍharma directly from the Veda ; all later good men derive their ideas, not always from the Veda directly, but from these only through the help of the Smṛiṭis ; so that the difference between the authoritative character of the two lies to the same extent as that between the character of the Smṛiṭi—compilers and the good men of later days.

16. In this connection, *sūṭras* 15-32 consider the character of certain popular local customs ;—The idea being that local customs, if at all authoritative, in howsoever limited a manner, must owe that authority to the Vedic texts ;—it is argued that if the customs have only *local* authority, then the Vedic texts upon which they are based must also have only local (and limited) authority ; and thus the very keystone of the Mīmāmsaka's position—the '*universal*

authority of the Veda'—becomes shaken. The final conclusion upon this point is that the Vedic Injunctions assumed in support of such customs cannot be qualified by any specifications of time or place;—firstly because the specifications generally spoken of—'in the east,' 'in the north-west,' and so forth,—are only relative, and do not refer to any particular country or people; what is 'eastern' to one is 'western' to another;—and secondly because the customs are not found to be observed by *all* men of any limited area; nor are they found to be *not* observed by *all* men of other parts of the country. Says Prabhākara*—

'There being no fixity to any specification, no limitation is possible. That there is no fixity is proved by the fact—(1) that the Injunction does not impose any such limitation; as all that an Injunction can do is to indicate that a certain act has to be done; (2) that the names of the customs themselves, *holāka* and the rest, cannot indicate any such limitation, as all that they signify is a certain act;—(3) nor is there anything else that could specify the place or time; as there are no words indicative of any *quality*, *genus*, *position* or *place*.'

17. The next *Adhikaraṇa*—*Sūtra* 10—raises a rather interesting question:—There are certain words, even in the Veda, that are not current in *Āryāvarta*; but are in use among *Mlechchhas* or Foreigners; with regard to these there arises a doubt as to whether they should be accepted to have that signification which is sanctioned by foreign usage, or some other meaning should be deduced from them etymologically,—the words themselves in their entire form being in this case regarded as meaningless. The *Pūrvapakṣa* according to Prabhākara, as usual, is that such words contained in the Veda are meaningless, and that for this reason, the Veda in its entirety cannot be regarded as affording valid knowledge of Dharma,—thus vitiating the main thesis of

* *Bṛihatī*. MS. p. 34.

Aḍhyāya I, put forward in *Sūṭra* 2; and hence, in order to avoid this meaninglessness, some signification should be deduced from the etymology of these words. The final conclusion, however, is that, inasmuch as in the case of all words we accept the meaning assigned to it by usage among men, we shall be fully justified, in the case of the words in question also, in accepting the usage of the foreigners, in the absence of any other source of information. Says Prabhākara*—

'For this reason, in the understanding of the meaning of the Vedic passage, we shall certainly be guided by such usage of the foreigner as is *not* found to be opposed to any *Ārya* usage.'—

As to whether or not the form of the word current among foreigners is the correct one, that is always doubtful; but when we find the word in the Veda to be exactly the same as that in use among foreigners, we must unhesitatingly accept the signification assigned by this usage; specially in the case of such words as denote things found in the foreign country only. A recourse to the etymology of the word for finding out its meaning would be justifiable only in cases where no meaning can be got at though the help of any usage in any part of the world,—the meaning assigned by usage always having precedence over the derivative meaning—'*Yogāḍrūdhirbalīyasī*.'

18. The difficulty raised above in connection with the correct *meaning* of words leads us on directly to the question of the correct *form* of words, and the rules regarding these forms as embodied in Grammar. What bearing the trustworthiness of Grammar has upon the authority of the Veda is thus explained by Prabhākara† :—

'The students of Veda hold that all such words as *gauḥ*, *ashvaḥ*, and the like have definite meanings; in fact, it is only

* *Bṛihaṭī* MS. Page 33b.

† *Bṛihaṭī* MS. Page 34.

when these and other words contained in the Veda have definite meanings that any explanation or comprehension of Vedic passages is possible; and this definiteness of meaning is possible only if the Science of Grammar is authoritative and trustworthy; as in the absence of this, there would be no reasonable basis for accepting any definite meaning; and the meaning of the whole Veda becoming thus indefinite and uncertain, the Veda comes to have that untrustworthy character which is inseparable from all that is indefinite and uncertain. Hence in view of the fact that the correct forms of words, and their significations, can be ascertained only by the help of Grammar, it becomes necessary to enquire into the character of works dealing with Grammar, in order to ascertain which of these may be accepted as authoritative.'—

Thus here, as in all other *Aḍhikaraṇas*, the subject of Grammar is considered only as having a bearing upon the general authority of the Veda.

The *Pūrvapakṣa* arguments against the necessity of using only 'correct' forms of words,—and also against the Science of Grammar in general,—may be thus summed up*:—

(1) The word '*gāvī*' and such other vernacular 'corruptions' are as expressive of the *cow* and other things as the 'correct' word '*gauḥ*' and the like.

(2) The 'corruptions' are as *correct* as the so-called 'correct' forms.

(3) They are not 'corruptions'; because they are as perceptible by the ear as any other words.

(4) They are all equally 'eternal,'—as in the case of these also we cannot trace any beginning in time.

(5) No 'transcendental' result can follow from the use of the so-called 'correct' forms; as the use of these also only serves the ordinary purpose of denoting things; and also because they cannot form the subject of Vedic injunctions.

* *Bṛihaṭī* MS. Page 35. *Ṭanṭravārṭika*—Translation, Page 298.

(6) Grammar cannot be called 'Scripture,' because it has not got the form of the Veda,—the Science of Grammar not differing in any way from the ordinary explanations of vernacular words.

(7) Grammar cannot derive its authority from the Veda, as it does not treat of *actions*, which alone form the subject-matter of Veda proper.

(8) Grammar cannot be regarded as an integral part of the Veda, as is it not found to serve any useful purpose in matters relating to Ḍharma,—specially as in the expressing of their meanings—the words of the Veda do not stand in need of any help of grammar.

(9) The ordinary usage of words cannot be based upon grammar; as it is this latter itself that proceeds on the basis of *usage*.

In answer to the above the final conclusion is as follows:—Even though a certain word be found to be current in ordinary usage, there would be no ground for the belief that it has been in use from time immemorial; it is always necessary to enquire whether or not it is correctly expressive of the meaning which it is intended to convey; and it is this enquiring that the Science of Grammar makes it its business to undertake. As a matter of fact, for denoting one thing or idea, there can be only one verbal expression; and there can be no justification for assuming endless synonyms. Words and phrases are used for the sole purpose of enabling us to talk of things; and so long as this purpose is served by a single verbal expression, no synonyms are permissible. In some cases however, we have to accept synonyms, as they are found sanctioned by usage in the Veda and the Smṛitis. For the vernacular and other more recent forms of words however, there is no such sanctioning authority available; hence there can be no justification for assuming any denotative potency in these. 'Potencies' or 'forces' are to be postulated only when without them we cannot explain certain well-established facts; hence when the established fact—in the shape of our talking of the cow, *f.i.*—is found possible to explain through the potency of the word '*gauḥ*', which is found in the Veda, we have no reason for postulating a further potency for any vernacular forms of that word. Then as regards the fact that the vernacular forms of words are actually found to be expressive of the same thing as the correct forms,—this must be due to the simlarity of sounds the word '*gāvī*' for instance, being similar in sound to '*gauḥ*,' denotes the *cow*, not directly, but only through the latter word. As regards the Science of Grammar, it is true that all correct words are present in the Veda; but how would it ever be possible to collect all these words from out of the endless Vedic texts, unless we had the help of Grammar, which classifies and arranges the words in certain well-defined groups, through their derivation? As for the 'eternality' of this science, it is found as a matter of fact—(1) that we cannot think of any point of time where some sort of grammatical rules did not exist; and (2) that Vedic injunctions supply the requisite basis for all the six factors of science—*viz*: (*a*) the derivatiou of words, (*b*) the correct forms of words, (*c*) the injunction of using the correct forms thus ascertained, (*d*) the actual use of such words, (*e*) the prohibition of the use of words not so explicable; aud (*f*) the actual avoidance of such words. And from all this we conclude that these are eternal, having had no beginning in time. The continuity of the Science of Grammar is as unbroken as that of the making of the Sacrificial Post and other such sacrificial things; just as in the case of the latter, the making of an individual Post may have a beginning in time, but the Veda lays down an injunction with regard to it,—so in the same manner, even though a certain using of the correct words may have a beginning in time, yet the Veda can lay down injunctions pertaining to such using. Then again, as regards the vernacular words being expressive of their meanings,—whether or not a word is really expressive cannot be ascertained by usage alone, nor indeed by Grammar alone; it is only when the two conjointly point to a single conclusion that the word can be regarded as really expressive. It is for this reason that we accept as expressive only such words as are *correct*, that is, which are proved to be so by usage, as also by the Science of Grammar. As regards the *corrupt* words, on the other hand, their expressiveness is indicated by usage, it is true; but it is not countenanced by Grammar; and it has been shown above (§15) that *Smṛiṭis* have an authority superior to that of *usage*; consequently what rests solely upon usage cannot be accepted as true when it is opposed to *Smṛiṭis*. Hence the incorrect forms of words cannot be accepted as rightly expressive; the fact that they do denote the same thing as the correct word must be attributed to their similarity to these latter, as explained above. As regards the 'scriptural' character of the Science of Grammar,— even though it is found to bring about only ordinary perceptible results, it cannot be denied that there must be a transcendental result following from the use of the correct word, which could not be brought about by the use of the corrupt word,—the authority for the assumption of such a transcendental result consisting in those Vedic texts which prohibit the use of incorrect words. It is upon this prohibition too that the whole science of grammar is based. Being thus based upon the Veda, it must be regarded as 'scriptural.' The authority of grammar is also based upon the highest code of ethics: Truth always leads to supreme happiness; and Truth is of two kinds—that pertaining to facts, and that to words; consequently, just as the assertion of the true state of things is 'good', so also is the utterance of the true (*i. e.*, correct) word; and this latter character of the word can be ascertained by grammar alone.

19. The question as to whether a certain word is 'correct' or not having been settled by grammar, the next question that would arise would be as as to what that word signifies. This forms the subject-matter of *Sūtras* 30-35. Before entering into this question however, it becomes necessary to ascertain if the words found in the Veda are the same as those used in ordinary parlance; because most of the arguments propounded in this connection would proceed upon the basis of ordinary experience; as the Veda itself does not say anything regarding the signification of words; and ordinary experience can bear upon only such words as are in common use in everyday life; consequently if the words in the Veda were totally different from those in ordinary use, there would be no sound basis for ascertaining the meaning of Vedic passages, which would thus become absolutely untrustworthy. Says Prabhākara * :—

'It is from the trustworthy character of the Veda that we ascertain the purpose of the present enquiry; and this purpose is no other than the recognition of the fact that the words used, as also the things signified by them, in the Veda are the same as those in ordinary everyday life.'

The *Pūrvapakṣa* arguments in support of the view that the two are entirely different are put forward in the *Bhāṣya* and the *Bṛihaṭī*, in the shape of certain examples of words that are found in the Veda in a sense entirely different from that assigned to them in ordinary speech. This view of the *Pūrvapakṣa* however is not accepted by Kumārila, who bases the difference upon the fact that between the two sets of words there are distinct differences of pronunciation, accentuation and so forth; another reasou being that while the woman and the *Shūdra* cannot utter 'Vedic' words, there is no such restriction with regard to ordinary words.

In answer to the above, the final conclusion is that the words are the same in both cases;—firstly, because, if they

* Bṛihaṭī Ms. Page 36.

were different, there would be no means of ascertaining the meaning of the words of the Veda, which would thus become meaningless and hence untrustworthy; and secondly, because the form of the words is exactly the same in both.

20. From the above we are led to the question of the exact nature of the denotation of words: Does the word—'*gauḥ*' for instance—denote the *class*. or the *individual*, or *both*? The ground for doubt on this point put forward by the *Bhāṣya* is that—'while the cognition pertains to the *class*, the action laid down pertains to the *individual*.' This same view is accepted by Prabhākara, * who holds the *Anviṭābhiḍhāna* theory, according to which the denotation of a word is obtained only through its connection with some particular action; and as each sentence would naturally pertain to some individual thing, this theory would appear to lend support to the *Individualistic* theory. The above-mentioned ground of doubt however is not accepted by Kumārila; and his reason is that, as a matter of fact, the cognition is often found to refer to the Individual also (and not always to the Class, as the Bhāṣya asserts). Kumārila bases his doubts as to the true denotation of the word upon the fact that both Usage and Cognition are found severally to apply to the class *and* the individual, while works on grammar lend support to the Individualistic theory. The 'class' or 'class-character' has been defined by the *Bhāṣya* (page 79, bottom) as the *commonality of Substances, Properties and Actions*; and this is explained by Kumārila in the following words—

'At the time that we perceive certain cows,......we have an idea of a certain character that is common to all the various individnals perceived......and it is this *common character* or *commonality*—that constitutes the *class*.'

The Individual has been defined by the *Bhāṣya* as that which is *the receptacle or substrate of specific peculiarities.* The practical purpose of the present enquiry lies in the fact

* Bṛihaṭī Ms. Page 36 b.

that if all words denoted only individuals, there could be no differentiation of rules into *general* and *particular* (the general law and its exception); and thus it would not be possible for the former to be set aside by the latter;—this would give rise to much confusion.

The *Pūrvapakṣa* arguments on the point at issue may be thus summed up :—

(1) Words must denote individuals; because if they did not do so, no injunction of any action would be possible, either in the Veda, or in ordinary worldly activity.

(2) If words denoted only Classes, different 'numbers' and 'cases' of nouns would not be possible.

(3) If nouns denoted only classes; there could be no words expressive of *qualities* of objects, and thus there could be no co-ordination betweeu nouns and adjectives. This is the *Prābhākara* interpretation of the Sūṭra; according to Kumārila the form of the argument embodied in the *Sūṭra* is that—it is only when words denote individuals that there can be a co-ordination between nouns and adjectives.

Prabhākara, in his characteristic manner, turns this question also upon the authority of the Veda. The Pūrvapakṣa, according to him, is that it being doubtful whether the words contained in the Veda denote individuals or classes, the meaning of the whole becomes open to doubt, which vitiates the authority of the entire Veda.

In answer to the above, the final conclusion is that—there is no doubt as to the true meaning of words: *it is the class that is signified by the word, because it serves the purpose of actions* (Sūṭra 33). The reason for this, given by the *Bhāṣya* and by Prabhākara,* is that, if the noun denoted the individual, we could not explain such injunctions as 'the altar is to be built as *kite*'; because it could not possibly mean the making of an individual bird in the altar; it must

* *Bṛihaṭī* MS. Page 37-37b.

mean that 'with brick and mortar one should make an altar of the shape of the kite'; and as it would be impossible for *all* altars to be built like an *individual* bird, the word '*shyena*', '*kite*' must mean the *class* '*kite*'; and as that alone is the 'denotation' of the word which is found to be related to a sentence,—and here we find the *individual kite* incapable of being so related,—the word must denote the *commonality* or class-character. The *Bṛihaṭī* (p. 37b) adds that though all this may be true in the case of the particular sentence—'*shyenāchiṭam chinvīṭa*,'—in the case of other sentences, it is equally evident that the noun *cannot* denote the *class-character*; thus then, it being uncertain as to whether the words in the Veda denote the individual or the class, no trust can be reposed on the Veda, containing, as it does, words of doubtful signification. In answer to this, the *Bṛihaṭī* proceeds to point out that, as a matter of fact, we find that the injunctive function of an injunctive sentence cannot be accomplished until its words afford some idea of 'commonality'; consequently all *actions* must be related to that *commonality* or *class-character*, and *not* to the *individual*;—the idea of the individual, when necessary, being obtained indirectly, through the commonality, with which it is inseparably connected. This is what, according to Prabhākara is meant by the word '*kriyārṭhaṭvāṭ*' (in Sūṭra 33).

Not satisfied with the above exposition of the *Siḍḍhānṭa* Kumārila puts it forward in the following form—*It is the class that is denoted by the word*;——(1) because, as a matter of fact, whenever we hear a word, the first idea that it brings up before our mind is that of the *class*—'Cow' for instance—and not of any *individual* cow; (2) because if individuals were, denoted, then, inasmuch as these are diverse, there could not be any such single idea as is found to be actually presented to, the mind by the word 'Cow'; and even if this were possible, it would only be a conglomeration of all the specific characteristics of all individual cows; (3) because in the case of the denotation of *individuals*—(A) *all individuals* cannot be denoted; as that would necessitate the assumption of as many expressive potencies in the word as there are individuals denoted by it; and the conception of *all* individuals being an impossibility, the full signification of any word could never be grasped; (B) nor can an *aggregate of individuals* be denoted; as in this case also *all* individuals would have to be grasped, which is not possible; and further, all units of this aggregate being perishable, the aggregate also would be perishable; and thus there could be no eternality in the relationship of the word and its meaning; (C) nor lastly could a *single in lividual* be denoted; as the relationship of words and meanings would cease to be eternal; and as it could not be ascertained which particular individual is denoted, no business could ever be carried on.

Then as regards the *Pūrvapakṣa* argument,—that no sacrificial action would be possible with reference to a 'class', if it were the *class* that was denoted by the word,—it is declared (in *Sūṭra* 34) that all such actions are laid down for the purpose of bringing about certain transcendental results; and as the proper agents for the carrying out of the acts leading to these results are the *substances*, what the word denotes is the *class*, not indeed for the sake of the class merely, but only with a view to provide the requisite knowledge of the *substance*, which knowledge would not be possible until the pointing out of the *class* to which that substance belongs.

21. We have thus seen that due authority and trustworthiness attaches to all the more important factors of the Veda,—viz., Injunctive Sentences, *Arṭhavāḍas Manṭras* and Names,—as also to the Smṛiṭis, &c. based upon the Veda. *Apart from these however, we find in many cases that the true indication as to what should be done is afforded also by Supplementary Explanations and Indirect

* *Ṭanṭravārṭika*—Translation, Page 466.

Implications of the words contained in Vedic texts. In such cases, these also have to be accepted as authoritative; inasmuch as these also serve the useful purpose of settling doubtful points in regard to Ḍharma.

SECTION II.

Differentiation of Actions and Texts prescribing them.

Sub-section (1)—*Apūrva.*

1. In Section I, Jaimini has described the *means* of knowing Ḍharma. The first sub-section has shown that the Vedic Injunction is such a means *par excellence*, and the other sub-sections have shown that the character of being such means belongs also to *Arṭhavāḍas*, Names, *Mantrās* *Smriṭis*, Usage, Supplementary Explanations and Indirect Implications. Thus the first section has supplied the full answer to the question—'what are the means of obtaining the true knowledge of Ḍharma?' In answering this question, in detail, it has also been shown that the true character of Ḍharma belongs to such actions as (for instance) the *Agnihoṭra* and the *Jyoṭiṣṭoma* (directly enjoined in the Veda), the *Aṣṭakā* (laid down in the *Smriṭis*), the *Holāka* (as established by custom), and so forth. But in the preceding section, these actions have been mentioned only by way of exemplifying the general principles therein discussed; and the detailed question of the individual character of these actions was left over for the second section. Thus the second section supplies the detailed answer to the second question propounded by the *Bhāṣya*—'what is Ḍharma?—that is to say, what are the particular acts that are to be regarded as Ḍharma?' Or as Prabhākara, with his usual desire for turning the entire body of the *Sūṭras* upon the *Veda* itself, states the subject of the aḍhyāya:—'What are the *several* texts that lay down the various acts that constitute *ḍharma*?'—Hence according to Prabhākara the subject-matter of Aḍh. II consists of difference among the texts prescribing the actions, and not among the actions directly, these latter being regarded

as different according to the difference of the texts prescribing them. This view of the subject-matter of Aḍh. II has been red-argued in the *Shāsṭraḍīpikā*, in the beginning of Aḍh. III. The third question—'What are the *Sāḍhanas*—the means of accomplishing—of Ḍharma?'—is reserved for the third section.*

2. In order to find out each individual act laid down as Ḍharma, it becomes necessary to have some basis for proceeding with the enquiry as to differentiating one action from the other—from among a number of actions laid down in the Veda, &c.; and it is this basis that is discussed in the present section, where it is shown that one action is to be known as different from another when the two are found to be mentioned by different words and so on (*see below*). Then again, inasmuch as one action cannot be regarded as entirely different from another, unless the transcendental results—*apūrvas*—proceeding from them be also different, we have here an explanation of the difference among the *apūrvas* also. Lastly, so far it would seem that for each act there is a distinct *Apūrva*; so in order to set aside this view, we have the further distinction of Actions into 'primary' and 'subsidiary,' in connection with which it is shown that it is only the 'primary' action that leads to an independent *apūrva*, while those actions that are 'subsidiary tend merely to complete that 'primary' action to which they are subsidiary; and as such have no distinct *Apūrvas* of their own. But this distinction between the '.primary, and the 'subsidiary' action is merely mentioned here,—its detailed consideration being left over to sections (3) and (4); the fourth section deals with the *motives* of actions; section (5) is devoted to the subject of the *order* in which certain actions have to be performed; and the question of persons entitled to the performance of sacrifices is dealt with in section (6); sections (7) to (12) deal witht he

*See *Shāsṭraḍīpikā*—Page 193.

subject of the *Transference* of details from one action to the other. Thus we find that all the subsequent sections—from (3) to (12)—turn upon the *Difference* among actions, which, for that reason, forms the subject of section (2).

3. Before proceeding with the grounds of difference among actions, Jaimiui devotes the whole of *sub-section* (1) to what has been called by the commentators an 'introduction' to the main subject. This *sub-section* deals with such matters as—(*a*) which is the word in the injunctive sentence to which the *apūrva* resulting from the enjoined action is related *sūṭrās* 1-4); (*b*) Is there any such thing as '*Apūrva*'? (*sūṭra* (5); (*c*) Division of actions into 'primary' and 'subsidiary' (*sūṭrās* 6-8), aud so forth. In connection with this last subject, the further question is raised as to whether verbs are always injunctive of some action (primary or subsidiary), or sometimes they serve other purposes also; the conclusion on this poiut being that in many cases, where it cannot, under the peculiar circumstances, enjoin an action, the verb has to be regarded as merely expressive of a certain act, which it recalls as being the one at the performauce of which the passage (in which the verb occurs) can serve a useful purpose by being recited. As this is fouud to be the case with *Manṭrās* mostly, the *Bhāṣya* has interpreted the *aḍhikaraṇa* as proving the fact that *Manṭrās* are never purely *injunctive*. In connection with *Manṭrās*, in the preseut context, the Sūṭrās supply us with definitions of the three principal kinds of Mantras.*

4. As the existence of *Apūrva* must be proved before we consider the question of the word to which it is related, we shall change the order of treatment adopted in the *Suṭrās*, and begin with the question of *Apūrva*. The *Pūrvapakṣa* argument agaiust the assumption of *Apūrva* is thus stated by Prabhākara †:—

*See above—Section I, sub-section (1), § 12 and 13.

† *Bṛihaṭī*, MS. p. 47*b*.

'The injunction imparted by the injunctive word only urges the agent to the performance of a certain *action*, and not towards anything desired by him; the *action* is something ephemeral, and is not present immediately before the attainment of heaven by the agent; hence in order to meet these difficulties we must accept the Sacrifice itself to be either everlasting, or bringing about a certain faculty in the agent, or the favours of the deity; and there is no reason for assuming any such thing as the *Apūrva*.'

In answer to the above, he continues—

'At the very outset you commit a mistake in assuming that the Injunction prompts the agent to *action*; what the Injunction really does is to prompt him to *exertion*; and the particular *action* denoted by the root is only the *object of that exertion*. [Thus then, what is denoted by the injunctive sentence is the '*niyoga*' (decree or mandate); this 'mandate' urges the man to *exertion*; and this 'exertion' pertains to some sort of action (denoted by the verb).] The assumption that the action itself is everlasting is against all evidence; the Self also is, by its very omuipresence, inactive; hence what brings about the final result cannot abide in the Self.'

The above passage from the *Bṛihaṭī* is not quite clear; nor has it been possible for us to obtain a manuscript of this portion of the commentary, *Ṛijuvimalā*. But the whole subject is discussed, from the *Prābhākara* stand-point, in the *Prakaraṇapañchikā* (page 185 *et seq.*), from which the following may be gleaned:—

'There can be no doubt as to the ephemeral character of the Sacrifice itself; it is borne out by everyday experienee. Nor can the sacrifice be held to be laid down for the purpose of obtaining the favour of the deity; as there is no evidence in support of this; as a matter of fact also, Sacrifices are never performed for that purpose; the deity is only one to whom the offering is made; and we could please a deity by only such acts as could reach it; then again, it is not possible for any deity to get at all the offerings made by different men at all times; specially because no deity is either eternal or omnipresent. Nor can we accept the view that the verb with the injunctive affix expresses an action tending to produce, in the agent, a certain faculty, which is the immediate cause of the final result. This is the view favoured by *Kumārila*. * We cannot accept this view; as there is no proof for the postulating of the appearance of any such faculty in the agent. That the sacrifice produces such a faculty is not proved either by Perception or by Inference, or even by Verbal Authority,—there being no Vedic texts pointing to any such faculty; specially as we find that the *action* is brought about by the *exertion* of the agent; and therefore the causal potency must reside in this *exertion*,—which *exertion* therefore should be denoted by the injunctive sentence. The assumption of the faculty in question might be said to be proved by Presumption, based upon the consideration that the action cannot be the cause of the final result, without some such faculty lasting during the time intervening between the completion of the action and the appearance of the result. But what presumption can justify us in assuming is some faculty or potency *in that thing itself which is found to be incapable* in the absence of that faculty; so in the case in question, the Presumption can only point to some faculty in the *Action*, and not in the *Agent*; what appears in the *Agent* cannot be regarded as belonging to the *Action*; hence what is brought about by the faculty abiding in the *Agent* cannot be regarded as produced by the *Action*.'

The whole matter of what the *Bhātta* calls '*Apūrva*' and the *Prābhākara* '*Niyoga*', is thus explained in the *Prakaraṇapañchikā* (p. 187):—

* *Tantravārtika*, Translation, p. 504.

(1) The second aphorism of *aḍhyāya* I has shown that what the Injunctive Sentence denotes is *kārya, something to be brought about.* (2) In the beginning of *aḍhyāya* VI, it has been shown that, of this *kārya* denoted by the sentence, the *Niyojyā—i.e.* the person prompted to its bringing about—is one who is desirous of acquiring for himself some desirable result in the shape of Heaven and the like,—this person being denoted by the sentence, by virtue of his being related to that *kārya.* (3) In the *Bāḍaryaḍhikaraṇa* (III—i-3) it has been proved that it is this *kārya* that is the direct cause of the production of that desirable result which is desired by (and as such, qualifies) the *prompted* person. (4) In the *Ḍevaṭaḍhikaraṇa* (Sū. IX—i—9) the *Bhāṣya* has shown that this *kārya* cannot be the *act* (of *sacrificing*, for instance); as this *act* cannot possibly be the direct cause of the final result; nor could it be held to lead to the result through the favour of the deity to whom the sacrifice is offered; nor can it be regarded as leading to the result through a certain potency in the agent; and it is well known that either the act itself, or any potency abiding in itself, does not last long enough to bring about the result. (5) In the *Apūrvāḍhikaraṇa* (II—i-5) we have the final conclusion led up to by all the above *aḍhikaraṇas*: That which is denoted by the injunctive affix and other factors of the Injunction is the *kārya* inhering in the agent, who is *prompted* by the sentence, and as connected with whom the *kārya* is indicated; as this *kārya* is not cognisable by any other means of knowledge, it has been called *apūrva, something new, not known before.* The connection of this *kārya* with the *agent* and the *action* may be thus traced :—The *kārya* by its very nature is something brought about by *kriṭi*, or operation; and this *operation* is none other than the *exertion* of the agent. In the *Bhāvārṭhāḍhikaraṇa* (II—i—1) again, it is shown that no such exertion is possible, independently of some *act* denoted by the verbal root. Hence what the

injunctive sentence denotes, in this connection, is the *Niyoga* or *prompting*, relating to that *act*. This *act*, thus being the object of that *prompting*, comes to be spoken of as the *instrument* by which that *prompting* is accomplished, as shown under III—i—3. Even though the *kārya* is brought into existence at a time other than that of the appearance of the final result, yet, inasmuch as it is inseparably related to the *prompted* agent,—in whom the desire for that result is present,—and this agent is present at the time of the result,—there is nothing incongruous in regarding that *kārya* as the direct cause of the result. This *kārya* has been called *apūrva* by the *Bhāṣya* by reason of its being *something new* to all other means of knowledge, save the Injunctive sentence; but the name given to it by Prabhākara is *Niyoga* or *prompting*, by reason of the fact that it acts as an incentive to the *prompted person* (*Niyojya*) and makes him put forth an *exertion* towards the accomplishment of the action denoted by the verbal root. This *kārya* or *Niyoga* is expressed neither by the verbal root, nor by the injunctive affix, nor by any other word in the sentence; but it is denoted by the *sentence as a whole*; all other necessary factors being expressed by the several words of the sentence individually, what the sentence *as a whole* expresses is this *Niyoga* as related to the *prompted* person expressed by one of the words in the sentence (*i. e.*, the word signifying the *result*, the person desiring which is the *prompted* person). That the *Niyoga* is thus expressed by the sentence is also proved by the fact that the general rule is that, that which is the principal thing made known by the sentence forms its denotation; and there is no doubt that of all things made known by the sentence, the *Niyoga* is the most important; for even though the final *result* has all the appearance of the most important factor, yet it is the *Niyoga* that is really such, because it is the direct and immediate cause of the result, and it is also the immediate effect of the action performed; and further because the result also has to be regarded as subservient to the *Niyoga*, in view of the fact that the *result* enters as one of the factors uecessary for the making up of the full character of the *Niyoga*. To explain—the *Niyoga* caunot be a true *Niyoga*, until there is a *Niyojya*, the person to be prompted to exertiou; as without exertion there can be no *Niyoga*; then again, without the *agent* there cau be no exertion; nor cau an agent put forth exertion—and be a *Niyojya*—until he is entitled to the uudertaking resulting from that exertion; aud lastly, it is only the person desiriug the result issuiug from the uudertaking that is entitled to its performance; thus iudirectly, through the ageut, the result becomes a necessary factor in the *Niyoga*; this relation between the *Niyoga* and the *result* being similar to that between the master aud servant: without the servant the master cannot be a true 'master,' and yet it is the master that is the more importaut person of the two.

The *Prakaraṇapañchikā* raises an interestiug question here:—"Grauted that the iujuuctive senteuce—'oue desiring heaven should perform the *Jyotiṣtoma*,'—expresses the *Niyoga* as proceediug from the actiou of *Jyotiṣtoma* Sacrifice, and as being the direct cause of attaining heaven. But just as the sacrifice being an effect, has only au ephemeral existeuce, and caunot contiuue till tbe appearance of the result,—so in the same manner, the *Niyoga* also, as an effect, could not but be transieut, and as such unable to coutinue till the appearauce of the result. Thus the very purpose for which the hypothesis of the *Niyoga* has been put forward, fails to be accomplished by it. This cuts off the ground entirely from under the whole fabric of the *Niyoga* or *Apūrva*." The author fails to answer this objectiou satisfactorily. All that he says is that the *Niyoga* does not bring about the result immediately ofter it itself comes iuto existence, because in its action towards the bringing about of the result, it stands in need of certain auxilliaries, which are not always available, and until whose appearance the result cannot appear. This explanation does not meet the difficulty that the *Niyoga* itself cannot, and does not, exist at the time that the result appears. He has explained in another place that, it is through the *prompted* agent, that the *Niyoga*, though itself appearing at the present time, brings about the result. This however is as much as to say that the *Niyoga* produces something *in the agent*, which latter something brings about the result; and thus this much-vaunted theory of the *Prābhākara* is found to be less acceptable than the *Bhātta* view, by which the action,—of sacrificing—itself produces a certain faculty in the agent, which faculty brings about the result at the proper time; while Prabhākara appears to assume a *Niyoga* intervening between the *action* and the *something lasting* that is produced in the agent, he does not call it 'faculty,' but which comes to be the same.* In order to meet the difficulty, Shālikanāṭha has been forced to call in the aid of 'Fate'; he says that it is only when the *Niyoga* is aided by *Fate* that it briugs about the result. This after all is a very poor explanation to be offered by the '*Mīmāmsān'ṣṇāṭā*' as he has called the followers of Prabhākara.

Another question arising in this connection is that, what has been said above may be all right so far as those actious are concerned which are laid down as to be performed with a view to a certain result; but how would it apply to those actions which are to be performed merely in fulfilment of a duty incumbent upon all persons, without reference to any result?,—or to those passages that lay down the *non-doing* of certain acts? The answer to this is that, in the explanation of *Niyoga*, the *Prābhākara* has brought in the *result*, not as something desired by the agent, but only as something the presence of which makes a person entitled to the performance of a certain act; in the case of those actions then,

* Herein lies the only justification for Prabhākara's views being regarded as 'gauravāḍ-dūravāntam.'

that are laid down as *necessary* duties to be performed *throughout life,*—any person *who is endowed with life* being entitled to the performance of those acts, the character of the 'Agent' becomes fully accomplished; and this is all that is needed for the explanation of the *Niyoga.*

By Kumārila's view the *Apūrva* is 'a capability in the principal action, or in the agent, which did not exist prior to the performance of the action, and whose existence is proved by the authority of the scriptures'.* Before the sacrifices laid down as leading to heaven are performed, there is in the Sacrifices themselves, in the first place, an incapability of leading to heaven, and in the second place, in the agent, that of attaining to heaven. Both these *incapacities* are set aside by the performance of the sacrifice; and this performance creates also a positive force or capacity, by virtue of which heaven is attained; and to this latter force or capability we give the name '*Apūrva.*' The proof for the existence of such an *Apūrva* lies in Presumption,—based upon the fact that without some such force many Vedic passages are wholly inexplicable. For instance, there are many passages declaring that certain sacrifices lead the sacrificer to heaven,—the idea being that he goes to heaven, not indeed immediately on the completion of the sacrifice, but after death. The question then arises that, as a general rule the effect comes into existence while its cause is still present, or immediately after the cause has ceased to exist; but in the case in question, the sacrifice ceases to exist at the present time, while the attainment of heaven comes ten or twenty years later. This can be explained only by the hypothesis that the sacrifice, on its completion, produces directly a certain potency or faculty in the agent, which resides in him, like many other faculties, throughout life, at the end of which it leads him to heaven. Without some such intervening potency—as the connecting link between

* *Tantravārtika*—Translation, page 504.

the sacrifice and its ultimate result—the causal relation between these two cannot be explained. *Apūrva* thus is nothing more than a force set in motion by the performance of the action,—this force being the direct instrument whereby, sooner or latter, the action accomplishes its result. There is nothing incongruous in this hypothesis; as every action is actually found to set going certain forces, either in some substance, or in persons connected with those substances; and the force thus set going accomplishes its result, as soon as it reaches its full development with the aid of attendant auxilliaries. The whole process is thus briefly stated systematically in the *Nyāyamālāvistara*:—

'(1) The sentence—"one desiring heaven should perform sacrifices"—lays down the fact that the *sacrifice* is instrumental in the bringing about of the attainment of heaven. (2) Then arises the question—how can the sacrifice, which ceases to exist at the moment that it is complete, bring about the result at a much later time? (3) The answer to this is that the sacrifice accomplishes the final result through the agency of the force called *Apūrva*. (4) A further question arises—how is this *apūrva* brought into existence? (5) The answer is—by the performance of the Sacrifice.'

In all simple sacrifices, there is a single *apūrva* leading to a single result. But there are certain elaborate sacrifices which are highly complex, being made up of a number of subsidiary sacrifices; such, for instance, as the *Ḍarsha-Paurṇamāsa* sacrifices. In all such Sacrifices, there are as a rule four kinds of *apūrva*:—(1) The *Phalāpūrva*—that which brings about the result directly, and which is the immediate cause of the result; (2) the *Samuḍāyāpūrva*—in the *Ḍarsha-Paurṇamāsa* sacrifices, the three sacrifices performed on the New Moon day form one group, and the three performed on the Full Moon Day another group; each of these groups occurring at different points of time could not have a single *apūrva*; hence each group has a distinct *apūrva* of its own, the two *apūrvas* combining to produce the final *Phalāpūrva*; and each of these distinct *apūrvas* is called a '*Samuḍāyāpūrva*'; (3) the *Uṭpaṭṭyapūrva*—i. e., the three *apūrvas* following from each of the three sacrifices forming the '*Ḍarsha*' group; these three *Apūrvas* lead to the *Samuḍāyāpūrva* of the group; which, when combining with the *Samuḍāyāpūrva* of the '*Paurṇamāsa*' group, leads to the final *Phalāpūrva*; (4) the *Aṅgāpūrva*—each of the three sacrifices of the group is made up of a number of minor acts, each of which in its turn, must have a distinct *apūrva* of its own; as otherwise the act could not help in the final *Phalāpūrva*.

5. The general law having been established, that every action enjoined in the Veda brings about an *apūrva*, the *Sūṭras* proceed to note certain exceptions. These exceptions form the subject-matter of *Sūṭrās* II—i—6 to 8;—which also deal with the distinction of actions into 'primary' and 'secondary.' The chief basis of this distinction may be thus explained:—Every action is related to a certain material substance; and hence the material has been regarded as serving the visible purpose of accomplishing the action. In certain cases, the action mentioned turns upon itself and imparts an aid to the material; as for instance, in the case of the *threshing* which cleans the corn; while in some cases the action rests upon itself entirely, its sole purpose being its own fulfilment,—*e. g.* the performance of a sacrifice. In this latter case, there naturally arises a desire in the mind of the agent to know what useful purpose would be served by the action; and where no visible purpose is found to be served by it, we have to assume a transcendental result in the shape of the *apūrva*. Where, however,—*e. g.* in the case of the *threshing* of the corn—the action is found to serve a distinctly visible purpose, we have no reason for assuming any transcendental result; specially as the injunction of the action is quite justified by a visible end. From the

above distinction it follows that—*those actions that do not tend to make a material are 'primary' actions* (Sūtra II—i—7). And the reason for this is that these actions—which do not serve to bring into existence any material substance, or to produce a certain peculiarity in a substance already extent —cannot but be regarded as bringing about transcendental results, and as such being 'primary.' *Those again are 'secondary' actions which are meant to make material substances*—(Sūtra II—i—8),—such actions, for instance, as the consecrating of the sacrificial fire, the appointment of priests at a sacrifice, the threshing and grinding of the corn, and so forth. It may be noted here that the distinction of actions into 'primary' and 'secondary' is distinct from the subject of '*aṅga*' or '*sheṣa*' (Subsidiary) and '*aṅgin*' (Principal); as the former refers to *actions* alone, while the latter is a relationship subsisting between *actions* on the one hand and Substances, Qualities and Purifications on the other. This latter forms the subject-matter of section (3).

6. Having proved the existence of the *apūrva*, we now proceed to consider the question—Which is the word in the injunction of an action with which the result of that action is related, and which would, on that account, indicate the difference or non-difference among the *apūrvas* leading up to the results, and thence also among the *actions* themselves. The first step in the answer to this question is—that the result is related to only *one* word in the injunctive sentence;—and the second, that it is related either to the *noun* or to the *verb*. This then leads to the final question—To which of these two—the noun or the verb—is the result related? The answer to this is contained in what has been called the '*Bhāvārthādhikaraṇa*' * (Sutras II—i—1 to 4). That the result cannot be related to the noun follows from the very nature of nouns: Nouns are the names of things already *accomplished*, and not standing in need of

* *Bṛihatī*—MS. pp. 44—47; *Tantravārtika*, Translation, pp. 473—96.

any thing else,—being self-sufficient in their denotation. That word, on the other hand, to which the main result is related, must, as a matter of fact, be something that has yet *to be accomplished*, and as such stands in need of such agencies as would help in its accomplishenent. It is only *Verbs* that are found to be expressive of things that donot already exist at the time, but have got to be accomplished with the help of certain agencies. And inasmuch as the *Apūrva* also is something that is yet *to be accomplished*, it is to the Verb that it must be closely related.

As to how the *Apūrva* is related to the verb, this may be thus explained :—Every verb in an injunctive sentence is found to be made up of a verbal root and the injunctive affix. This affix denotes what has been called 'viḍhi' or, more technically, '*bhāvanā*', by which is meant *the activity of the agent towards a certain course of action.* That is to say, the injunctive affix in the word '*yajeṭa*' signifies that 'the agent must put forth his effort towards a definite end.' This is what has been called the '*Ārṭhī bhāvanā*'; while the factor of *prompting* that accompanies the injunctive is called the '*Shābḍī bhāvanā*.' But in the present connection it is the *Ārṭhī bhāvanā* that concerns us.

As soon as we have realised the above import of the *bhāvanā*, we are confronted by the following three questions—(1) *what is* it that is to be accomplished by the effort of the agent ? ,(2) *by whit* is it to be accomplished ? and (3) *how* is it to be accomplished ? (1) As for the *first* question it naturally follows that it is the desirable result mentioned in the sentence that has to be accomplished ; as regards the *second*, the answer is supplied by the particular action expressed by the verbal root in connection with which the injunctive affix appears ,—in the case of the word '*yajeṭa*', the action of *Yāga, Sacrifice*, denoted by the root '*yaji*'; and lastly, as regards the *third* question, the answer is supplied by the details of procedure laid down in the Veda in connection with the action. Thus it is to the verb alone that the result can be related ,—both grammatically and materially; and hence it is the injunctive verb alone that can show whether or not any two *apūrvas* are different; and from this it would follow as a corrollary if any two actions expressed by the two verbs are one and the same or different. *

This leads us on to the main subject of the section—the Difference among Actions.

SECTION (2)—*Sub-section* (2).

DIFFERENCE AMONG ACTIONS.

1. Before proceeding with the question of what differentiates one *action* and *apūrva* from another, we shall explain the different kinds of action. † I. The first division of actions is into—(1) *Laukika*—worldly, and (2) *Vaiḍika*—Vedic, pertaining mainly to the other world. II. Vedic Actions are classed under three heads:—(1) Positive or Action Proper, the performance of an act, (2) Negative, or Avoidance of an act, (3) Positive-Negative, or Partaking of the character of both Performance and Avoidance, also called '*Paryuḍāsa*.' Another division of Vedic Actions is into—(1) *Guṇakarma* or Secondary (Auxilliary) Action, and (2) *Praḍhāna* or *Arṭha-karma* or Primary action. III. Of Positive Actions the three main divisions are into the three kinds of 'Sacrifice' —(1) '*Yāga*' Sacrifice Proper, the offering of a certain substance to a deity, (2) '*Homa*' offering of the substance into fire or water, and (3) *Ḍāna*—the waiving of one's own proprietary right over a thing in favour of another person.‡ Kāṭyāyana§ draws a further distinction

* In connection with the *Shābḍī bhāvanā*, what is *accomplished* is the activity of the agent; it is accomplished *by* the injunctive word in the Veda; and *by means* of the idea of the excellence of the activity afforded by the *Arṭhavāḍa* passages.

† *Mīmāmsābālaprakāsha*, pp. 81 *et. seq.*

‡ See last chapter, on 'Sacrifice.' *Mīm. Sū*, IV—ii—28.

§ *Shrauṭa-Sūṭra*, 1-27, 28.

between *Yāga* and *Homa*,—the former being that in which the offering is made by a man *standing* and pronouncing the syllable '*vaṣat*' at the end of the *manṭra*, while in the *Homa* the man is *sitting* and pronounces the syllable '*svāhā*.' Positive Action is divided into another three classes, by the followers of Kumārila (specially by Pārṭhasāraṭhi Mishra) :—(1) *Kraṭvarṭha*—accomplishing something tending to the fulfilment of the Sacrifice, for instance, all Subsidiary Actions, called '*guṇakarma*.' (2) *Puruṣārṭha*—accomplishing something desired by the agent, for instance, all Primary Actions, also called '*Arṭhakarma*,' that which produces the *Apūrva* directly; and (3) those that are neither *Kraṭvarṭha* nor *Puruṣārṭha*, for instance, the *Agnyāḍhāna*. These three divisions have been mentioned by Parṭhasāraṭhi in the *Ṭanṭraraṭna*, under the *aḍhikaraṇa* on *Ḍravyārjana*.* Prabhākara however accepts only the first two of these; nor is there any authority for the third division, either in the *Bhāṣya* or the *Vārṭika*. The two-fold classification, as accepted by Shabara as well as by Prabhākara and Kumārila, is based upon the authority of the Sūtra itself. IV. The *Kraṭvarṭha* Action is divided into—(1) *Āraḍupakāraka*—helping the Sacrifice indirectly, through distinct subsidiary *apūrvas*,—*e.g.* the *Prayājas*; and (2) the *Sannipaṭṭyopakāraka*, helping the Sacrifice directly. V. The *Sannipaṭṭyopakāraka* Action is of three kinds :—(1) that which fulfils a visible purpose; (2) that which accomplishes an invisible or transcendental purpose; and (3) that which fulfils both visible and invisible ends. The *first* of these again is of two kinds—(*a*) that which brings about something visible in substances *to be used* at the Sacrifice, and (b) that which effects some visible result in that which *has been used*,— this latter action being called '*Praṭipaṭṭikarma*.' The *second* kind of the *Sannipaṭṭyopakāraka* is also of three kinds :—(1) That which affects the substance that *has been used*—*e. g.*,

*Mim. Sū. IV—i—(*Fourth Varṇaka*).

the burning up of the substances out of which the offerings have been made; (2) That which affects the substance *to be used*—*e. g.* the sprinkling of water over the Corn; and (3) that which is performed aud affects the substance at the time that it is *being used*,—*e. g.* the offering of the cake without turning the vessel. Another division of the *Kraṭvarṭha* Action is into the following four kinds:—(1) *Uṭpaṭṭi* or Productive Action—*e. g.* the kneading of the dough, which *produces* the eake; (2) *Prāpṭi* or Approaching,—*e. g.* the milking of the cow, whereby the milk is *got at*; (3) *Vikṛiṭi* or Modificatory,—*e. g.* the threshing of the corn, which changes its shape; and (4) *Samskṛiṭi* or Purificatory,—*e. g.* the sprinking of water over the corn.

Another classfication of Vedic Actions is into the following four classes:—(1) *Pṛakriṭi* or Archetypal,—*e. g.* the *Agnihoṭra*; (2) *Vikṛiṭi* or Ectypal,—*e. g.* the *Māsāgnihoṭra*; (3) *Prakṛiti—Vikṛiṭi*, partaking of the character of both,—*e. g.* the *Agnīṣomīya*, the *Savanīya* and the like, the former being the *ectype* of the *Ḍarshapurṇamāsa*, but the *archetype* of the *Savanīya* (see *Mīm. Sū.* VIII—i—14); and (4) That which is neither *archetypal* nor *ectypal*,—*e. g.* the *Ḍarvihoma*; that this is neither the one nor the other has been explained in the last *adhikaraṇa* of the VIII *aḍhyāya* of Mīm. Sū.

The most well-known classification of Vedic actions is into—(I) *Niṭya*, Absolutely Necessary,—*e. g.* the performance of the daily *Sanḍhyā*; (2) *Naimiṭṭika*, Necessary but for certain specified occasions,—*e. g.* the performance of the *Jyotiṣ* sacrifices on the advent of spring (see *Mīm. Sū.* VI); and (3) *Kāmya*, Performed for a specific worldly end,—*e.g.* the *Kārīrī* sacrifice, performed for obtaining rain.

The above are the main divisions of the Positive Action. The Negative Action— Cessation from Activity, or Non-performance—is of two kinds:—(1) *Kraṭvarṭha*,—*e. g.* the *non-holding* of the *Ṣodashin* vessels at the *Aṭirāṭra* sacrifice; and (2) *Puruṣārṭha*—*e. g.* the non-killing of animals.

The third kind of action,—which is neither Positive nor Negative—is also of two kinds:—(1) *Kraṭvarṭha,*—*e. g.* the reciting of the '*yeyajāmaha*' hymns at the performance of the main sacrifice, and their non-reciting at the *Anuyājas*. and (2) *Puruṣarṭha,*—*e. g* the vow to *not see* the rising one.

2. Having explained the more important divisions of Action, we shall now turn our attention to the main question of the *Section*—what are the means by which we ascertain the difference or non-difference among actions? There are *six* means of ascertaining the fact that one action is different from another *:—

(1) *Difference in words*—when two actions are found to be mentioned by two distinct words, there is no doubt that they are intended to be regarded as entirely distinct; specially so when the difference is between the verbs, the roots whereof are directly expressive of the *action*. 'As the *Niyoga* or *Apūrva* is related to the verb, as shown above, we must accept as many distinct *apūrvas*, and hence *actions*, as there are *verbs* in the sentence'—says the *Bṛihaṭī* (page 52 b).

(2) *Repetition*—When the verb is found to be repeated—*e.g.* in the passage '*Samiḍho yajaṭi, ṭanūnapāṭam yajaṭi,* &c., &c.' †—each '*yajaṭi*' is regarded as mentioning a distinct sacrifice.

(3) *Mention of number*—when it is distinctly laid down that there should be '*three* libations,' each of these three must be regarded as a distinct action.

(4) *Difference of names*—in the passage '*eṣa vishvajyoṭiḥ eṣa sarvajyoṭiḥ,* &c.,'—it is clear that each of the names '*vishvajyoṭiḥ*' and '*sarvajyoṭiḥ*' pertains to a distinct action.

(5) *Difference of material*—The sentence '*Vaishvaḍevī āmikṣā*' speaks of the offering of the *āmikṣā* to the Vishve-

* *Mimāmsāparibhāṣā*—Page 45. *Mimāmsā-Sūṭra*—Aḍhyāya II, Pādas 2 and 3

† A passage referring to certain offerings to the Seasons,—occurring in the *Shaṭāpaṭha-Brāhmaṇa* 1. 5. 3. 9 *et seq.*

ḍevas ; and the sentence '*Vājibhyo vājinam*' similarly speaks of the offering of the *vājina* to the Vājins ; and from this it is clear that the offering of the *Āmikṣā* is one action and that of the *Vājiṇa* another.

(6) *Difference of context*—we find the sentence '*Upasaḍbhishcharitvā māsamagnihoṭrañjuhoṭi,*'—'Having performed the *Upasaḍ* sacrifices, one performs the *Māsāgnihoṭra,*'—in a context entirely different from that of the ordinary *Agnihoṭra* ; and this fact shows that the *Māsāgnihoṭra* Sacrifice herein laid down is an action that is entirely different from the ordinary *Agnihoṭra,*—even though the details of the two sacrifices are entirely alike. In this connection the *Mīmāmsā-Sūṭra* (Aḍhyāya II, Pāda 4, Sūṭras 8 to 32) raises the question as to whether or not the '*Agnihoṭra*' mentioned in a passage of the *Māḍhyanḍina* Rescension of the Yajurveda is the same as that mentioned in a passage of the *Kāṇva* Rescension ; and the final conclusion is that the two are one and the same ; mentioned in different Rescensions for different sets of readers. It is only when actions are mentioned in different contexts of the same rescensional text that they are to be regarded as different.

SECTION (3)—SUB-SECTION (1).

Mutual Superviency among Actions.

1. The difference among actions having been established, the next question that arises is—is each and every action expressed by verbs occurring in the Vedic texts an independent act by itself, bringing into existence a distinct *Apūrva*?—or, are some subordinate to, and subserve the various purposes of, some others?—and if the latter,—what actions are subservient to what? Though this is what forms the main subject of section (3), yet it will be shown here that it is not only *actions* that are subservient or subsidiary to *actions*, but that under the word 'subsidiary'—,*sheṣa,*' '*aṅga,*' '*āshriṭa*'—are also included Substances and

their properties. The consideration of this point is all the more important, as the subject-matter of all the rest of the *Sūtras* (sections 4 to 12) are, directly or indirectly, based upon this relationship of the 'principal' and 'subsidiary' among actions, as says Kumārila*—

शेषस्यैवाधिकारोऽत्र युक्तो, नान्यस्य कस्यचित् ।
शेषधीसिद्ध्यपेक्षत्वात् अन्यलक्षणवाग्धियाम् ॥

2. The 'Subsidiary'—'*Sheṣa*'—is defined as *that which is for the sake of another* (III—i—2); that is to say, that which is indicated by direct assertion, &c. *as aiding some action towards the fulfilment of its Apūrva*; this latter qualification being necessary in order to preclude mere verbal relationship. This *being for the sake* of another does not necessarily *in itself* imply that the Subsidiary should in some way help the Principal; but such help is assumed on the strength of Presumption. For instance, in the case of the action of *sprinkling water* on the corn, the fact of its having been laid down in connection with a sacrifice leads to the presumption that it must accord some help to that sacrifice. Similarly in the case of the *Prayājas*, laid down in connection with the *Ḍarshapūrṇamāsa* sacrifice, we find that these latter stand in need of some help; and also that there are certain other actions laid down (in the shape of the *Prayājas*), which stand in need of some other action to which they could accord help; and this mutual need leads us to the presumption that the *Prayājas* subserve the *Ḍarshapūrṇamāsa*.

3. Before proceeding further we shall stop a while to discuss a question that has led to some confusion in the minds of all students of *Pūrvamīmāmsā*. In the Mimāmsā-sūṭra, II—i—7, 8, we have a division of actions into 'primary' and 'secondary,' the two *Sūtras* providing us with

* *Ṭanṭravārṭika*—Text, p. 655 and 660.

the definitions of the two kinds. The question arises—' Inasmuch as the ' secondary ' action will be necessarily *subservient* to the 'primary,' where is the use of raising the question at all, in *aḍhyāya* III ?'

There are two answers to this question :—(1) that the Sūṭras in *aḍhyāyā* II have taken note of *actions* only, and those also only such as are actually found to fulfill only visible ends ; while the third *aḍhyāya* takes up, not only *all* actions—serving visible as well as invisible ends—but *substances, manṭras* and such other details also. This answer is rejected by Kumārila* on the ground that, in that case, the subject of *aḍhyāya* II would be only a part of what is dealt with in *aḍhyāya* III ; the answer that he proposes is as follows :—(2) that the actions mentioned in the second *aḍhyāya*—the threshing of the corn for instance,—are ' subservient ' can be ascertained only from what the *Sūṭras* say in the third *aḍhyāya* ; what has been said in the second *aḍhyāya* therefore is only this, that those actions cannot be regarded as leading to an *apūrva*, for the simple reason that they are found to accomplish only visible purposes ; 'and under the circumstances, if they were to produce an *apūrva* also, they would be bringing about two results'—adds the *Ṛijuvimalā* (MS. Vol. III, page 11).

According to Prabhākara,* the connection between the two *aḍhyāyas* is thus explained :—What has been explained in the second *aḍhyāya* is only the difference among injunctive texts ; that is to say, it has been shown there how two texts are to be regarded as different, by reason of the difference in their *results*—*apūrva*—spoken of in each, and also of the difference in the several adjuncts of these ; and as ' action ' is one of the most important of these *adjuncts*, the difference among actions has also been explained in that *aḍhyāya*,—but this last only as the basis of differentiation among

* *Ṭanṭravārṭika*, page 670.

† *Bṛihaṭī* page 65, and *Ṛijuvimalā*, Vol. III, page 1.

the texts; and thus the *difference* therein dealt with is that based upon the consideration of the connection among the words of the injunctive texts. While the *difference* upon which the subject-matter of the third *aḍhyāya* is based is that of the *Niyoga* or *apūrva* resulting from actions.* The distinction herein drawn will be made clear from the example of the sentence '*graham sammārṣti*'; here the relationship between the *graha* (vessel) and the *washing* expressed by the words is only that of the *vessel* being the 'objective' of the action of *washing*; while the relation of 'subserviency' between the two is based upon the fact that the *washing* is 'subservient' to the *vessel* as leading to some other result. Thus it is found that what is dealt with in the third *aḍhyāya* is closely connected with what has gone before in the second *aḍhyāya*.

4. The answer to the question—what is it that can be the 'subservient' or 'subsidiary'?—is supplied by the *Sūṭras* III—i—3 and 4, wherein it is stated that the character of the 'subsidiary' can belong to—(1) 'substances, (2) accessories (*i. e. manṭra* and deity) and (3) purifications' (these three only, according to Bāḍari—*Sūṭra* 3; but according to Jaimini, also to) (4) 'actions, (5) results, and (6) human agents.' (*Sūṭra* 4). (1) That *substances* are subservient to Sacrifices follows from their very nature; they exist, because they subserve some purpose. (2) *Manṭras* and *Deities* also are necessary appendages to the Sacrifice. (3) Such *purificatory* or *preparatory acts* as the threshing of the corn come to be regarded as 'subservient' to Sacrifices, in view of the fact that Sacrifices need some substances out of which the cake and such other things could be made; the cake, for instance, must be made of some corn; but no entire corn can make it; the grains have to be threshed and cleaned, so that it may be used for the making of the cake to be used at the Sacrifice. (4) *Actions* (Sacrifices) also are 'subservient'

* See *Ṛijuvimalā*—Vol. III, page 3.

to their result; as it is *for the sake* of the result that the action is performed. (5) The *result* is 'subservient,' because it is *for the sake* of the human agent that seeks it, and accomplishes it by means of the action. (6) The *Human Agent* is 'subservient' to the actions,—being the 'performer' who will accomplish the action, *for the sake* of which, therefore, he would exist. The 'subserviency' of the agent to the action is expressed by the word enjoining the act; for instance, of the word '*yajeṭa*' the 'Sacrifice' forms the principal factor in the denotation; and as no such action as the 'Sacrifice' would be possible without an *agent*, the agent also must be regarded as implied by the same word. Apart from this, there are cases where the human agent occupies the most subordinate position; *e. g.* in the case where the man is required simply for the purpose of measuring the height of the sacrificial post.

The above is the view of Jaimini as interpreted by the Bhāṣya; which quotes the interpretation of the 'author of the Vṛiṭṭi' (Upavarṣa),—the sense of which may be thus stated:—It is only *Substances, Manṭras and Deities* and *Purificatory Acts* that can, by their very nature, be 'subservient' to sacrifices as held by Bāḍari; as it is only these that can *never* be 'principals'; and the reason for this view, says the *Bṛihaṭī* (p. 66b), lies in the fact that the *Niyoga* or *Apūrva* is accomplished by the Sacrifice, which, in its turn, is accomplished by Substauces, Manṭras and Deities and Purificatory Acts, which latter alone are forces contributing to the ultimate result.—'To the other three things, mentioned by Jaimini, the *subserviency* can belong only relatively; for instance, the *Sacrifice* (mentioned in *Sūṭra* 4) is *principal* in relation to the *substance*, but *subservient* in relation to the *result*; the *result* (mentioned in *Sūṭra* 5) is *principal* in relation to the *Sacrifice*, but *subservient* in relation to the *agent*; the *human agent* (mentioned in *Sūṭra* 6) also is *principal* in relation to the result, but *subsidiary* to such acts as the *measuring of the sacrificial* post.' (*Shabara Bhāṣya*, page 211).—

The meaning of this is that the first three—Substance and the rest—are *always* 'subsidiary'; they are never 'principal'; while the latter three—Result and the rest—are both 'principal' and 'subsidiary' in relation to one another.

फलयागनराणाञ्च द्रव्यादीनामङ्गत्वम्परस्परम्*

5. 'Subsidiaries' or '*Aṅgas*' have been divided by Kumārila and his followers† into two classes—(1) the Direct and (2) the Indirect. Those subsidiaries which, either directly or indirectly, help in the fulfilment of the Sacrifice, and, *only through that sacrifice*, the ultimate *Apūrva*, are called 'Direct'; *e.g.*, the *substance* corn, and its *purificatories*, the threshing and water-sprinkling, the *deity* and the *mantras*; the sprinkling of water produces, in the corn, a certain peculiarity not otherwise possible; the threshing helps by removing the chaff from the grain; the corn itself helps by constituting the cake; the *mantras* help by recalling, and consecrating, the deity: and lastly, the deity helps directly by being one to whom the offering is made; and unless there is such a deity, there can be no 'Sacrifice', which is only the offering of substances *to a deity*. Those on the other hand, are called 'Indirect' subsidiaries which produce distinct *apūrvas* of their own,—these *apūrvas* appearing in the soul of the performer,—and which, through these *apūrvas*, help the ultimate *apūrva* of the Sacrifice.

Prabhākara and his followers ‡ proceed on a somewhat different line, as regards the classification of Subsidiaries; their classification is more logicial and exhaustive; it is into the following four heads:— (1) 'Jāṭi' or Class-character, (2) 'Guṇa' or Quality, (3) 'Ḍravya' or Substance, and (4)

* *Ṭanṭravārṭika*—Page, 675.

† *Mīmāmsaparibhāṣā*, pp. 16-17, also Shāsṭraḍīpikā, p. 202.

‡ Prakaraṇapañchikā pp. 202-5.

'Bhāvārṭhāṭmaka' or such things as are denoted by verbs, *e.g.*, actions. The last of these is subdivided into the *Sannipaṭṭyopakāraka* or Direct and the *Ārāḍupakāraka* or Indirect. That which produces its direct effects in a certain thing that is a *Kāraka* in,—*i.e.*, conducive to—the fulfilment of the Sacrifice, is its *Sannipaṭṭyopakāraka* (p. 202); *e.g.* the *Sitting* of the *Sacrificer*, the *thumping* of the material *object* offered, &c.; these have no *apūrvas* of their own, but are related to the final *Apūrva* of the Sacrifice to which they are 'subsidiary.' The *Sannipaṭṭyopakāraka* again is divided into the following four kinds (p. 202)—(*a*) that which brings into existence a certain substance,—*e.g.* the kneading of the flour, which brings into existence the dough that did not exist before; (*b*) that which leads to the acquisition of a certain substance,—*e.g.* the milking, which leads to the acquisition of the milk that existed already; (*c*) that which produces some modification in the substances,—*e.g.* the boiling of ghee which changes the solid into the liquid form; and (*d*) that which purifies,—*e.g.* the sprinkling of water over the corn, which does not produce any material change in the corn, but adds to it something invisible and transcendental.

By the *Bhātta* view, the *Sannipaṭṭyopakārakas* have no distinct *apūrvas* of their own,—their full effect lying in the accomplishment of certain material substances; they have thus only visible effects, (*see* Ṭranṭravārṭika Translation, p. 526) and help the final *apūrva* of the Sacrifice only through the aid that they impart to the material fulfilment of that sacrifice. But even though the subsidiaries themselves do not bring about an *apūrva*, it is held by the *Bhātta* that a distinct *apūrva* does proceed from the recourse that is had to the particular subsidiary. Says the Shāsṭraḍīpikā (p. 203)—'*Niyamāḍrisṭanṭu kalpanīyam, ṭaḍ varamekameva ḍrisṭārṭhāvaghāṭaniyamāḍ aḍrisṭam kalpiṭam.* For instance, the visible effect, the removal of the chaff, for which the *thumping* of the corn is laid down, can be fulfilled by many ways; and so even though the *thumping* itself may not produce an *apūrva*, the choice that the performer exercises, in having recourse to the *thumping* out of the several other ways of removing the chaff, does produce an *apūrva*. The reason for this is that, according to Kumārila, every Vedic injunction must, by its very nature, be related to an *apūrva*; and as the *thumping* is *enjoined*, it must be related to an *apūrva* but as the action of thumping itself is found to be productive of only a visible result, in the shape of the removal of the chaff, the *apūrva* to which it is related must be due to the choice of that particular method of removing the chaff, in preference to others; and the real reason underlying all this lies in the fact that a Vedic Injunction must lay down a *Ḍharma*; and an injunction that would not have what it enjoins conducive to an *apūrva*, would lose its character of 'Injunction of Ḍharma'; and as the action itself is found to be conducive to only a visible end, we must accept an *apūrva* proceeding from the choice that is exercised; it is for this reason that these injunctions have been called 'Restrictive.'

The above view is traversed by the *Prābhākara* in the following manner:—In the case of the thumping of the corn, we find that the words of the text enjoining it, the thing (the corn) itself, the nature of the thing and the action enjoined, —all point to the fact that the only result that can be brought about is the removal of the chaff from the grain. Now if over and above this result, an *apūrva* were assumed, we would fall into the absurdity of a single action being related to, and bringing about, two results. Then as to how there can be a Vedic Injunction of that which refers to some material substance that already exists,—the explanation is that what the injunction lays down does not refer to the mere *shape* or *material form* of the corn, but to the action of *thumping*; and this thumping of the corn *in relation to the Sacrifice*, can not be known by any other means except the injunction; hence the injunction can not be called 'restrictive', but purely 'original,' laying down, as it does, something not otherwise known; because what the injunction means is that the Sacrifice is to be related to *that corn which has its chaff removed by thumping*; and the *restriction* and *specification* of the particular method of removing the chaff is only a Secondary *purpose* served by the injunction, and not itself the *object* of the injunction. This may be thus explained:—If the *thumping* had not been laid down in connection with (and as subsidiary to) a certain *apūrva* (the *apūrva* of the Primary Sacrifice),—but simply for the sake of the visible result of removing the chaff, which would be all that was meant as necessary for the preparation of the cake,—then, inasmuch as this visible purpose could have been fulfilled by the tearing of the corns with the nails also, there would be no necessity for the *thumping*; while, if the *thumping* is laid down in connection with a transcendental result of the sacrifice, in the shape of the *apūrva*, then, as in view of this injunction, the *apūrva* could not be brought about if any other method of removing the chaff were adopted,—the specification of the process becomes necessary; and thus this specification is only the *motive* of the injunction. And as for the fact of the *thumping* being related to the *apūrva*, this is not known by any other means save the injunction in question; and thus in view of this also, the injunction lays down something not otherwise known and hence must be regarded as an 'original' and not a 'restrictive' injunction.

Though the *Sannipaṭṭyopakāraka* is *related* to an *Apūrva* (that of the Sacrifice), it does not *produce* any *Apūrva* of its own; as all that the action does is the bringing about of something visible;—*e. g.*, the removal of the chaff; and yet it is a fit object of injunction, as it does, indirectly through the fulfilment of the sacrificial performance, help in the accomplishment of the final *Apūrva* of that sacrifice. That is why such actions have been called '*sannipaṭṭyopakāraka*'—*yāgasvarūpe eva sannipaṭṭya ṭasyāpūrvasiḍḍhāvupakurvanṭi*. This relationship to the *Apūrva* is ascertained from the proximity of the sentence to the sentence laying down the Principal Sacrifice as bringing about the *apūrva*,—and not upon the words of the sentence themselves. This explanation is objected to on the ground that, in this manner, as the principal fact of the action (of thumping) being related to the *apūrva* would not be expressed by the sentence itself, the sentence would become practically meaningless. Prabhākara's answer to this objection is that it is not necessary that every Vedic sentence *must* speak of some purpose to be served; it is merely a question of facts; a sentence that does *not* speak of a purpose cannot be *made* to speak of it. But in the case in question, the sentence does not, as a matter of fact, become meaningless or purposeless, as it serves the purpose of laying down a certain method of doing a certain thing; and it is only the connection of this method with the *apūrva* that is left to be implied by the said 'proximity;' and that 'proximity' forms one of the bases of syntactical connection is admitted by all philosophers. Thus the *Prābhākara** concludes that,—(1) all *Sannipaṭṭyopakārakas* are 'subservient' to the *apūrva* by direct assertion; (2) they are 'subservient' to the *object* conducive to the sacrifice (the corn) by the nature of their use; (3) they are 'subservient' to the *sacrifice* which is instrumental in the accomplishment of the *apūrva*, by virtue of their constituting the material offered at the sacrifice.

As regards the second class of 'subsidiary' *actions*, the *Ārāḍupakārakas*, these are of two kinds :—(a) That which fulfills only an *unseen* purpose; and (b) that which fulfills *seen* as well as *unseen* purposes. To the latter class belongs the *Payovraṭa*,—*i.e.*, the living on milk alone,—of the sacrificer and his wife, during the performance of the *Jyoṭiṣṭoma*. To the former class belong such actions as are laid down by sentences

**Prakaraṇapañchikā*, page 209.

like '*samidho yajati*,' which do not speak of the action as producing any effect in any of the *kārakas*—the substance offered, or the human agent—helping the action ; and as it is only effects produced in these that could be *seen*, the action cannot but be regarded as bringing about an *unseen* result. But all such actions produce an intermediate *apūrva*, through which they aid in the final *apūrva* of the principal sacrifice, to which latter, on that account, they are regarded as being 'subsidiary.' As such actions do not help in the principal Sacrifice in any perceptible manner,—if they were not accepted as producing an *Apūrva*—then, in as much as they will have been destroyed long before the fruition of the final *Apūrva*, they would not accord any help to the principal sacrifice. It is for this reason that in such cases Prabhākara admits of intermediate *apūrvas* resulting from subsidiaries.

These *Apūrvas* or *Niyogas* are expressed by the injunctive affix itself; and do not belong to the principal Sacrifice. Thus being related to the Sacrificer only through the principal sacrifice, these subsidiaries do not stand in need of the assumption of the fact of the Sacrificer desiring some result. This admission of intermediate *apūrvas* might give rise to the doubt that this result would necessitate a further enquiry and seeking after the method by which these *apūrvas* are to be brought about; but with a view to this, the Prābhākara* draws a subtle distinction between the '*anuṣtheya*' and the '*kārya*',—the former being that which is recognised by the agent as something to be brought about independently, by itself—*e. g.*, the final *apūrva* ; while the latter is that which is recognised as to be brought about only for the sake of the accomplishment of the former ; and as a rule the question of details of procedure can arise only with regard to what is *anuṣtheya*, and not with regard to what is *kārya* ; and thus no question can arise with regard to the intermediate

**Prakaraṇapañchikā*, pp. 214—215.

Apūrvas, which are recognised only as helping in the accomplishment of the final *Apūrva*. It may be noted here that the Prābhākara is rather strict in the matter of postulating *apūrvas*; so long as he can find any perceptible result to justify an act, he will not assume an *apūrva* or *adṛiṣta*; Kumārila, on the other hand, postulates au *apūrva* with every injunction. Being an *Anviṭābhiḍhānavāḍin*, Prabhākara does not accept the law—'*shābḍi ākaṅkṣā .shobḍenaiva pūryaṭē*'—by which the *iṭikarṭavyaṭā* or details of procedure can be sought after only for the sake of a result in the shape of the *apūrva*, and not for the sake of a substance which is already in existence;* this law necessitates the assumption of an *apūrva* with every injunction, each of which, by this law, must be self-contained, having all its needs as an injunction supplied by itself; hence even the *apūrva*, which is one of the factors in the *bhāvanā* denoted by the injunctive verb, has to be got out of every injunction, even of the *Sannipaṭṭyopakārakas*,—if not with the action itself, at least from the *Niyama* or choice of the particular method. Prabhākara, not accepting this law, takes every injunction along with all that it is found to be related to; and thus the *subsidiary* action mentioned in the injunctive sentence being found to be expressive of the accomplishment of some material, it becomes related to the injunction of the *principal* Sacrifice in the following manner:—the *apūrva* of the principal action enjoined by the principal injunction is to be accomplished by meaus of the principal action performed with materials brought into existence in accordance with the subsidiary action enjoined by the subsidiary injunction; thus there is no necessity for assuming an *apūrva* for the latter,—the objective of these injunctions resting in the particular materials brought into existence according to them, and not in any *apūrva*.

---

* *Nyāyamālāvisṭara*, page 423.

Section (3)—*Sub-section* (2) *.

Means of ascertaining what is 'Subsidiary' to What.

1. The six means of ascertaining what is 'subsidiary' to what are the following :—(1) *Shruṭi* or Direct Declaration in the Veda;—*e.g.*, There are certain *manṭras* sacred to certain deities, which are named '*Niveshana Saṅgamana*,' '*Ainḍrī*' and so forth ; with regard to these we meet with the following declaration in the *Vājasaneya Samhiṭā* XII. 66 :—'The *niveshana-sañyamana* belongs to the Vasus, and with the *Ainḍrī* one should worship the *Gārhapaṭya* fire'; here the question arising as to whether the *Ainḍrī manṭra* is to be used in the worshipping of Indra,—in virtue of the name '*Ainḍrī*' ('pertaining or belonging to Indra'),—or in that of the *Gārhapaṭya* fire,—in obedience to the aforesaid declaration in the Veda ;—the conclusion is that the *manṭra* should be used in the worshipping of the *Gārhapaṭya* fire, and is therefore to be regarded as 'subsidiary' to that worshipping. (*Mīm. Sū.* III—ii—3, 4).

(2) *Liṅga*' or Indirect Implication.—It is laid down in the Veda that at the *Soma* sacrifice, the juice that is left after all the offerings have been made, should not be thrown away, it should be drunk ; in connection with this drinking we meet with the *manṭra*—'*bhakṣehi*, &c.' (*Ṭaiṭṭirīya Samhiṭā* 3-2-5-1)—called the *Bhakṣānuvāka* ; in regard to this the conclusion is that the *manṭra* is to be used, not only in connection with the *eating* or *drinking*,—as the words of the *manṭra* directly express,—but also with all those other actions without which the drinking would not be complete ; *e.g.*, the taking up of the juice in the hand, examining it, swallowing it and digesting it, and so forth—all of which collectively go to make up the 'drinking.' In accordance with this conclusion, the whole of the *Bhakṣānuvāka* is broken up into four parts,—each part being employed with

* **Including Pāda iii also.**

each of the four above-mentioned acts; and this is due to the *indirect implication* of all these acts in the act of 'drinking.' (III—ii—24, 25).

(3) *Vākya* or Syntactical Connection.—In connection with the *Jyoṭiṣtoma* we meet with the declaration (*Shaṭapaṭha Brahmaṇa*, 4-4-6-16, and 4-6-17-18)—'the *Ṛik* should be recited loudly, the *yajuṣ* not loudly'; the question arises as to what is meant by the words '*ṛik*' and '*yajuṣ*' in this connection? do they mean the *Ṛigveḍa* and the *Yajurveḍa*? or the *metrical* and the *prose* passages? In the latter case those *manṭras* which are in the *metrical* form, even though they be *manṭras* of the *Yajurveḍa*, would have to be recited *loudly*; while in the former case, all that appears in the text of the *Yajurveḍa* would be recited *not loudly*. The conclusion on this point is that the words refer to the two *Vedas*, and not to the *passages*; and this on the ground that, in the earlier part of the passage at the end of which we have the direction in question, we meet with the declaration—'Three Vedas came into existence, the Ṛigveḍa from Agni, the Yajurveḍa from Vāyu, &c., &c.'; and as the aforesaid direction with regard to the *loud* recitation of the '*Ṛik*,' &c., is a continuation of this same sentence, there is a *syntactical connection* between the two parts of the sentence, by virtue of which it is clear that the words '*ṛik*' and '*yajuṣ*' in the latter part of the sentence must refer to the *Vedas* spoken of in the former part; and in accordance with this conclusion, the metrical passages occurring in the text of the *Yajurveḍa* only, cannot be recited loudly (III—iii—i).

(4) *Prakaraṇa* or Context.—In the *Shruṭis* we meet with the passages—'one desiring heaven should perform the *Ḍarshapurṇamāsa* Sacrifices,'—'He should perform the *Samiḍ* sacrifice,'—'He should perform the *Ṭanūnapāṭ* sacrifice.' (*Shaṭapaṭha-Brāhmaṇa* 1·5·3·9); we also find that there is no *syntactical connection* among these three passages, each being an independent sentence by itself; and as such capable

of being regarded as the injunction of a distinct sacrifice; nor is there anything in the *indirect implication* of the sentences which could indicate any sort of dependence or connection of the *Samiḍ* and *Ṭanūnapāṭ* sacrifices with the *Ḍarshapūrṇamāsa.* We find, however, that no result is mentioned along with the *Samiḍ* and the *Ṭanūnapāt*, as 'heaven' is along with the *Ḍarshapūrṇamāsa*; and we also recognise the fact that being enjoined in the Veda, those Sacrifices also must lead to some desirable end; but at the same time no such end is found to be mentioned; all this leads to the conclusion that the injunction of these sacrifices is wanting in that factor, as without the end to be accomplished, no injunction is complete (see above, Sec. 2). Then as regards the *Ḍarshapūrṇamāsa,* we find that all the information that the injunction of that sacrifice affords is that—'if one desires heaven he should perform the *Ḍarshapūrṇamasa*',—and it says nothing as to the procedure or method to be employed in the performance of that sacrifice; and this shows that this injunction also is wanting in one factor,—the *method* or *procedure,* without which also no injunction can be complete. Now then, looking into the two sets of injunctions, we find that, if taken together, they supply the need of each other, the factor wanting in the one being supplied by the other, and *vice versa*; that is to say, 'the attainment of heaven' mentioned in the injunction of the *Ḍarshapūrṇamāsa* becomes recognised also as the *result* to the accomplishment of which the *Samiḍ* and the *Ṭanūnapāṭ* Sacrifices lend some help; and that these sacrifices go to form the *procedure* or *details* of the *Ḍarshapūrṇamāsa.* This *supplying of mutual need* is what has been called '*Prakaraṇa*', 'Context.' The conclusion thus is that the *Samiḍ* and the *Ṭanūnapāṭ* Sacrifices—called collectively '*Prayājas*'—are 'subsidiary' to the *Ḍarshapūrṇamāsa.* In this case, the two sets of injunctions cannot be regarded as a single *sentence,* because there is no syntactical connection among them,—*syntactically* each injunction being complete in itself. (III—iii—11).

(5) '*Krama*,' or '*Sthāna*,' *Order* or *Position*.—In the section of the *Darshapūrṇamāsa* we meet with the *mantra*—'You are the missile—may I remain unhurt—may you wound *so and so* (my enemy),' (*Taittirīya Sam*, 1-6-2-4). There is no *direct declaration* as to where this *mantra* is to be used; nor is there anything in the *mantra* to show, by *indirect implication*, how it is to be used. But we find that the three sacrifices—the *Āgneya*, the *Upāmshu* and the *Agnīṣomīya*—are mentioned in a definite order; aud later on we find three *mantras* mentioned in conuection with these three sacrifices; aud as the three sacrifices are mentioned in a definite order, and the three *mantras* also appear in a definite order, the natural conclusion is that the first of the *mantras* is to be used at the first of the sacrifices, the second with the secoud, and the third with the third. The *mantra* in question happens to be the second of these, and heuce it is used at, and is 'subsidiary' to, the *Upāmshu* Sacrifice. (III—iii—12).

(6) '*Samākhyā*' or Name.—There are many *mantras* mentioned as to be recited by the various priests at the performance of Sacrifices; no distinct injunctions are found as to which *mantra* is to be recited by whom; but the confusion that might otherwise arise under the circumstances is averted by the *names* given to the *mantras*,—such as (1) '*hautra*' indicating that the *mantras* (mainly those of the *Rigveda*) are to be recited by the *Hotṛi* priest, (2) '*ādhvaryava*,' the *mantras* of the *Yajurveda*, to be recited by the *Adhwaryu*, (3) '*audgātra*,' the *Samāveda mantras* to be recited by the *Udgatṛi*. Thus the fact of the *Hautra mantra* being recited by, and hence being 'subsidiary' to, the *Hotṛi* priest is ascertained by the *name* of the *mantra* (III—iii—13).

*2. (*a*) In a case where there is struggle for supremacy between *Direct Declaration* and *Indirect Implication*, it is the former that supersedes the latter. That is to say, when we have a Vedic declaratiou laying down that a certain 'Subsidiary'—*Mantra* for instance,—is to be employed at a certain sacrifice, while the words of the *mantra* itself indicate that it is to be employed in connection with another, we have to accept the former and reject the latter. The principle underlying this supersession is that, in all matters relating to *Dharma*, nothing can be regarded as authoritative except what is laid down in the Veda. In the case of *Direct Declaration* we have it directly stated by the Veda what should be done; in the case of *Indirect Implication*, on the other hand, even when its indication is accepted, the course of action implied is accepted as authoritative only after, on the strength of that implication, a Direct Declaration to the same effect is assumed. It is for this reason that whenever there is difference between the two, the *Direct Declaration*, which is self-sufficient, accomplishes its purpose long before the *Indirect Implication* can do its own, through the intervention of the assumed Direct Declaration. As an instance of this difference aud supersession, we have the text—'with the *Aindri Mantra* one should worship the Gārhapaṭya fire' (*Vājasaneya Sam. XII.* 66); this is a *Direct Declaration* laying down the use of the *Aindrī* verse in the worshipping of the Fire; ou the other hand we have the words of the *mantra* itself—'*Kaḍā ca nasṭarīrasi nenḍra sashchasi ḍāshuṣē*,' 'O Indra, you never harm anyone,—in fact you do good to one who makes offerings to you' (*Ṛigveḍa Sam* 8, 51, 7.)—imply that the verse should be used in the worshipping of Indra. But before this latter can be accepted as authoritative, we have to assume, on the strength of this implication, a direct injunction to the effect that *the Ainḍīri ṛik should be used in the worshipping of Indra*; but the

* *Mīmāmsā-Sūtra*, III—iii—14.

road to this assumption is blocked by the above-mentioned *Direct Declaration* to the effect that the *manṭra* is to be used in connection with the worshipping of Agni.* (*b*) *Indirect Implication* in its turn is more authoritative than *Syntactical Connection.* In connection with the *Ḍarshapūrṇamāsa* we find the *manṭra*,—' *Syonanṭe sadanam kriṇomi ghriṭasya ḍhārayā suṣevam kalpayāmi—ṭasmin sīḍāmriṭe praṭiṭiṣtha vrīhīṇām meḍha sumanasyamānaḥ*', 'O Cake, I prepare a nice seat for thee, with Ghee I make it comfortable! O Essence of Corn, may thou, with a peaceful mind, take thy seat upon this'! (*Ṭaiṭṭi—Brāhmaṇa* 3-7-5-2);—here the words, as *syntactically* placed, make, of the two parts of the *manṭra*, a single sentence; and this would imply that the whole is to be used in the preparing of the Kusha-bedding for the Cake. But the words of the two sections distinctly imply that the first section of the *manṭra* is to be used in the *preparation of the bedding*, and the second section in the *placing* of the Cake upon it. What makes this latter implication more authoritative than the former is that in the case of the former, before we can assume the *Direct Declaration* to the effect that 'the whole *manṭra* should be used in the preparation of the bedding', we have to assume the *Indirect Implication*, by the words of the *manṭra*, of the act of *preparing*; while in the case of the latter, the *Indirect Implication* directly leads to the assumption of the necessary *Direct Declaration*. And thus being one step nearer to the necessary *Direct Declaration*, *Indirect Implication* is regarded as more authoritative than *Syntactical Connection*. † Prabhākara adds one more reason for *Indirect Implication* being more authoritative: As to how a certain *Yajuṣ-manṭra* is to be employed depends upon the useful purpose served by it; what this purpose is can be learnt,—in the absence of *Direct Declarations* to the effect,—

* *Bṛihatī*.—page 78 *b*.

† *Bṛihatī*.—pp. 79—79*b*.

only from the significance of the words composing the *mantra*; thus then, the use indicated by the *implication* of these words is based directly upon what forms the very foundation of the usefulness of the *mantra*; the *Syntactical Connection*, on the other hand, indicates the use of the *mantra* purely on the verbal basis of grammatical construction afforded by the words, independently of any useful purposes served by it. Thus *Indirect Implication* is much nearer to the basis of usefulness than *Syntactical Connection*. (c) *Syntactical Connection* is more authoritative than *Context*. In the *Sūkṭavāka* mentioned in connection with the *Ḍarshapurṇamāsa*, we read—'*Agnīṣomāviḍam havirājuṣeṭām ...Inḍrāgnī iḍam havirājuṣeṭām*' (Ṭaiṭṭi. Brā. 3-5-10-3); as this *manṭra* occurs in the *Context* of the *Ḍarshapurṇamāṣa*, it would follow from this that on the *Amāvāsyā* day, the word '*agnīṣomau*' should be dropped, and similarly on the *Paurṇamāsi* day, the word '*inḍrāgnī*' should be dropped. But before this is accepted as authoritative, it would be necessary—(1) to assume, on the strength of this *Context* the *Syntactical Connection* (which is not present) between the two sets of words '*havirājuṣeṭām*' and '*indrāgnī.*';—(2) to assume, on the strength of this *Syntactical Connection*, the *Indirect Implication* of Indra, &c., by the words of the first section of the *manṭra*;—and (3) to assume, on the strength of this *Implication*, the *Direct Declaration* to the effect that the *manṭra* should be used in making offerings to Indra-Agni. On the other hand, we find that *Syntactical Connection* indicates that the words have to be retained in both cases,—inasmuch as each is syntactically connected with the word that follows: and for the acceptance of this procedure, as the *Syntactical Connection* is already present, we have to assume only the *Implication* of the deities and the *Direct Declaration*. Thus being one step less removed from the ultimate *Direct Declaration*, *Syntactical Connection* is regarded as more authoritative than *Context*. Another reason for this given by Prabhākara * is that what is indicated by *Syntactical Connection* is based upon the meaning afforded by the natural construction and interpretation of the words of the *mantra*; while what is indicated by *Context* would, at best, be based upon some construction or interpretation forced upon the words, in view of circumstances outside the limits of the *Mantra* itself. (*d*) *Context* is more authoritative than *Order* or *Position*. Under the *Rājasūya* we find many 'principal' sacrifices, one of which is the *Abhiṣēchanīya*; close upon the injunction of this last sacrifice we find the injunctions of such actions as *gambling* and the like. The proximity of these latter to the *Abhiṣēchnīya* would indicate that the *gambling* is 'subsidiary' to it; whereas the fact that the *gambling* is mentioned in the Context of the *Rājasūya* would indicate it to be 'subsidiary' to the *Rōjasūya*; under the circumstances, the *gambling* is accepted as 'subsidiary' to this latter. The reason for preference is the same as in the preceding cases,—*Context* being one step nearer to *Direct Declaration* than *Order* (Position or Proximity). According to Prabhākara,† the *Context* consists simply in the mutual need between a certain act and a *mantra*; so when the *Context* indicates that the *mantra* is to be used at a certain sacrifice, it is more direct in its operation than *Order*; because the connection between the action and the *mantra* is indicated by *Context*, or Mutual Need, directly through the Syntactical Connection established, through that *mutual need*, between the words of the *mantra* and the words denoting the action; while the *Order*, for establishing such a connection, stands in need of many more intervening factors; for instance (1) the *Order* indicates the *Mutual Need*, (2) which indicates the *Syntactical Connection*, (3) which last again indicates the connection between the *Mantra* and the *Act*. (4) *Order*

* *Bṛihatī*—page 79 *b*.

† *Bṛihati*, pp. 79b—80.

is more authoritative than *Name*. The *mantra*—'*Shundhadhvam daivyāya karmaṇe*—(*Taitti. Sam.* 1·1·3·1)—is met with in the chapter knowu by the *name* of "*Paurodāshika*'; this fact would imply that the *mantra* is to be used in the purification of the Cake (*purodāsha*). But the *mantra* is found in close proximity to the mention of the *Sānnāyya* vessels ;—on the strength of which the *mantra* is used in the cleaning of these vessels. The reason for this also lies in the fact that *Order* is one step nearer to *Direct Declaration* than *Name*; and also (according to Prabhākara)* in the fact that while *Order* is something *Vedic* or Scriptural, the *Name* is more or less *laukika* or worldly.

3. In connection with 'Subsidiaries,' Jaimini (*Mīm. Sū.* III—vii—18 to 20) raises the question as to whether the Sacrificer himself is to perform the Subsidiaries also, or it is necessary for him to perform the Primary Sacrifice only, the Subsidiaries being performed for him by priests appointed by him. The conclusion is that he may have the Subsidiaries performed by others, and yet, as being the *prime mover* in these actions also, the results of all actions—primary as well as subsidiary—will accrue to him.

The rest of *Adhyāya* III is taken up by discussions of cases of particular 'subsidiaries'; such for instance as the nature of the '*Pratipattikarma*'; those actions that are mentioned only incidentally in the Veda; the duties of the Sacrificer, and so forth.

4. There is au interesting matter in connection with *Adhyāya* III: after Sūtra 9 of *pāda* iv, the *Tantravārtika* has six *Sūtras* that are not found in the *Bhāṣya*. There are various reasons assigned for this omission :—(1) The author of the *Bhāṣya* forgot to comment on these *Sūtras*; (2) his comments on these have been lost; (3) he omitted them as they were not of much importance; (4) he did not accept

* *Bṛihatī*—page 80.

them as having been written by Jaimini, on the ground that the intervention of these *Sūṭras* makes it impossible to connect *Sūṭra* 16 with *Sūṭras* 1 to 9, a connection apparently intended by Jaimini. This last is the view accepted by Prabhākara,* who also omits the *Sūṭras* in question, and connects *Sūṭra* 16 directly with *Sūṭras* 1-9. Kumārila, on the other hand, regards the *Sūṭras* as genuine and makes four *aḍhikaraṇas* out of them. The interception of connection between *Sūṭra* 16 and *Sūṭras* 1-9, he points out, is nothing unusual; as we often meet with such intercepted connection between *Sūṭras,—e. g. Sūṭra* III—iv—38 is connected with III—iv—34, even in the presence of an entire *aḍhikaraṇa* (Sūṭras 35-37) intervening between them. This omission of the Sūṭras by Prabhākara has been noted by later writers also,—*e.g.* by Viḍyāraṇya in his *Vivaraṇaprameyasaṅgraha*, (page 4). It may be noted that the *Ṛijuvimalā* also does not make any mention of these *Sūṭras* ; it does not even seek to traverse the arguments propounded by Kumārila in favour of their inclusion.

SECTION (4).

The 'Motive' of Actions.

1. After the Principal and 'Subsidiary' character of Actions has been ascertained, we proceed to consider the question of '*Prayukṭi*' or *Motive* ; the question dealt with being—' What is it that affords the occasion for a certain action ? What is it for whose accomplishment an action is to be performed, or a thing to be brought into use' ? This question follows upon the preceding section, because as a rule it is the Principal Action that incites, or provides an occasion for, the Subsidiary. There are some actions however for which the sole motive or inciting cause is afforded by the desirable result ; while there are others, not directly accomplishing anything desired by the agent, which are yet performed

* *Bṛihaṭī*—page 82.

for the purpose of helping in the fulfilment of some other action that accomplishes something desired by the agent Hence the question of the *motive* of an action necessarily turns upon the question as to whether the action by itself fulfills something in connection with another action; the former would be called *'puruṣārṭha'* and the latter *'kraṭvarṭha.'* For this reason, before proceeding with the main question of Motive, it becomes necessary to ascertain what is meant by actions being *'puruṣārṭha'* and *'kraṭvarṭha.'*

2. The *'kraṭvarṭha'* is that which is laid down as making up the *procedure* of the *bhāvanā* of a certain enjoined action; that which is laid down for the accomplishment of something pleasing and desirable to the agent being called *'puruṣārṭha.'* As an instance of the *'kraṭvarṭha'* action we have the *Prayājas*, which enter into the procedure of the *Ḍarshapūrṇamāsa* Sacrifices, and do not themselves bring about any such result as the attainment of heaven and the like. (1) The *Ḍarshapaūrṇamāsa* Sacrifices and also the results accomplished by them belong to the *'Purūṣārṭha'* class, as they fulfill something that is pleasant and desirable for the agent; specially as these latter do not accomplish anything towards the help of another sacrfice, as the Prayājas do for the *Ḍarshapūrṇamāsa.* (2) All material substances, also their preparations and purifications, are regarded as *'kraṭvarṭha'* even in cases where some reults are mentioned as following from the use of such substances; the mention of such results being regarded as *'Arṭhavāḍa'* (IV.—iii—I). (3) There are certain things that may be regarded as both *'kraṭvarṭha'*—and *'purūṣārṭha'*; for instance *Ḍaḍhi* is, in one place, mentioned only as a material to be offered (where it is *'kraṭvarṭha'*), but in another place, it is mentioned as a substance an offering of which makes the sense-organs of the performer efficient (where it is *'puruṣārṭha.'*). (IV—iii—5 to 7).

The above is one interpretation of the Sūṭra IV—i—2; by which it is made to provide us with a definition of what is '*puruṣārṭha*' and '*kraṭvarṭha*'. On the definition of the '*puruṣārṭha*' as herein provided, the *Ṛijuvimalā* (Vol. II, p. 369) makes the following observations :—

'*Puruṣārṭha* cannot be defined as that which brings happiness, as this would not include the *Niṭya* actions; nor can it be that to the performance of which only a person with some desire would be entitled; as this would not apply to such acts as Vedic Study and the like. It must therefore be defined as that which subserves the Principal Sacrifice and the purposes of the agent, *by itself*, and not through being employed in another action, and through this latter aiding the Principal Action ;—those of this latter kind being '*kraṭvarṭha*.'

By a second interpretation, this same *Sūṭra* is made to declare that the result of actions, which is desired for its own sake, and to which men are, by their very nature, attracted, do not, and need not, form subjects of injunctions; as an injunction only urges one towards something towards which he would not direct his attention without such an injunction; to the desirable result the attention is directed by the very fact of its being desirable in itself.

This interpetation of the *Sūṭra*, propounded by Kumārila as Varṇaka II, is not accepted by the *Prābhākara*; as we find that the *Ṛijuvimalā*, while accepting all the other three *varṇakas* (I, III and IV) propounded by Kumārila, makes no mention of the second *varṇaka*.

By the third interpretation, the *Sūṭra* is made to lay down the fact that in such cases as—'the water should as a rule be fetched in cups, but in the milking vessel for those who desire cattle'—the *milking vessel* is '*puruṣārṭha*', inasmuch as, while the mere act of *water-fetching* could be done by other vessels also, the particular result, obtaining of cattle, could be obtained only if water were fetched *in the milking vessel*.

By the fourth interpretation the *Sūṭra* declares that the *acquiring of money* is '*puruṣārṭha*', inasmuch as it is necessary for livelihood; and it is only because it is '*puruṣārṭha* —by supplying the means of livelihood and thereby making *living* possible,—that the acquiring of money can help the performance of sacrifices also; as unless the man *lives*, he cannot perform any sacrifices.

3. As regards 'Motive' that which is '*puruṣārṭha*' contains its own motive within itself; whereas that which is '*kraṭvarṭha*' would have its motive in that particular action towards whose accomplishment it helps, or of whose *procedure* it forms a part. It is with the *Sūṭra* IV—i—21 that Jaimini begins to consider in detail the question as to what is the 'motive' of what. We shall cite here only one instance, in order to show the method of reasoning adopted. We have the declaration that 'when curd is put in hot milk, there is found the *āmikṣā* (the solid curdled pieces) which is for the Vishveḍevas; and the *vājina* (the liquid let loose) is for the Vājins'. The question arising as to whether it is the *Āmikṣā* or the *Vājina* that forms the *motive* of the action of putting curd into hot milk, the conclusion is that it is the former, the latter follows only incidentally. Says the *Bṛihaṭī* (page 93 b) :—

'The action is not for the accomplishment of the *Vājina*,—which is found to be brought about by something else,—here it is the *āmikṣā* for the sake of which the action is principally done.'

4. The whole of *pāḍa* i, and also the greater portion of *pāḍa* ii, contain discussions as to the 'motive' of actions, and towards the end of *pāḍa* ii, some actions are noted which have no 'motive', but are performed only for the sake of *setting aside* things that have been used,—*e.g.*, the removal of the horn that, during the Sacrifice, has been held by the Sacrificer in his hand (IV—ii—19).

4. In course of the enquiry as to the 'motive' of actions, we find that there are some actions which are enjoined, and yet they neither effectively help some other actions, nor lead to any desirable result themselves; such for instance is the making of the *Juhū* of leaves. Such an action is regarded as purely '*kraṭvarṭha*'; and the results mentioned along with these,—such for instance as the *absence of ill-fame*—must be regarded as *Arṭhavāḍa* (IV—iii—1). To the same category belong also those actions which tend only to purify certain material substances used at sacrifices; these purificatory actions, it is argued, render help to the performance of the sacrifice, inasmuch as without those purifications the substances could not be used; and in the absence of the substance, the sacrifice could not be performed. Of the same doubtful character is the *Vishvajiṭ* Sacrifice which is enjoined, but neither as part of another Sacrifice, nor as in any way helping in the preparation of a material substance, nor, lastly, as bringing about a desirable result with regard to such actions;—the conclusion is that they must be regarded as leading to the universally desirable result, in the shape of attainment of heaven, and as such being '*puruṣarṭha*.' But this law, called the '*Vishvajinnyāya*',—whereby in cases where no result is mentioned, *attainment of heaven* is assumed as the result,—is applicable only to cases where no kind of result is found to be mentioned or implied by even supplementary *Arṭhavāḍas*; where any such is found, the action must be accepted as accomplishing, and preformed for the sake of, that result. *

Similarly the *Rāṭrisaṭra* is regarded as leading to *praṭiṣṭhā* (respectability), which is found to be mentioned in an *Arṭhavāḍa* passage in close proximity to the injunction of that action. The *Ḍarshapūrṇamāsa* Sacrifices are mentioned as accomplishing *all* that is desirable; thus these are '*puruṣārṭha*' leading to all these results. But a single

* *Bṛihaṭī*,—Page 97.

performance of these sacrifices can bring about a single result; and for each particular result, the performance has to be repeated (IV—iii—27, 28). As regards those actions which are distinctly spoken of as accomplishing results pertaining to this physical world, the conclusion is that in every case, where there may be no obstacle in the way of the fulfilment of the result, the same result should be regarded as its 'motive'; but if in any case there be some insuperable obstacles in the fulfilment of the result, we must accept the action as bringing about superphysical results,—thus in either case they retain their '*puruṣārṭha*' character. The fact is that results are to be regarded as pertaining to another world only in cases where it is found absolutely impossible for them to be experienced in this world; *e.g.*, the enjoyment of the pleasures of heaven. But as for such results as can be experienced in this world—*e.g.*, the obtaining of cattle —there is no ground for regarding them as pertaining to any other world than this. There are some actions laid down as bringing something desirable, not to the Sacrificer himself, but to his son; *e.g.*, the *Vaishvānara* sacrifice These also are classed as '*puruṣārṭha.*'

5. The rest of *pāḍa* iii and *pāḍa* IV are devoted to the consideration of the question of certain Sacrifices being subsidiary to other actions, and as such being '*kraṭvarṭha.*' To this category belong the *Saūṭrāmaṇi*, the *Gāmbling* at the *Rājasūya* and so forth.

SECTION (5).

The Order of Performance of Actions.

1. In section (2) we had an account of *difference* among actions, which showed that certain actions, being different from one another, were to be performed separately; in section (3) we gave an account of *subserviency*, where it was shown that certain actions, or things, were to be performed, or brought into use, in connection with certain other actions or

things; in section (4) also, where we had an explanation of the *motive* of actions, what we have dealt with is something to be performed on account of—*i. e.*, incited or occasioned by—a certain other action or thing. Thus then, the preceding sections having dealt with what is to be *performed;* the present section procceds to deal with the *order* in which it is to be performed.

There is a difference of opinion between the *Bhātta* and the *Prābhākara* as to whether or not the *order* comes within the purview of injunction; according to the *Bhātta* * it does form an object of injunctions; while according to the *Prābhākara* † it cannot do so. The reasoning of the latter is that in the case of all injunctive sentences, apart from the enjoined *action* itself, we should be justified in accepting that alone as the further object of the injunction, without which the enjoining of the action itself would remain incomplete; as a matter of fact, the *order* of performance does not come under this category; as whether we perform the action at one time or the other, it would be *performed* all the same; and the purposes of the injunction would be fulfilled; thus then, *order* not being an integral factor in the action, it cannot as a rule be an *object* of injunction; in some cases however it is the order itself that is enjoined, the action having been enjoined by another injunctive sentence; for instance, the *drinking* or *eating* of the sacrificial remnant having been enjoined, the *order* in which the priests have to do this drinking is found to be enjoined by another sentence *vaṣatkarṭuḥ praṭhamo bhakṣaḥ*'—'One who pronounces the syllable *Vaṣat* is the first to drink'; such cases however are rather rare; as a rule, the injunctive sentence says nothing as to the *order*; and even if it does in a few cases, it does so, not by means of the *injunctive word*, but by some other word, ending in the past participial affix.

* *Nāyamātavistara* V—i—i.

† *Brihaṭi*—pp. 100—100 b; *Ṛijuvimalā* pp. 497 *et. seq.* and *Prakaraṇapañchikā*, page 220.

2. There are six means of ascertaining this *order* :—

(1) *Direct Declaration*, in the Veda itself—*e.g.* 'The *Aḍhvaryn* should initiate the Brahman after having initiated the Master of the House'. (V—i—1).

(2) The order in which the injunctive texts occur in the Veda; *e.g.* the *Ṭanūnapāṭ* sacrifice is to be performed after the *Samiḍ* sacrifice, because the sentence enjoining the former —'*Ṭanūnapāṭam yajaṭi*'—comes after that laying down the latter—*samiḍho yajaṭi*' (*Shaṭapaṭha Br.* I-5-3-9). (Mim Sū. V—i—47). Herein again, the order indicated by the order of the *manṭras* has preference over that indicated by the order of the injunctive *Brāhmaṇa* passages. (V—i—16).

(3) The Use or Purpose,—*e.g.* the cooking of the *Yavāgū* is done simply for the purpose of the performance of *homa*; consequently that cooking is to be done before the *homa*; even though the sentence '*yavāgūm pachaṭi*' occurs after '*agnihoṭrañjuhoṭi*'. (V—i—2).

(4) The Order of Commencement;—*e.g.* Seventeen animals have to be consecrated for seventeen offerings to Prajāpati; this 'consecration' consists of a series of actions done in connection with the animal; the first action of these series may be done with any of the seventeen animals got together; but when once this commencement has been made, the other actions must be done to the animals in the same order in which the former action has been done. (V—i—8, 12).

(5) Position,—In the *Jyoṭiṣtoma* sacrifice, there are three animals to be killed on three different days; the first animal called the '*Agnīṣomīya*' is killed on the day preceding the sacrifice (see chap. IV, §67); the second called the '*savanīya*' on the day of the *Suṭyā* or Soma-juice-extraction (ch. IV, §70), and the third called the '*anubanḍhya*' or the last or *Avabhriṭha* day. Then there is another sacrifice called the '*Sāḍyaska*' which is a *vikriṭi* or

modification (*i. e.* ectype) of the *Jyoṭiṣtoma*; but in connection with this sacrifice, it is laid down that all the aforesaid three animals are to be killed *together* on the same day, *i.e.*, the Second or *Suṭyā* day; now as the point of time, or day, laid down for the killing of all the three animals, pertains *par excellence* to the *Savanīya* animal (as at the Jyoṭiṣtoma, it is the *Savanīya* that is killed on the Suṭyā day)—when the actual killing comes to be done, it is the *Savanīya* that is killed first, then the *Agnīṣomīya* and the *Anubanḍhya*. (V—i—13).

(6) The Order of the Principal,—In connection with the *Ḍarsha* sacrifice, the subsidiary details of the *Sānnāyya* are performed before those of the *Āgnēya*; but in spite of this, inasmuch as between those two themselves, it is the *Agnēya* that is performed before the *Sānnāyya*,—when it comes to the performance of certain subsequent rites, it is the rites connected with the *Āgnēya* that have precedence over those connected with the *Sānnāyya*. (V.—iv—2).

3. In the performance of the Subsidiaries, the order indicated by the order of the injunctive sentences is regarded as of greater authority than that indicated by the Order of Principals (V—i—15). In cases where there is none of the aforesaid six means available, any order may be adopted. (V—i—3). There is no fixed order among a number of Sacrifices performed for the obtaining of desirable results pertaining to this world,—when these do not form part of any one Sacrifice, but are performed independently of one another. When each is independent of the other, it may be performed at any time when the Agent happens to have a desire for the result accomplished by it. (V—iii—32). Nor can any definite order be ascertained as between the *Soma* and the *Iṣti* Sacrifices* as such; as while in some cases, the *Iṣti* is dependent upon the *Soma*, in

* See Chap. IV, § 4.

others, it is the other way; so there can be no definite order of sequence. (V—iv—5).

Section VI—*Sub-section* (1).*

Who is entitled to the Performance of Sacrifices?

1. Having dealt with the Sacrifices and the Order in which they are to be performed, we proceed to consider the question as to who is entitled to perform them. The general principle that presents itself is that, in the case of all sacrifices accomplishing definite results, any person who is desirous of attaining a particular result is entitled to the performance of the Sacrifice accomplishing that resul' (VI—i—1). To this the most natural exception is that even if a person is desirous of attaining a certain result, if he is absolutely incapable of performing the Sacrifice laid down as accomplishing that result, he cannot be regarded as properly entitled to its performance (VI—i—4, 5.)

2. Having thus dealt with the most general principle and its most general exception, we proceed to consider special cases. Women are as much entitled to sacrifices as men (VI—i—6), with this exception, however, that the recitation of the Vedic *manṭras* cannot be done by them. In the case of married men, neither the man *alone*, nor the woman *alone*, is entitled to the performance; it is the two together that can perform sacrifices. The *Shūḍra* cannot perform any sacrifice, for the simple reason that he cannot study the Veda, and as such cannot take an active part in any Vedic Sacrifice. Though this reason might be regarded as applying, with equal force, to the case of women also,—at least in accordance with later authorities,—yet the very fact of Jaimini differentiating the *Shūḍra* from the *woman* in this respect would indicate that in ancient times women of the first three castes were allowed to study the Veda; that this was so is proved by a passage in the

* Includes also the subject matter of Aḍh. VI—pāḍa VI.

Bṛihaḍāraṇyaka Upaniṣaḍ also. This however would militate against what Jaimini puts forward in VI—i—24 as a reason for the *man*, and *not the woman*, reciting the *Upasṭhāna* and other *manṭras*; the reason here given is 'want of knowledge of the Veda.' But this is a reason which, in the case of the *Shūḍra*, precludes him from all sacrificial performance; but not so in the case of the *woman*; so it would seem that it is only in cases of both husband and wife jointly performing the sacrifice, that those *manṭras* are to be recited by the husband, and not by the wife. It may also be noted in this connection that the Sūtra itself does not contain any mention of the 'want of knowledge of Veda' in the case of *women*,—as it does in the case of the *Shūḍra* (Sū. 26, 33); it has only been added by later commentators, who, by this interpretation, raised for themselves the difficulty mentioned above, which they have failed to explain satisfactorily;* there was, in reality, no ground for this difficulty in the *Sūṭra* itself; it originated with the *Bhāṣya* declaring (page 620, lines 20-21) the 'Woman as inseparably connected with Aviḍyā' ('want of knowledge'); the reason for this lay in the fact that later writers could not bring themselves to take the same liberal view in regard to women that Jaimini had taken.

3. Of incapacitating circumstances, only two are mentioned—(1) want of necessary wealth, and (2) some disease that disables the man. As regards the former, it is not regarded as an insurmountable obstacle, as the poor man can with a little effort get together wealth enough for a particular sacrifice. As regards the latter, if the disease is an incurable one, the person cannot partake, in any sacrifice; if it is curable, he can do so after the cure. (VI—i—39 to 42).

4. The question as to who is entitled to perform sacrifices is dealt with more systematically by Kāṭyāyana †:—

* Vide *Shāsṭraḍīpikā*, pp. 443—44, for an attempt at an explanation.

† *Shrauṭasūtra*—I, 3 to 12.

In *sūṭra* 3 he puts forward the position that all beings—animal, human and divine—are equally entitled to the performance of sacrifices. *Sūṭra* 4 rejects this view, and declares that *human* beings alone can be so entitled; as it is they alone that can perform sacrifices; the gods cannot do so,—the commentator, Karka, adds,—because they have all their desires already fulfilled, and do not stand in need of anything which they would seek to accomplish by means of sacrifices; and also because apart from the gods themselves, there are no 'deities' to whom they could make offerings; the *Rākṣasas* and *Pishāchas* cannot perform sacrifices, as they are, by their nature, impure, and as such unfit for sacrificial performances; nor can animals do it; as they are devoid of the requisite Vedic knowledge.

There are however certain exceptions. These are mentioned in Sūṭra 5 :—Sacrifices can not be performed by one who has one or more limbs wanting, who is devoid of Vedic knowledge, who is sexless, or who is a *shūḍra*. These exceptions, Karka adds, are implied in the 'incapacity' mentioned in the preceding *sūṭra*; for instance, one who has no legs cannot perform the *walking* involved in the *Viṣṇukrama*, * the blind cannot do the '*avekṣaṇa*' or 'examination' of the *ghee*, † the dumb cannot recite the *manṭras*; and a sacrifice in which these details would be absent would be much too deficient to deserve the name. One who is devoid of Vedic knowledge is not entitled to any performances, because he does not know how it is to be done. The sexless person is not entitled, because the Scriptures have declared him to be 'impure' by his very nature. The *shūḍra* also is not entitled. On this point, both the *sūṭra* and the commentary are silent; they do not put forward any 'reasons' in support of this exception. *Sūṭra* 6 declares that the Brāhmaṇa, the Kṣaṭṭriya and the Vaishya alone are entitled to sacrifices,—because

* Mentioned in *Shaṭapaṭha Brā.* 1.1-2-13 ; 6.5-2.10 ; 6.6 4-1.
† Ibid. 1.3.1.18.

of declarations in the Veda to this effect'; the Veda, the commentator adds, has laid down the 'consecration of fire' as to be done by the three higher castes only; and as no sacrifices can be performed withont 'consecrated' fire, this precludes the *shūḍra* altogether. Kāṭyāyana does not, like Jaimini, exclnde the *shūḍra* merely on the gronnd of 'want of knowledge'; as this absence wonld exclude the ignorant Brāhmaṇa jnst as mnch as the ignorant Shūḍra; and also becanse, if that were the sole reason, it would exclnde women of the highor castes also, as pointed ont above. *Sūṭra* 7 distinctly lays down that women are as mnch entitled to the performance of sacrifices as men; specially as it is fonnd that the Veda lays down directions for the 'initiation' of the *sacrificer as well as his wife*—'the former being initiated with the *mekhalā* and the latter with the *yokṭra* (Sūṭra 8). Though snch is the liberal view taken by Kāṭyāyana, Karka conld not resist the influence of the later age; he has added that women are entitled,—bnt *only as accompanied by their husbands*, and not independently by themselves; he bases this qnalification npon a latter *Smṛiṭi* text which declares that 'there is no independent sacrificing for women.' He appears to have lost sight of the fact that the *man* also is not entitled to the performance of sacrifices, apart from his wife—in view of the declaration, '*yaṭ karṭavyam ṭaḍanayā saha.*' In *Sūṭras* 11 and 12, Kāṭyāyana takes acconnt of those Vedic declarations that speak of the '*Raṭhakāra*' and the '*Niṣāḍasṭhapaṭi*' as entitled to the 'consecration of fire'; '*Raṭhakāra*' is the name given to one who has his mother born of a *Shūḍra* mother and a *Vaishya* father, and his father is born of a *Vaishya* mother and a *Kṣaṭṭriya* father; the Commentator remarks that for snch a person, the 'consecration of fire' is only for the pnrposes of his pnrification, and not for that of sacrificial performances. The *Niṣāḍasṭhapaṭi*, the *Niṣāḍa* chief, is entitled to a particnlar *Iṣṭi* sacrifice which is performed for the preservation of cattle; but this is to be performed in the *ordinary*, and not in the 'consecrated' fire, (*Sūṭra* 14).

5. The sixth *paḍā* of *aḍhyāya* VI deals with the subject of persons entitled to the performance of *Saṭras*.* The *Saṭra* differs from an ordinary *sacrifice* in that—(1) it cannot be performed by one man, (X—vi—45 to 50; and X—vi—59 to 60),—and (2), all priests are from among the 'Sacrificers' themselves (X—vi—51 to 58). For this same reason, the services of the priests at the *Saṭra* are not 'bought' or 'exchanged' for any promised 'fee' (X—ii—35 to 38); and the gift of 'a mare, or a slave girl or a cow', that is laid down in connection with the *Sārasvaṭā Iṣti* (which forms part of the 'procedure' of the *Saṭra*) must be regarded as fulfilling a transcendental result, and not the ordinary result of such gifts, which has been shown (X—ii—22) to consist in the priests being won to service. (X—ii—44). If one of the Sacrificers at the *Saṭra* should happen to die during the performance, his bones are to be kept wrapped in deer-skin; and his place taken up by a person nearly related to him; and at the end of a year, the Sacrificers should perform, for the sake of their dead partner, a special sacrifice called the '*Samvaṭsara-yāga*' (X—ii—47, 48).

All the (seventeen) persons undertaking the *Saṭra* should belong to the same Brāhmaṇa sub-class—*i.e.* they should all be followers of the same '*Kalpasūṭra*' (VI—vi—1 to 11). But in the *Kulāyayajña*, it is permissible for the King and his priest to belong to different '*Kalpas.*' (Sū. 12—15). *Kṣaṭṭriyas* and *Vaishyas* cannot perform *Saṭras*, to which *Brāhmaṇas* alone are entitled; and of these also, only those who belong to the *Vishvāmiṭra Goṭra*; and of these last, only such as are guided by the same '*Kalpa*' (Sū. 16-26). All persons partaking in the *Saṭra* must be regular performers of the *Agnihoṭra* (Sū. 27—32). To the *Sāmiḍhenī* however, all 'ḍvijas' are equally entitled

* For a discussion as to the 'result' of Saṭras, see below, Sec. 6, Sub-sec. 2, § 1.

(Sū. 36—39). The *Juhū* and the other implements used at the *Saṭra* should be kept common among all the sacrificers, and none should belong exclusively to any one person; as if it did, then, if the person to whom it belongs were to die, he being an *Agnihoṭrin,* all his sacrificial implements would have to be burnt along with his body; and thus there would be a discrepancy in the sacrificial performance, for want of the implement thus burnt. (Sū. 33-35).

6. To the performance of the '*Vishvajiṭ*' only such persons are entitled as can afford to give 1200 pieces of gold. (VI—vii—18 to 20).

SECTION 6—*Sub-section* (2).*

Certain Miscellaneous Questions in regard to Sacrifices.

1. In the above connection, Jaimini treats incidentally of certain other matters, related to the main question of persons entitled to sacrificial performance. For instance, in *Sūṭras* 1 and 2 he raises the question of *Saṭras,*†—sacrifices performed by a number of persons (generally 17), and not by only one person. The question is whether the result of such *communistic* sacrifices accrues to each person severally or to all of them collectively. The conclusion is in favour of the former view, for the reason that, even though acting only in the group, each of the group is as much a 'Sacrificer' as any single Sacrificer; and as results are said to accrue to the 'Sacrificer,' it is only natural that it should accrue to each and every person that is a 'sacrificer,'—no matter whether he be so alone or in a group. Says *Prabhākara* ‡—

'The conclusion indicated by the Scriptures is that each one of the group is an independent Sacrificer.'

---

* Including also the matter of *pāda* viii.

† Dealt with in *Shaṭapaṭha Br.* III and IV; and *Mim. Sū.* Aḍh. VI, pāḍa vi

‡ *Bṛihaṭi*—p. 112b.

Then there arises the question as to whether or not such collective performance is possible in the case of the well-known sacrifices of the *Ḍarshapūrṇamāsa* and the like. The text laying down the *Ḍarshapūrṇamāsa* uses the injunctive verb in the singular number—'*yajeṭa*'; hence the conclusion is that these sacrifices must be performed by a single Sacrificer. (VI—ii—3 to 12).

In regard to the Sacrifices laid down as bringing about visible results—cattle, rain &c.,—when the Sacrifice has been once begun, it must be carried to its end, even if the result desired should happen to be accomplished before its completion; as the Veda deprecates all unfinished acts, and prescribes expiatory rites for leaving sacrifices incomplete; and also because learned men decry men who begin a certain act and do not carry it to its end.* (VI—ii—13 to 15). But this rule does not apply to such purely *worldly* acts as the building of a house; because the aforesaid deprecation of unfinished acts is based upon the consideration that when a sacrificial performance has been begun, an expectation of receiving offerings has been raised in the mind of the deities concerned; so if the prescribed offerings were not made, it would be a breach of promise. Such is not the case with purely worldly acts; specially as the aforesaid deprecation is based upou the fact that the Veda prescribes expiatory rites for unfinished *sacrifices*—which could not apply to the worldly acts. (VI—ii—16 to 18) (*Bṛihaṭī* p. 113 b).

2. With regard to the *prohibited* acts,—such as the *eating of Kalañja*,—there arises the question as to whether or not the prohibition—'one should nor eat the Kalañja'—is to be regarded as a *positive injunction* of taking a vow never to eat the *Kalañja*, just like the vow of the Brahmachārin not to look at the rising sun,—thereby making this

---

* *Bṛihaṭī*. p. 113b.

action of the *taking of the vow*, a *ḍharma* leading to Heaven (by the 'Vishvajiṭ Law' enunciated under *Mim. Sū.* IV—iii—10). 'The reason in favour of the view that the sentence should be taken in the sense of prescribing a positive action, is that, all injunctive verbs laying down actions for the fulfilment of something desirable for the agent, the prohibitive sentences also,—which are in the form of *injunctions*,—must be regarded as laying down something *to be done*,—a mere *avoidance* in this case,—which would fulfill some desirable end',—says Prabhākara.* The final conclusion however is that such prohibitions can not be treated on the same level as the prohibition of the looking on the rising sun, &c., the reason given being that in the prohibition—'*na kalañjambhakṣayēṭ*',—the negative word must be taken as enjoining *the negation or cessation of that act of eating*,—and not any positive act; all injunctions of positive acts lay down *something to be done;* but the sentence in question does not prescribe any thing *to be done;* therefore it can not be regarded as the injunction of a positive act. Nor would such a prohibition be entirely purposeless; as it would serve the useful purpose of saving men from the troubles of hell which would be their lot if they ate the *Kalañja*. This interpretation saves us from the necessity of assuming a result for the avoidance (by the 'Vishvajiṭ Law'); it is one who fears hell that is entitled to the cessation from the eating of *Kalañja*, and not one who desires heaven. For these reasons, Prohibitions can not be regarded as leading to any desirable results; they must be regarded only as saving from undesirable ones and from this it follows, as a necessary corrollary, that that which is prohibited leads to undesirable results. It may be argued, here that the syntactical argument, based upon the connection of the negative particle with the Verbal root, applies with equal force to such prohibitions as 'one

* *Bṛihaṭi*—p.—113 b.

should not look at the rising sun'; and yet these latter have been taken (IV—i—3 to 6) as laying down the positive act of taking the vow not to do the act mentioned—such vow leading to a desirable result. There is however a great difference between the two cases. These latter prohibitions are found to be prefaced by the words '*aṭha vraṭam*'—'now then a few observances to be kept by the Brahmachārin',—and then follow the prohibitions of certain acts; these prefatory words distinctly show that the prohibitions are not prohibitions of acts leading to undesirable results, but they lay down the *desisting* from certain specified actions,—this *desisting* constituting an *observance*, bringing about *desirable* results; they say nothing as to any undesirable results proceeding from the prohibited acts; specially so because the *looking on the sun* is nowhere spoken of in the Veda as *sinful*, and as such leading to undesirable results. In the case of the prohibition of the *eating of Kalañja*, on the other hand, we do not find any such prefatory words; hence the prohibition necessarily implies that what is prohibited is so because it brings about undesirable results.

As for the duties laid down for the *Brahmachārin*,—such as approaching the Preceptor, studying under him, and so forth,—the conclusion is that these duties become binding, not upon all men, but only upon those of the higher castes who are entitled to Vedic Study; and upon these also, not as soon as they are born, but only when their *Upanayana* has been performed (VI—ii—21, 22); and those duties continue binding, not indeed throughout life, but only during the time specified for the purpose (*Bṛihaṭī* p. 118).

3. The performance of the *Agnihoṭra* being laid down as *lifelong*,—the question arises as to whether this means that, throughout his life,—at all points of time, from morn till eve—the man is to be performing the *Agnihoṭra*, and hence doing nothing else; or that the performance is to be only at stated times,—*e. g.* some offerings in the morning, and

some in the evening. The conclusion is that the performamce is not be continued incessantly through day and night; because in connection with the acts laid down as making up the *Agnihoṭra*, it is distinctly declared that some are to be performed 'in the morning' and some 'in the evening.' Hence the expression 'throughout life'—'*yāvajjīvam*'—must mean *on all mornings and evenings during one's earthly existence.* (VI—ii—23 to 26). Similarly with the *Ḍarshapūrṇamāsa*, these also are laid down as 'lifelong'; but the offerings are to be made only on the New Moon and the Full Moon days. Three duties have been laid down as calculated to pay off the three kinds of debts:—(1) the *performance of sacrifices*' whereby debts owing to the *Gods* are paid; (2) *Vedic Study*—paying off debts owing to the *Riṣis*; and (3) the *begetting of children*—whereby debts to the *Piṭṛis* are paid. These acts may be supposed—on the basis of the 'Vishvajiṭ Law'—to be prescribed as leading to certain desirable results; and as such the idea would be that only those persons are to perform these actions who may be desirous of attaining that result; and of these also, only *Brāhmaṇas*; inasmuch as the actions are prescribed along with such others as the *Soma* and other Sacrifices which are meant for *Brahmāṇas* only. But the conclusion is that all these actions are *necessary duties* and as such, to be performed by *all persons* of the three higher castes—irrespective of any desire for results. (VI-ii—31).

4. In *Paḍā* viii, we have certain minor sacrifices dealt with. In regard to the *Chaṭurhoṭra Homa*, it is stated that only such persons are entitled to its performance as are *not Agnihotrins*; for such persons therefore the 'sacrificial fire' could not be the regular *Agnihoṭra fire*; it must only be that fire in which have been poured the libations in connection with the *Upanayana*. (VI—viii—II to 19). Similarly the sacrifice performed by the *Niṣāḍa* chief must be offered in the *ordinary fire*; as in his case, there is neither the

Agnihoṭra nor the *Upanayana* fire (Sū-20—21). So also the *Avakirṇī* offering is to be made in the *ordinary fire;* as this is an offering that is to be made by the *Brahmachārin,* for whom the regular *Agnihoṭra* fire is not possible; as this can be 'laid' only by 'the husband and wife' together, and the *Brahmachārin* has no wife.

5. All religious performances, connected with the Gods,—such as the *Chudākaraṇa,* the *Upanayana* and the like,—should be performed during the 'Northern Solstice' of the Sun; and then also only during the brighter half of the month. (Sū. 23, 24).

6. In connection with the *Jyoṭistoma,* the *Payovraṭa* (living upon milk) by the Sacrificer and his wife should be kept in all cases, and not only when milk is the material offered. (Sū. 28). For Agni-Soma the only animal that can be offered is the *goat.* (Sū. 30—42.)

SECTION (6)—*Sub-section* (3.) *

Capability of Sacrificers.

1. The question as to whether or not a person is entitled to the performance of Sacrifices naturally leads to the enquiry as to whether or not he is *able* to perform them; and in course of this we have to consider the chances of a man completing the undertaken Sacrifice under difficulties of sorts, and so forth.

In regard to the *Ḍarshapūrṇamāsa,* the *Agnihoṭra* and other such *necessary* and *life-long* performances, it is held that, in case one is not capable of performing all their

* Including *pāḍas* iv and v also. The only MS. of the *Bṛihaṭī* that has been available closes with *Aḍh.* VI, *pāḍa* ii; consequently henceforward we shall not be in a position to give any references to Prabhākara's own work—and as to what is pu forward here is the actual 'Prābhākara' view, the sole authority that we have is an indirect one: as Prabhākara, as a rule, agrees with the Bhāṣya in its apparentt interpretation; all points where there is the slightest difference are noted in the *Mimāmsanyāyamālāvisṭara.* On some points however we have the direct authority of the Prakaraṇapañchikā.

detailed subsidiaries, he need perform only the Principal Sacrifice in full, and omit the minor subsidiaries ,—but only in case he is absolutely and really incapable, beyond all help. (VI—iii—1 to 7). This however applies only to the case of the *necessary* (*niṭya*) actions; in the case of *Kāmya* actions—those performed with a view to certain desirable results,—the *entire* procedure has to be gone through scrupulously; as even the slightest omission would weaken the force of the action, which would be so far incapacitated to bring about the desired result. (VI—iii—8 to 10).

With regard to the materials of the Sacrifice, it sometimes happens that the substance that has been prepared and got ready for the offering gets spoilt or spilt or otherwise rendered uufit for use; aud in such cases, even in the middle of the performance, if one of the prescribed substitutes of the substance is available, and is used in the remaining offerings,—that does not spoil the sacrifice in any way (VI—iii—11 to 17). But the substitute must be some thing similar to the original; for instance, the *yava* for the *vrīhi* (Sū. 27.) If however another supply of the original substance is available, this must have preference over all substitutes (Sū. 35.) But in no case can we substitute a substance the use of which is prohibited,—such substances for instance, as the *māṣa*, the *chaṇaka* and such other substances, called '*ayajñīya*,' 'unfit for sacrifices.' In the case of the offering of cakes, if in the baking, it should get spoilt, or burnt, another cake is permitted to be used, but only after certain expiatory rites have been performed (VI—iv—17 to 21). If the fire is extinguished, it should be kindled again, with all the due rites of the *Agnyāḍhāna*. (VI—iv—26, 27).

Though substitutes are allowable in the case of *subtances*, it is not so in the case of Deities or Manṭras; if these happen to be wrongly named or recited, that performance is spoilt, and cannot be remedied. (VI—iii—18, 19). Lastly, as regards the Sacrificer, if anything happens to him that disables him from taking part in the performance, then the action fails entirely, no substitute being allowable for the Sacrificer (VI—iii—21). In the case of *Saṭras* however, where there are a number of Sacrificers, if one happens to be disabled, his place can be taken by another; the reason for this is that in the case of *Saṭras*, all Sacrificers take part in the performance, not only as 'sacrificers' or 'masters,' but also as 'priests' (there being no other officiating priests at the *Saṭra*); and as even during the performance, a change of priests is permissible, the Sacrificer, who has been also acting as a 'priest,' can, on that account, be replaced (Sū. 22). But such a substitute can be regarded as a 'Sacrificer' only for the purpose of making up the prescribed number 'Seventeen'; and he does not partake in the result. (Sū. 23). The real reason for this exception to the general principle of the *non-replacement of Ṣacrificers* appears to lie in *expediency*; in the case of a single Sacrificer, his incapacity spoiling the performance, this failure as pertaining to himself would be easily allowed; but in the case of *Saṭras*, there being seventeen 'Sacrificers,' if only one of them happens to be disabled during the performance, the other sixteen would not be willing to forego the elaborate Sacrifice and its much coveted result; and further, as there was a greater likelihood of one out of the 17 being disabled, some latitude had to be allowed in this case. In case any one of the persons taking part in a sacrifice should wish to go away after the performance has been begun, he may do so; but he should have to perfom the *Vishvajiṭ* sacrifice in expiation of his failure. (VI—v—25 to 27).

2.* In *pāḍa* iv, we find two *aḍhikaraṇas* devoted to the 'Eating of Remnants.' It having been laid down that of the substances offered, if something is left, the remnant

* See Chap. IV, § 75.

shonld not be thrown away, it should be eaten,—this 'eating of the remnant' being regarded as a '*pratipattikarman*'; the qnestion arising as to who should eat it, the conclnsion is that the priests shonld do it (VI—iv—4 to 9),—those who have taken part in the offerings and libations, as well as those who have helped in the extracting of the Soma-jnice (Sū. 24, 25). Bnt the Soma-juice can be eaten by the *Brāhmaṇa* only; for which the principal reason is that all *priests* mnst be *Brāhmaṇas* (XII—iv—42 to 47); and every eater mnst eat ont of the cup named after himself (III—v—22); it natnrally follows that a Brāhmaṇa alone can eat it. The Sacrificer also being entitled to the eating of remnants, if he is a Brāhmaṇa, there is no difficulty; bnt if, as in the case of the Soma sacrifices, he happens to be a *Kṣaṭṭriya,* instead of the remnant of the Soma-juice, they give him in its place, a preparation of Vata-seeds mixed with cnrds (III—v—23). Bnt in case the remnant gets spoilt, or rendered inedible, it shonld be thrown into water (VI—v—48). If, after the priest has eaten it, he shonld vomit it, he has to make an offering of the *Somenḍra-charu,* as an expiatory rite (III—iv—38).

3. *Pāḍa* 5 deals with certain mishaps. For instance, the *Ḍarsha* sacrifices are to be performed on the day that the moon is entirely invisible; if, however, by miscalcnlation of dates, the sacrifices are commenced on a wrong day,—and the moon becomes visible after the materials have been dnly prepared,—then, these materials need not be thrown away, bnt they shonld be offered to some deity other than those prescribed for the *Ḍarsha*; and the details of the *Ḍarsha* itself begnn over again on the proper date (VI—v—1 to 9).

4. From *Sūṭra* 28 onwards, the snbject of Initiation is taken np. In connection with the *Ḍarshapūrṇamāsa* the nnmber of initiations prescribed are varions—1, 2, 3, 4, and 12; and the conclnsion according to Shabara is that in all cases there should be 12 initiations; bnt according to

Kumārila, the exact number depends upon the option of the Sacrificer, so far as the *Ḍarshapurṇamāsa* itself is concerned; but at the *Ḍvāḍashāha* Sacrifice, they must be 12. (VI-v—28).

From the day that the Initiation for the Soma Sacrifice begins, either on the *fifth* or the *seventh* or the *eighth* day, there is the extraction of the juice *,—this day being on that account called the 'Suṭyāha.' On the same day there is also the 'bath'; but if for some reason the bath is postponed, then the duties of the Initiate,—such *e.g.* as the making of no gifts—continue to be incumbent on him, until the bath has been performed, as it is the bath that forms the concluding item in the Initiation. (VI—v—38, 39).

The rest of *pāḍa* V deals with mishaps in connection with the moving of the priests out of the *Havirḍhāna*. It is laid down that they should go out in a fixed order, each holding the end of the cloth worn by one in his front †. If this order happens to be broken, certain expiatory rites have to be performed (VI—v—49 to 56).

SECTION 6—*Sub-section 4.*
The Vishvajiṭ Sacrifice.

1. The whole of *pāḍa* vii is devoted to the consideration of certain details in connection with the *Vishvajiṭ* Sacrifice. This sacrifice can be performed only by such persons as can afford to give 1200 gold pieces, which is the least that can be meant by the '*sarvasva*' (all one's belongings) which is the prescribed 'fee' in connection with this sacrifice (Sū. 18—20). In this connection, it is further laid down that when the Veda enjoins the giving away of *all one's belongings* at this sacrifice—by 'all belongings' here are meant only the *riches* of the Sacrificer, and not such things as his parents, for instance (Sū. 1—2); but of the 'riches'

* Chapter IV, §70 *et. seq.*
† Ch. IV, §73.

also no landed property is to be given (Sū. 3), nor horses (Sū. 9), nor such slaves as may be actually in attendance upon the master (Sū. 6). Where the Veda speaks of the giving of 'immeasurable riches', any number beyond 1000 (of gold pieces, presumably) is intended (Sū. 23-25). Similarly, where '1000 years' are spoken of as 'the period of the *Vishvajiṭ*', it is 1000 *days* that are meant. (Su. 31-40).

SECTION (7).*

Transference or Extended Application of Details.

1. The first six *aḍhyāyas* have dealt with what has been called '*Upaḍesha*'—the Direct Mention, or Indirect Implication, of what is required to be done, in connection with *Ḍharma*. The *seventh aḍhyāya* takes up the subject of '*Aṭiḍesha*'—Transference, or Extended Application, of certain details from one action to the other. There are many sacrifices with regard to which the Veda does not prescribe all the necessary details; but lays down simply that 'such and such a sacrifice is to be performed in a manner similar to such and such another';—*e. g.* with regard to the *Iṣu* Sacrifice, after having mentioned what is peculiar to it, the texts declare—'the rest is like the *Shyena* sacrifice.' In such cases the Shyena would be called the '*Prakṛiṭi-yāga*,' the *Archetype*, 'original Sacrifice,' and the *Iṣu* the corresponding '*Vikṛiṭi*' or 'Modification' or the *Ectype*. The *transference* then, of the details of the 'Archetype' to the 'Ectype' is what is called '*Aṭiḍesha*';—defined as 'that by which the details of performance are transferred, or extended, from one *archetype* to other sacrifices similar to it'...(quoted in the *Mimāmsānyāmālāvisṭara*, p. 374); the definition given by the *Prakaraṇapañchikā* (p. 227) is that it is 'that through which the *Ectype* becomes connected with the details of the *Archetypal* Sacrifice'; it

* Including *aḍhyāyas* VII and VIII.

goes on to add that 'the extension of the details of one sacrifice to another ,—when there is no incongruity in snch extension—is called *Aṭiḍesha.*

2. Before proceeding with the main snbject of *Transference,* Jaimini pauses to consider a qnestion, upon the consideration whereof the enqniry into Transference depends ;—viz. The *Prayāja* Sacrifices which are mentioned as the 'snbsidiary details' of the *Ḍarshapūrṇamāsa,*—are these 'snbsidiaries' laid down for this latter sacrifice only, or for *all* Sacrifices ? This enqniry becomes necessary at this stage, becanse if the details laid down in one section are intended by the Veda for *all* Sacrifices, then those details belong as mnch to one Sacrifice as to the other; that is to say, the details laiḍ down in the *Shyena* section belong as mnch to the *Iṣu* Sacrifice as to the *Shyena* ; and thus the details belonging eqnally to all sacrifices, by Direct Declaration, there wonld be no need for any 'transference'; in fact there would be no snch thing as 'transference'; bnt in case the details mentioned in connection with one sacrifice are intended by the Veda to belong to only *a few* sacrifices, then those sacrifices to which they do not belong, and which have no details of their own, wonld be wanting in those details ; and for the snpplying of this want they wonld be dependent upon those sacrifices to which the details belong directly ; and in this case alone, the former wonld be the '*ectype*' of the latter ; and then alone wonld there be an occasion for considering the qnestion of 'transference' of details (dealt with under *aḍhyāyas* VII and VIII), as also those of *Ūha* (Aḍh. IX) and *Bāḍha* (Aḍh. X).

3. The question of the details of the *Ḍarshapūrṇamāsa* belonging to all sacrifices or to only a few, tnrns npon the question as to whether the performance of the details is simply for the sake of accomplishing sacrifices, or for that of bringing about an *apūrva* ; becanse, in the former case, as all sacrifices are equally 'sacrifice,' what are mentioned 'for accomplishing

sacrifices' would be related equally to *all* Sacrifices; while in the latter case, they would be related to only one definite *apūrva*; and this one *apūrva* could not but be the one mentioned as following from the Sacrifices in whose connection the details are mentioned; as it is only of such Sacrifiees that the details are 'aṅga' or 'subsidiary'—as explained in aḍhyāya III; and thus the details would belong directly only to these sacrifices, and could be connected with other sacrifices only by 'transference.'

The conclusion on this point is that the details are related to the *apūrva*;—(1) because between the *apūrva* and the *sacrifice* in general, it is the former that is the predominant factor, inasmuch as it leads directly to something desirable, while the mere 'Sacrifice' in general does not, independently by itself, bring about anything desirable; and (2) because it is only by such interpretation that the requirements of 'Context' are fulfilled,—the details being connected with that sacrifice in whose 'Context' they are mentioned. In the other case, no significance could attach to 'Context.' (VII—i—1 to 12).

4. Before taking up the special cases of 'Transference,' we shall offer a few observations on the general character of 'Transference'. At the very outset, it has to be noted that we have *Transference*, not only of *actions* or *procedure of action*, but also of other sacrificial details, materials and so forth; says the *Prakarṇapañchikā*:—'*Aṭiḍeshaḥ prakāasya ḍharmāṇāñchaiva yujyaṭē*'—'there is *transference* of the procedure of action as also of the accessory details'—(p. 227, shl. 13); it is only of the result that there is no *transference* (VIII—i—20 to 22). The only rule in regard to *transference* is 'the *ectype* is to be performed in the same manner as the *original archetype*,'—*e. g.* the '*Sau ya*' sacrifice is to performed in the manner of the '*Āgneya*,' the '*Iṣu*' like the '*Shyena*,' and so forth; what is meant by this

is that all those details and accessories for the performance of the *Iṣu*, which are not directly laid down specifically as to be employed at it, are to be brought in from the *Shyena*. It is true, as the *Prakaraṇapañchikā* remarks (p. 226) that the first of the details that come up for *transference* are the *procedure*; but that is not all; if the *offering material* is not laid down, we have to bring in that material; and so also any accessory that may be found wanting. Nor does this in any way militate against the first *aḍhikaraṇa* of *aḍhyāya* X; as there we have the denial of the 'transference' of only such details of the *archetypal* sacrifice as have had their purposes entirely fulfilled, and which, on that account, could serve no useful purpose in the *ectype*; similarly under V—i—19, we have an instance of the details of the *archetype* not being transferred to its *ectype*, in virtue of Direct Declaration, whose authority is above everything,—also abovo the general law with regard to the transference of the details of the *archetype* to the *ectype*. Thus then, the 'Transference' being due to the needs of the sacrifice, the *need* or *motive* that prompts this 'transference' may lie either in some transcendental result expected out of what is *transferred*, or in some purely visible result, expected to be accomplished better by what is *transferred* than by any other means. (*Prakaraṇapañchikā* p. 227, shl. 18). The question then that we have to deal with here is—in what cases is this 'transference' possible or desirable? and in what cases is it not so? It is on this question that the whole of the second part of Jaimini's *Sūṭras* (Aḍh. VII—XII) turns; that is why it is taken up here.

5. 'Transference' is regulated and controlled by—(1) *Prakaraṇa* Context), and (2) *Sṭhāna* (Position). For instance, —(1) a certain sacrifice will have its details transferred to another only if the two are found enjoined in the same context; this is the reason why the details of the *Shyena* are transferred to the *Iṣu*, and not to the *Saurya*. (2) In this

'Transference', that which occnpies the 'position' of the *Ḍevaṭā* or Deity at the original sacrifice is to take the same 'place' when transferred to the other sacrifice; what appears in the former as the *offering material* is to be used in the same capacity at the latter also. In cases where the mention of the Deity indicates the 'transference' of the properties of one substance, while the nature of the *offering material* points to the properties of another,—preference is given to the latter. For instance, in the injnnction 'for Indra one shonld prepare the *one-pan* substance', the *deity* 'Indra' indicates the 'transference', to this *baking or preparing of the Cake*, of the properties of the *Sānnāyya* (mixtnre of milk and cnrd) which is specially sacred to Indra; while the natnre of the snbstance 'that which is baked npon one pan' points to the 'transference' of the properties of the *Cake*; and it is this latter 'transference' that is accepted (VIII—i—32 to 34).

6. There are primarily fonr kinds of Transference—(1) Transference by Direct Injnnction,—*e.g.* with regard to the *Iṣu* sacrifice, we have the direct injnnction 'the rest is to be done in the same manner as the *Shyena*', which lays down the *transference* of certain details from the *Shyena* to the *Iṣu* sacrifice. (VII—i—13 to 16). (2) Transference by *inferred* or *presumed* injunction,—*e.g.* In connection with the *Saurya* sacrifice we find no accessory details laid down; we know at the same time that no sacrifice can be performed withont certain details; knowing also that the *Saurya* bears a close relationship to the *Ḍarshapurṇamāsa*, we are led to the natnral presumption that the details necessary for the performance of the *Saurya* have to be *transferred* to it from the *Ḍarshapurṇamāsa*; and this presumption leads ns to the inference of an injnnction laying down such transference. (VII—iv—1). (3) Transference by the name of sacrifices—*e.g.* The *Māsāgnihoṭra* has not all its details mentioned in connection with itself; these

details have to be *transferred* to it from among these of the Ordinary *Agnihoṭra*,—simply because the *name* '*Agnihoṭra*' is common to both.* (VII—iii—1 to 4). Transference by the name of *samskāras*,—*e.g.* in connection with the *Varuṇapraghāsa* sacrifice, we find the '*Avabhṛiṭha*' bath enjoined; this '*Avabhṛiṭha*' which, in this connection, is only a *Samskāra* or purification, leads to the *transference* to the bath of the *Varuṇapraghāsa*, of the details of the bath in connection with *Agniṣtoma* sacrifice,—to which latter bath the name '*avabhṛiṭha*' specifically belongs. (VII—iii—12 to 15). In this connection we may note that some writers have a third kind of name,—the 'name' applying to the sacrifice in its literal signification,—the literal signification of the names of sacrifices being, according to these writers, a guide as to the transference of details to it; but this is denied by the older writers, specially by Kumārila, who says†—'*yaugikam nāṭiḍeshakam*,' 'no name, in its literal signification, can indicate transference.' ‡

7. 'Transference by presumed injunction' is of three kinds—(a) the Transference of injunction,—an example of this we have already cited under (2) above. (b) Transference of substrate,—an instance of this is found under II—ii—25, 26, wherein it is shown that the sentence—'one should make an offering of curds if the sacrificer be desirous of acquiring effcient sense organs'—enjoins only a particular substance, 'curds'; as to what action or sacrifice is to be the *substrate* of an offiering of that substance—*i. e.*, 'the sacrifice at which the curds could be offered'—this is got at by *transference*; the *Agnihoṭra* being such a sacrifice. (c) Transference of substitutes,—an instance, of this has been mentioned under III—v—47 to 51. In the case of sacrifices

* That the *Māsāgnihoṭra* is entirely different from the *Agnihoṭra* has been shown under II—iii—24.

† *Tuptīkā* VII—i—5, page 156.

‡ *Mīmāsābalaprākāsha*, pp. 118—19.

being performed by the *Ksaṭṭriya* or the *Vaishya*, it is laid down that when these people, as 'sacrificers' wish to eat the 'remnant,' they are to be given, not the 'remnant of the soma-juice,' but a decoction of Vata-seeds and curds ; from this injunction of the 'Substitute of Soma-juice,' it is *inferred* that the decoction is to be substituted, not for the eating only, but also for the offering ; that is to say, in case of the sacrifice being performed by a *Ksaṭṭriya* or a *Vaishya*, the offerings also are to be of the same decoction, in the place of the offerings of Soma-juice.

In a case where only a portion of the details of the *archetype* is intended to be *transferred* to the *ectype*, it is the first of these details that are to be transferred; for instance, for the *Āgnēya* sacrifice 'eight pans' are prescribed ; while for the offering to '*Ḍyāvāpṛiṭhivī*,'—which is an *ectype* of the *Āgnēya*—we need only one pan ; the particular pan used at the latter has to be the *first* of the eight pans used at the *Āgnēya*. (X—v—1 to 6).

Section 8. *

Ūha or Modification.

1. In the last section we dealt with cases where the details of one sacrifice are 'transferred' to another ; this 'transference', we have seen, is not of actions only, but also of *manṭras*; in connection with the latter however, it may so happen that the exact details—*e.g.* the words of the *manṭra*,—as used at the *Archetype* are not quite applicable to the conditions of the *ectype* to which it comes by 'transference ;' and in such a case certain alterations in the *manṭra*, —in virtue of the altered conditions of the sacrifice,—would seem to be called for. It is the subject of this alteration or modification of *transferred manṭras* that we proceed to consider now.

* Corresponding to Aḍh. IX.

In this connection it becomes necessary to consider what particular *detail* is related to, and regulated by, what particular factor of the sacrifice; and it is only after we have ascertained this that we can be in a position to judge whether or not a certain *transferred detail* is in keeping with the factors of the *ectype*. Jaimini has laid down the following correlations:—(1) all the details of the *Agnihoṭra* are meant to be related to the *apūrva* (IX—i—1). (2) So also is the washing of the Sacrificial implement. (Sū. 213 and also 11—89). (3) The loudness or otherwise of the recitation of the *manṭra* is related to the Final *apūrva* (Sū. 3). (4) The details connected with the Result and the Deity are controlled by, and related to, the Apūrva (Sū. 4, 5). (5) The details are not dependent upon the nature of the Deity (Sū. 6—10). This is the 'Ḍevaṭāḍhikaraṇa'; and herein we meet with the pronounced opinion of the Mīmāmsaka against all idea of the Deities having a corporeal form, &c., &c., &c. (6) The '*Upāmshuṭva*' enjoined in connection with the *Jyoṭiṣtoma* is dependent upon the intervening minor *apūrva* (Sū. 20—25).

The greater part of *pāḍas* i and ii of Aḍh. X is devoted to distinctions drawn between the simple '*Ṛik*' *manṭra*, that has only to be recited, and the same *manṭra* set to music and called '*Sāman*'. We have already explained this distinction above (in section I, sub-sec. 1, § 10 *et. seq.*)

* 2. *Ūha* or Modification is of two kinds:— (1) one that is directly laid down; as when it is declared that a certain corn in the *ectype* has to be thumped only *once*, and not as many times as may be necessary for the removal of the chaff—as is done in the *Archetype*; and the manṭra accompanying the thumping has to be recited only once. (2) That which has to be inferred or reasoned out. This latter is of three kinds—(*a*) the *Ūha* of *Manṭras*,—*e.g.*, In the *Āgneya* sacrifice, *Vrīhi* is the material offered, and the offering is made to

Agni, and the *manṭra* used is '*Agnaye ṭvā juṣtam nirvapāmi ......vrihiṇām meḍha sumanasyamānāḥ* (*Vājas. sam.* I. 13); this *Āgneya* is the 'Archetype' of which the *Saurya* is an 'Ectype'; but at this latter, the corn used is the *nīvāra*; and the offerings made to *Sūrya*; in virtue of these facts some alteration in the *manṭra* also is found to be necessary; consequently, even though no such alteration is laid down in the Veda, we infer the necessary injunction and read the *manṭra* as *sūryāya ṭvā juṣtam nirvapāmi......nivārāṇām meḍha sumanasyamānāḥ* (IX—iii—1,2). (*b*) *Ūha* of Sāman,—*e.g.*, for the *Vaishyasṭoma*, the *Kaṇvaraṭhanṭara* Sāman is prescribed; while in the original sacrifice as performed by the Brahmaṇas, of which the *Vaishyasṭoma* is an ectype, the *sāmans* used are the *Bṛihaṭ and the Raṭhanṭara*. The question then arises as to whether the *sāman* at the *Vaishyasṭoma* is to be sung in the manner of both the *sāmans* of the archetype, or of one of these two only; in the answer to this question, there is a marked difference between Shabara and Kumārila: according to Shabara, it has to be sung in the manner of both;—there being an option only with regard to such details of singing in which the *Bṛihaṭ* is directly opposite to the *Raṭhanṭara*; as for instance, while the *Bṛihaṭ* is to be sung *loudly*, the *Raṭhanṭara* is not sung loudly; according to Kumarila, on the other hand, there is an option with regard to all the details of singing; that is to say, when singing the *Kaṇvaraṭhanṭara* at the *Vaishyasṭoma*, one should sing it either *wholly* like the *Bṛīhaṭ*, or *wholly* like the *Raṭhanṭara* (IX—ii—48). (*c*) *Ūha* of *samskāra*,—For the *Vājapeya* sacrifice, the *nīvāra* corn is prescribed, while at its 'archetype' the corn used is the *vrīhi*, in connection with which *washing, thumping* and such other 'purifications' are laid down; though no such purificatious are directly prescribed for the *Nīvāra*, yet they have to be done in connection with this latter also; for the simple reason that without such 'purification,' the corn would not be fit for use at any sacrifice (IX—ii—40).

The *ūha* of *manṭra* again is of various kinds; the *Mīmāmsābālaprakāsha* notes the following ten:—(1) *alteration of the basic noun,—e. g.*, the change of '*āgnayē ṭvā*' into '*sūryāya ṭvā*';—(2) of the *gender,—e. g.* the *manṭra* '*Vasiyasí ruḍrāsi*' (*Vājas. Sam.* IV—21) addressed to the heifer is changed to '*Vasvasi ruḍrosi*' when addressed to the calf;—(3) of *number,—e. g.* the *manṭra*, '*Chhāgasya vapāya mēḍhasaḥ*, &c.' is changed into '*Chhāgānām*, &c.' at the *Prājāpaṭya* sacrifice, where there are many goats;—(4) of the *basic noun and gender,—e. g.* the change of '*agnayē juṣtam*' into '*aḍiṭyai juṣtam*';—(5) of the *basic noun* and *number,—e. g.* of '*agnayē juṣtam*' into '*vishvebhyo ḍēvēbhyo juṣtam*';—(6) of *number and gender,—e. g.* in '*Prāsmai aginm bharaṭa*', the masculine singular '*asmai*' is changed into the feminine plural '*ābhyaḥ*';—(7) of the *basic noun gender and number,—e. g.* for the consecration of water for the washing of the corn we have the *manṭra* '*āpoḍēvīḥ shuḍḍhāḥ sṭhaḥ*' where '*apoḍēvīḥ*, &c.' is feminine plural; this same *manṭra*, when used for the consecration of ghee, is read as '*Ghṛiṭaḍēva shuḍḍhamasi*';—(8) the alteration in the form of repeating the whole of the original twice over,—*e. g.* in the cutting of the skin, the manṭra is '*ēkaḍhā*', when there are two skins, the same *manṭra* is '*ēkaḍhā-ēkaḍhā*' (IX—iii 29 to 31);—(9) alteration of a *ṭaḍḍhiṭa* word,—*e. g.* the *manṭra*, '*Miṭrāvruṇaū ṭvā uṭṭaraṭaḥ*, &c.' (Vājas-Sam, II-3) is changed into '*Miṭrāvaruṇau ṭvā purasṭāṭ*, &c.'; (10) of *indeclinables,—e. g.* the *manṭra* '*agnim grīhṇāmi......shvo-yajñyāya ramaṭam*' is changed into '*......aḍya*, &c.' where for '*shvaḥ*' in the original we have '*aḍya*' in the modification.

It has to be noted in this connection that the *manṭras* in their *altered* form are no longer regarded as 'manṭra' in the strict sense, even though they serve the purposes of the *mantra*; they are regarded as mere 'auxiliaries' to the *mantra*; the reason for this is that the learned do not regard the altered *mantra* as 'mantra'; and it is upon the usage of the learned that it depends whether or not a certain passage is to be regarded is '*mantra*.' (*Bṛihaṭī* on II—i...34, page 50 b).

SECTION 9.

Annulment or Suspension of Details.

1. 'Alteration' having been dealt with in the foregoing section, we proceed to consider the question of '*Bāḍha*' or 'Annulment' or 'Suspension'; *i.e.* the question,—'in what cases are the details and accessories of Sacrifices, as indicated by a general rule or by 'transference', to be *suspended* in certain performances, at which they may not be found to be permissible?' There are two kinds of this 'Suspension':* (1) '*Prāpṭabāḍha*' or '*Prarmeyāpahāra*' (as called by Pārṭhasārathi Mishra),—*i.e*, the Suspension of the alteration that is indicated by Transference;—this Suspension being due to the alteration being such as, by its very nature, cannot be allowed. (2) '*Aprāpṭabāḍha*' or '*Mūlochchheḍa*,'—*i.e.* Suspension of an alteration not indicated by any of the valid forms of 'Transference'; which is, by its very nature, not allowable. The '*Prāpṭabāḍha*' is again divided into two kinds:—(a) Suspension or Annulment by the six ordinary 'means of right knowledge,' and (b) Annulment by 'Scripture.' Of these latter again there are many subdivisions. For example,—(1) that which is laid down as to be done always (*niṭya*) is annulled by what is laid down as to be done by reason of some special circumstances (*naimiṭṭika*); *e. g.* fifteen *sāmiḍhēnī* verses are laid down as to be recited at the *Ḍarsha* sacrifice;† but when the sacrifice is performed by a *Vaishya*, the number 'fifteen' is *suspended*

* See *Mimāmsābālaprakāsha*—p. 131 *et seq.*

† *Shaṭapaṭha.* 1, 3,5,7.

in favour of 'seventeen,' which is the number laid down for the *Vaishya*. (2) That which is enjoined as merely helping in the accomplishment of the sacrifice is annulled by that enjoined as accomplishing something desirable for the agent; *e. g.* with regard to the *sāmiḍhenī* verses, it is laid down that in case the Sacrificer is desirous of acquiring 'fame' or 'honour,' the number of verses should be 21; this number thus *annulling* the 15 and 17 spoken of above. (3) That which goes before is annulled by what comes after it; in connection with the going out of the priests from the *Havirḍhāna*, it is laid down—'if the *Uḍgāṭri* priest breaks the line, the Sacrifice must be finished without any sacrificial fee......if the *Praṭihartṛi* breaks it, the Sacrificer should give away all his 'belongings;' now if it so happen that the line is broken by both these priests, the Sacrificer has to give away all his belongings; the later enactment annulling the earlier.

(4) In connection with the corn to be used at the *Ḍarshapūrṇamāsa* sacrifices, the Veda lays down certain acts as to be done with a view to remove the chaff from the grain; for the *Prājāpaṭya* sacrifice, which is one of the 'ectypes' of the *Ḍarshapūrṇamāsa*, we find that instead of the *vrīhi* corn, *grains of gold** are laid down for use; now in accordance with general law that 'the ectype has to be performed in the same manner as the Archetype,' it would be necessary to go through all the acts laid down for the removing of the chaff of the *vrīhi* corn, in connection with the *golden grains* also; but all these acts are annulled in view of the fact that they would be entirely useless, there being no chaff to be removed; and the only purpose served by those acts is the visible one of removing the chaff,—there being no transcendental *apūrva* spoken of as following from

* Each of these grains of gold—called '*Kṛiṣṇala*'—has to be one third of a *Karṣa* in weight. (*Vyavahārakhaṇḍa* of *Parāsharamāḍhava*, p. 116.)

them. (X—i—1 to 3). But this does not set aside the necessity of the golden grains having to undergo the process of 'cooking' or 'baking': it is directly enjoined that 'the golden grains have to be cooked in ghee'; and this shows that, even though the 'cooking' cannot produce any visible effect in the grains, yet, *as enjoined*, it must serve some other transcendental purpose (X—ii—1, 2); similarly in connection with these grains of gold the 'eating of the remnant' has to be done, as laid down in the Veda (X—ii—13 to 16). In the same manner, when the *charu* is the material offered, all those acts of *kneading the dough*, &c. that were necessary in connection with *Cake*, are *annulled* in favour of those acts that are necessary for the preparation of the *charu* (X—i—45 to 58). (5) Some details that are 'transferable' from the Archetype to the Ectype are found to be annulled by the Direct Assertion of the Veda itself negativing the use of those particular details; *e. g.* the 'appointment' of the *Hoṭri* priest is negatived in connection with the *Paiṭrī* sacrifice. (6) A substance transferable from the Archetype is set aside by the direct injunction of another substance for the same purpose; *e. g.* at the *Shyēna* sacrifice, *Kusha* is set aside in favour of the 'reeds'; and for the *Agnyāḍhāna*, the 'fee' prescribed is the *cow*, but at its Ectypes,—all subsequent *Agnyāḍhānas,*—the fee consists of an old cart duly repaired,—the former being set aside by this latter (X—iii—30 to 33). Similarly in a case where the acceptance of both is not possible—one being totally incompatible with the other,—we have the *annulment* of the *ectypal* details in favour of the *archetypal*; but where the two are compatible with each other, we have the 'combination' of both; *i.e.* both are to be used at the Ectype; the third pāḍa of Aḍh. X deals with particular cases of such 'incompatibility.' (7) What is laid down by the general rule is annulled by that laid down by the special rule; *e.g.* i connection with the *Varuṇapraghāsa,* we find a substance specially laid down, in the shape of '*Niṣkāsa*' (the water left after the removal of the curdled particles of milk); and this sets aside the use of the 'Cake' which would be the material for the *Varuṇapraghāsa*, only in accordance with the general law that 'the details of the Archetype are transferred to the Ectype.' (VII—iii—16). Another example of this is given under X—viii—16. (8) The *useless* is set aside by the *useful*; *e. g.*, among the *mantras* laid down as to be recited as '*nigadas*,' addressed to others, there are some '*yajuṣ*' also; with regard to the reciting of the '*yajuṣ*' it is laid down that it should be done silently,—not loudly; now if the sentence intended to be addressed to another person were recited *silently*, it would entirely fail in its purpose; for this reason, the 'silent recitation' of the *yajuṣ* is, in this case, annulled by the 'loud recitation,' which would serve a useful purpose when heard by the other person to whom it is addressed. (9) The *smaller* is annulled by the *larger*; *e.g.*, in connection with the *Pañchaḍasharāṭra* Sacrifice, when we come to consider the matter of 'names,' we find that the *single* name '*Agniṣtuṭ*,'—which would indicate the reciting of the *Āgnēyī Subrahmaṇyā* verse,—is set aside in favour of the many names '*Jyoṭiṣ*' and the rest, in virtue of which the *Aindrī Subrahmaṇyā* is recited. (10) That which has room for itself elsewhere is set aside by that which, if not adopted on the occasion in question, would have no place anywhere else; *e. g.*, with reference to the recitations preceding the *Agnīṣomīya* offering (Chap. IV, Sec. 67), it is laid down that they are to be done *silently*; but with regard to the *Ḍīkṣaṇīyā Iṣti* (Chap. IV, Sec. 44), a distinct 'accent' is laid down showing that the *mantras* have to be recited loudly enough to allow of the accentuation being marked; now as regards this latter recitation, the *silent* method is set aside in favour of the *louder*, in view of the fact that the *silent* method, if dropped at the *Ḍīkṣaṇīyā*, could still be adopted at the recitations on other occasions, while the particular 'accent,' if dropped at the *Ḍīkṣaṇīyā* recitation, could not be adopted at any other recitation; and thus it would be dropped out altogether, which cannot be allowed with regard to anything that is directly enjoined.

2. The 'annulment' hitherto described has been that of the details of the *Archetype* as transferable to the *Ectype*. There is yet another kind of 'annulment' which is more general in its character, to which the name '*Prasaṅga*' is given. There are five kinds of this form of 'Annulment':—(1) The annulment of the Principal Sacrifice,—*e.g.* the daily *Agnihoṭra* is set aside by the *Agnihoṭra* performed for the attaining of a certain result. The other four are the annulments of subsidiaries:—(2) The annulment of one enjoined subsidiary by another enjoined subsidiary, (for examples see 1 and 2 above);—(3) of the *transferred* subsidiary by the *enjoined* subsidiary,—*e.g.*, the *Prayāja*, &c. for the *Iṣṭi* performed at night are set aside by those performed for the *Ḍarsha*;—(4) of the *transferred* Subsidiary by that which is *transferred*,—*e.g.*, the *Prayāja* done for the *Purodāsha* is set aside by that done for the *Pashu*;—(5) of the *enjoined* by the *transferred*,—*e.g.*, the recitation of the *Sāmiḍhēnī* verses for one who is desirous of fame sets aside the recitation of the original *Sāmiḍhēnī* verses.

3. The above are instances of *compulsory* annulment. There are cases where it is purely *optional*,—*e.g.*, when the post is said to be of *Khaḍira* or *Bilva* wood; the one may be set aside, at option, in favour of the other.

4. In all the above cases, we had the 'annulment' of something that was, by some means or other, indicated as fit for being adopted. There are annulments also of such things as do not have their adoption indicated by any means. As there can be no limit to things not so indicated, the nnmber of annulments of this kind cannot be fixed. We

shall cite a single example of this kind :—When a direct injunction lays down a certain *manṭra*,—the *Aindrī* verse for instance,—to be used at the sacrifice to the *Gārhapaṭya* fire,—this *manṭra* annuls or sets aside the possibility of the *manṭra* being used at any other sacrifice,—that to Indra for instance,—at which it would have been used in virtue of certain words contained in the *manṭra* itself. Though in these cases, what is annulled is something that might be regarded as actually indicated,—*e.g.* by the indirect implication of the words of the *manṭra*,—yet it is called '*aprāpṭabāḍha*,' the 'annulment of that which is indicated,'—in view of the fact that in face of the Direct Injunction to the contrary, the 'indirect implication' of the word does not possess any indicative force at all ; so we have the annulment, not of what is actually indicated, but only of what might be indicated.

Shankara Bhatta* enumerates and exemplifies no less than 556 'annulments' of this class.

5. There are many cases where we have the 'Annulment,' not of *all* the details transferred from the Archetype, but of only a portion of these. This *partial* 'Annulment' forms the subject-matter of the fifth *pāḍa* of *Aḍhyāya* X. We shall cite here a few instances :—(1) For the baking of the cake dedicated to Agni, *eight* pans are prescribed in connection with the *Āgnēya* sacrifice ; in connection with its *Ectype*, the offering to *Ḍyāvāpṛiṭhivī*, only *one* pan is prescribed ; hence when transferring the pan from the *Āgnēya* to this latter we shall bring in only *one* pan—and that too only the first of the eight—and set aside the remaining *seven* (X—v—1 to 3).

In some cases, the order of the details in the *Archetype* is changed in the *Ectype* ; for instance, at the *Jyoṭiṣtoma*, there are certain cups dedicated to certain deities ; when

* *Mimāmsābālaprakāsha*, pp. 134—37.

these come to be held up, it is the one dedicated to Indra that is laid down as to be held up first; and so on; at the *Ectype*, the same cups are 'transferred'; but the order of the *holding* is changed, in virtue of the direct injunction that at the Ectype, the first to be held up is the cup dedicated to Shukra. (X—v—67 to 69). This change of order has been called '*Pratikarṣa.*' In some cases, the details transferred from the Archetype are not sufficient for the Ectype; for instance, at the Archetype only 15 *Sāmans* are sung; while for the Ectype 21 are prescribed; in this case the remaining six *Sāmans* have to be added over and above the 15 at the Archetype; and the number 21 is not to be made up by repeating 6 out of the 15 *Sāmans* of the Archetype. (X—v—15 to 25). Then again, the *Jyotiṣtoma* is laid down as to be performed by only one Sacrificer; the twelve-day *Satra* has this *Jyotiṣtoma* for its Archetype; but for the *Satra* it is directly enjoined that there should be many (17) *Sacrificers*; hence at this we have seventeen, and not only one, Sacrificer. (X—vi—45 to 50).

SECTION (9)—SUB-SECTION (2).

Samuchchaya or Combination.

1. The subject of '*Bādha*' naturally leads to that of '*Samuchchaya,*' 'Inclusion' or 'Combination' or 'Aggregation'; in virtue of which there is no 'Annulment' of actions and things, but only a 'Combination' of what is laid down for the Ectype specifically, with what comes to it from its Archetype. For instance, in connection with the *Nakṣatrēṣti*, certain additional libations are laid down as to be poured after the principal offerings,—these offerings being to *Agni*, the *Kriṭṭikās*, *Ambā* and *Dula*; while in its Archetype, the *Nāriṣtahoma* is not set aside by the offerings to Agni, &c.; but both sets of libations are offered; and the reason for this 'Combination' lies in the fact that the offerings laid down serving a transcendental purpose, there would be no justification for abandoning any of them. (X—iv—1).

2. Pāḍa VI deals with 'Annulment' and 'Combination' as pertaining to the singing of *Sāmans*; and *pāḍa* vii with those pertaining to the Animal Sacrifices.

SECTION (9) SUB-SECTION (3).

Meaning of the Negative Word.

1. In view of the fact that 'Annulment' is, in most cases, expressed by the negative word, Jaimini proceeds, in pāḍa VIII, to explain the various meanings of the negative word. (1) The negative denotes 'annulment,' and hence an *exception*;—*e.g.*, the 'appointment' of priests is laid down for the Archetype; this 'appointment' is negatived in connection with the Ectype; and here the negative modifies the Archetypal injunction to this extent that it comes to mean that 'at the Ectype one should make use of all archetypal details, *with the exception of the Appointment.*' (X—VIII—1 to 4). (2) The Negative denotes 'Option,'—in the case of two contradictory declarations;—*e.g.*, in the sentences 'the vessels are to be held at the Aṭirāṭra' and 'the vessels are not to be held at the Aṭirāṭra,'—the negative in the latter does not lead to any exception; it only modifies the original injunction to the extent that the holding of the vessel is made to be regarded as optional (X—VIII—6). (3) The Negative expresses praise of something other than what is negatived;—*e. g.* in connection with the *Agnihoṭra*, we meet with the passage 'one should offer the wild seasamum; ......these are *no* offerings'; now, how to reconcile the first part of this passage—where the wild seasamum is laid down as something to be offered,—with the latter part,—where it is spoken of as *not* to be offered? With a view to this reconciliation, we take the negative to mean that 'the *offering of milk* at the *Agnihoṭra* is so praiseworthy, that even such an excellent thing as the wild seasamum is not to be offered in its place,'—the negation of the seasamum indicating the praise of the milk (X—VIII—7). (4) The negative denotes

paryudāsa or Partial Rejection ;—*e. g.*, in connection with the *Jyotiṣtoma* we read,—'one who is initiated for the Sacrifice *should not give gifts, should not make offerings, should not cook,*'—which prohibits certain acts ; these same acts are also enjoined, in connection with the same sacrifice, as accomplishing certain desirable results ; these same acts again are also found to be *transferable* to the same sacrifice from the *Agnihoṭra*,—in which case those acts are meant to help the accomplishment of the Sacrifice. Now the question arises as to which *one* of these two sets of the actions concerned,—or both sets,—are meant to be negatived by the aforesaid prohibition ; and the conclusion is that both sets are not negatived ; it is only the set calculated to accomplish something desirable for the man that is negatived ; as the prohibitive sentence follows closely upon the injunction of this latter set. (X—VIII—12 to 15).

SECTION (10) SUB-SECTION (1).

The Methods of Ascertaining the Extent of the Archetype along with its Ectype.

1. The preceding section has dealt with 'Annulment' and 'Combination' ; by means of these we are enabled to ascertain the extent of the ectypal performances alone ; and we are led to consider the means of ascertaining the extent of the Archetype along with the Ectype. This subject lends itself to a twofold division :—(1) There are certain subsidiaries which, if performed once, effectually help, by that single performance, more than one action ; this help, accorded by a single performance of the subsidiary to many Primaries, has ben called '*Ṭanṭra*' ; (2) there are, on the other hand, some subsidiaries which have to be repeated in connection with each Primary to which they are related ; to this repetition of the Subsidiary with each Primary has been given the name of '*Āvāpa*.'

2. As a preliminary to the consideration of the question of *Ṭanṭra* and *Āvāpa*, it is necessary to consider whether, in the case of a sacrificial performance consisting of a number of Primaries and Subsidiaries, the specified result follows from any one of these, or from all collectively. It is only when the result follows from all collectively, that the question can arise as to whether a certain Subsidiary is to be performed in connection with every one of the Primaries, or not ; whereas if the result follows from each of the Primaries, it would be absolutely necessary for the subsidiary to be performed with every one of them, and as such there would be no possibility of '*Ṭanṭra*' ; as each Primary in this case, will have to be treated as a complete whole by itself. Herein lies the use of Aḍhi. (1) of aḍhyāya XI. The conclusion is that the result follows from all collectively.

3. The second and following Aḍhikaraṇas also deal with the question as to whether the Subsidiaries taken together, help their Primary, or each accords its share of help independently of the rest ; the conclusion is in favour of the former view ; so that in this case also we have '*ṭanṭra*' (XI—i—5 to 19). It is for this reason that the *Prayājas*—which are the subsidiaries of the *Ḍarshapurṇamāsa*—are to be performed once only (XI—I—29 to 37).

4. Another general question dealt with in this connection is with regard to the '*Kāmya*' sacrifices ; these have to be performed as often as one may desire the result proceeding from it (XI—i—20 to 25). Actions with only visible worldly results have to be repeated as often as it may be necessary for the accomplishment of that result. But in cases where the action is for invisible results, it has to be performed only once (XI—i—27, 28).

SECTION (10) SUB-SECTION (2).

Particular Cases of 'Ṭanṭra' and Āvāpa.'

1. Bearing upon the *Ḍarshapūrṇamāsa* sacrifices we find a number of texts—*e. g.*, (*a*) 'the Ḍarshapūrṇamāsa

should be performed on level ground,' (*b*) 'the Purṇamāsa should be performed on the Full Moon Day,' (*c*) 'there should be four priests at it,' and so forth. From these passages it would seem that one entire *Ḍarshapūrṇamāsa* should be performed on level ground, another on the Full Moon Day, and so forth,—the whole sacrifice to be repeated at each place and time mentioned. But the conclusion on this point is that the whole is to be performed only once; and that this one performance is to be done at the place and time laid down in the texts; and the reason for this is that the numerous actions composing the *Ḍarshapūrṇamāsa* are to bring about their result, as combining to make up the single performance of the sacrifice (XI—ii—1, 2). All the Subidiary Sacrifices that go to make up the single Primary Sacrifice are thus to be performed at the same time and place as that laid down for the Primary. This affords an instance of 'Ṭanṭra' (XI—ii—3 to 10). Another case of 'Ṭanṭra' we have in the well-known *Agnyāḍhāna*, which has to be done only once,—the same *consecrated* fire serving for all subsequent sacrifices. (XI—iii —2).

2. This same *Ḍarshapūrṇamāsa* sacrifice supplies us with an instance of '*Āvāpa*' also :—The Sacrifice consists of two sets of sacrifices—one group called the '*Ḍarsha*' and another the '*Pūrṇamāsa*' *; though the subsidiaries laid down for each group are nearly the same, yet they have to be repeated with each group; and the reason for this is that though the two groups together form a single sacrifice leading to a single resnlt, yet, inasmuch as the two are to be performed on two different days,—15 days apart from each other,—the subsidiaries performed with one would be performed on the day of that group; and thus they would not be performed on the day prescribed for the other group, which latter would therefore be left incomplete; so in such cases the subsidiaries have to be

* See Chap. IV, § 6.

repeated. (XI—ii—11 to 17). There are however certain subsidiaries which, by their very nature, and also by virtue of direct injunctions, cannot be performed on the same day as the Primary; for instance, the *making of the altar*, as prescribed for the day preceding the *Ḍarsha*, cannot be done on the same day as that sacrifice. (XI—iii—1).

SECTION (11)—SUB-SECTION (1).

Prasaṅga: an extended Ṭanṭra.

1. The subject of our last section is *Prasaṅga.* It is not the '*Prasaṅga*' that we have already noticed above (sec. 9, sub-sec. 2) as a particular form of 'Annulment'; it is something entirely different; it may be regarded as a sort of an *extended Ṭanṭra*: '*Ṭanṭra*' *proper* is the single performance of a subsidiary with a view to helping more than one Primary,—that single performance being prescribed and intended by the Sacrificer to help more than one Primary; a case of '*Prasaṅga*' however we have where the single performance of the subsidiary,—even though prescribed and intended to help a single Primary,—is accepted as helping another Primary also, when this latter is performed by the same man and at the same time and place as the former Primary. As for instance, the *Prayāja* and other subsidiaries performed in connection with the *Agnīṣomīya* animal-offering, helps the Cake-offering also. Even though we have no such injunction as—'what is done for the animal-offering helps the cake-offering also',—yet the circumstances brought into existence by the performance of the subsidiaries with the intention of helping one action, could not cease to exist and withdraw their help from another action also, which might happen to be performed at that same time and by the same agent (XII—i—1 to 6). Then again, when one has prepared the sacrificial altar, in connection with the *Agniṣtoma,* if he wishes to perform an *Iṣti* also,—

after that *Agniṣtoma*—it is not necessary for him to erect another altar; the same altar can be used for a number of sacrifices. (XII—ii—8, 9).

2. There are certain exceptions also: *e. g.* the *Ārambhaṇīyā Iṣti* is laid down as to be performed at the commencement of the *first Ḍarshapūrṇamāsa* that the person undertakes to perform, as shown under IX—i—34, 35; and though this sacrifice is meant to be simply purificatory in its character,—tending to purify the Sacrificer,—yet, inasmuch as a single performance of this cannot help *all* the sacrifices performed by the man during the *Ḍarshapūrṇamāsa*, it has to be repeated along with each of the Ectypes that the man performs; and the reason for this lies in the fact that the qualification 'lifelong' does not pertain to the *Primary Sacrifice*, but to the *Performer* of each Sacrifice (as shown under II—iv—1); and and thus there is no '*Prasaṅga*' in this case—(XII—ii—19 to 21).

SECTION (11)—SUB-SECTION (2).

Vikalpa : *Option*.

1. We now proceed to consider the case of Option or '*Vikalpa*', which may be regarded as an antithesis to the 'Combination' dealt with in Sec. 9, Sub-sec. (2). In a case of 'Combination' we have certain Subsidiaries to be performed together; but in a case of 'Option' only one of the many subsidiaries can be performed; and the choice lies with the Sacrificer. This comes after '*Prasaṅga*', as it is this latter that leads to a number of subsidiary details being accepted as *optional* alternatives.

2. Before taking the particular cases of Option, we shall offer a few general observations on the subject. An 'option' is not permissible exept under strict necessity; because its acceptance gives rise to *eight* undesirable contingencies; this is what is meant by the dictum we so often meet with in Sanskrit works—*vikalpasya aṣtaḍoṣa*

duṣṭatvāt? These eight undesirable contingencies may be thus briefly explained in reference to the case of the '*yava*' and the '*vrīhi*', both of which are prescribed as *optional* alternatives :—(1) If we use the *vrīhi*, and reject the *yava* we reject the authority of the text enjoining this latter ; (2) we assume the untrustworthy character of this text ; (3) if we use the *yava*, we reject the text prescribing the '*vrīhi*' and (4) assume the untrustworthy character of this text ; (5) and in this latter case we again accept the authority of the *yava*-text, which we had rejected before ; and (6) we also reject the assumed untrustworthiness of the *yava*-text ; (7) in using the *vrīhi* again, we accept the authority of the *vrīhi*-text which we had rejected and (8) we also reject the assumed untrustworthiness of that text.

It may be noted however that none of these objections apply to the *Options* that are *fixed* or *limited*, as shown under II—iv—8 to 32 ; nor in the case of those *Options* that depend entirely upon the wish of the agent.

3. *Options* have been grouped,* primarily, under three heads :—(1) Indicated by Reasoning ; (2) Indicated by Direct Declaration ; and (3) Depending upon the wish of the agent. Of the (1), there are eight sub-divisions :—(*a*) Option between two 'kinds',—*e. g.*, between the *kind* of corn called '*Yava*' and that called '*Vrīhi*.' (*b*) Between particular individual Substances,—*e. g.*, at the *Ḍarshapūrṇamāsa*, for the *Agnīṣomiya*, the cake offered may be one baked in eleven or twelve pans,—as mentioned in the texts of two rescensions (Vide II—iv—8 to 32). (*c*) Between Qualities,—*e. g.*, between the *black* and *red* colour of the goat at the *Agnīsomiya*. (*d*) Between Actions,—*e. g.*, at the *Jyoṭiṣtoma*, when the priests go out of the *Havirḍhāna* forming themselves into a line, if the line happens to be broken by one priest, one set of expiatory rites is prescribed

* *Mīmānsābālaprakāsha*, page 152.

if by another priest, another set; if both should happen to break the line simultaneously, there is an 'option' between the two sets. (VI—v—51 to 53). (*e*) Between the use of a *kind* and its entire abandonment,—*e. g.*, for the *Vājasanēyins* it is laid down that they may or may not recite the *Nakṣaṭra-manṭras*; here the recitation of the class '*nakṣaṭra manṭras*' may be done, or it may be omitted altogether. (*f*) Between the use of a particular individual and its abandonment,—*e. g.*, the particular *manṭra* '*Sambhāra*' may or not be recited. (*g*) Between a quality and its abandonment,—*e.g.*, for the altar of the *Ḍarsha Sacrifice*, a particular *size* is laid down; but at the same time, there is a declaration to the effect that 'there need be no exact measurement for the altar'; hence the size prescribed in the former may or may not be adopted. (*h*) Between an *action* and its omission,—*e.g.*, the holding and the non-holding of the *Ṣodashin* vessels at the Aṭirāṭra sacrifice.

All these eight 'options' again may be either '*kraṭvarṭha*'—helping in the accomplishment of the sacrifice,—or '*puruṣārṭha*'—accomplishing something desirable for the agent. All the examples cited above belong to the former class. As an example of the latter class, we have the following:—At the *Ḍarshapūrṇamasa* sacrifice, the water is fetched in a vessel which has a handle four inches long, and a cavity eight inches deep, and about 9 inches in diameter;—if one Sacrificer is desirous of acquiring 'brahmic glory', this vessel is, in one text, spoken of as to be made of the wood of a large tree, and in another as to be of *Kānsya* metal; and this gives rise to an 'Option.'

There are thus 8 kinds of '*kraṭvarṭha*' and eleven kinds of '*puruṣārṭha*' options *indicated by reasoning*,—making 19 in all.

Similarly, of *Option indicated by direct declaration* also, there are 19 kinds. As an example of one of these we have the one indicated by the text—'One who desires to sacrifice with *corns* or with *animals*, or with *Soma*, should sacrifice either on the New Moon or on the Full Moon Day,'—where we have an 'option' of *time*, as also of *materials*. In this connection we may cite an example from *Smṛiṭi* literature also; where it is laid down that 'the *Piṭṛis* remain satisfied for a month with offerings of seasamum, *yava*, &c.,'—if one is desirous of keeping his *Piṭṛis* satisfied for a month, he may offer any one of the materials herein mentioned.

Of the third main kind of *Option* also—that depending on the will of the agent,—we have the same 19 divisions, As an example of this we have the following:—In connection with the *Ashvamēḍha* a '*Brahmaṇa*' is laid down as to be sacrificed 'to *Brahman*'; this *Brāhmaṇa* sacrificed may belong to the '*Kauṇḍinya*' or to any other *goṭra*,—this depends entirely upon the wish of the agent.

4. Another division of 'Options' is into two: the two classes of—(*a*) *Vyavasṭhiṭa*—where among the alternatives there is *limit* or *fixity*; and (*b*) *Avyavasṭhiṭa*,—where there is no such limit or fixity. Each of these again is either *indicated by reason* or *pointed out by direct declaration*. As Options of this latter class, we have the examples already cited above. As an example of the *Fixed* or *Limited* kind *based on reasoning*, we have one from the *Smṛiṭis*, discussed by Kumārila under the *Smṛiṭi-pāḍa*. It has been laid down that the Brāhmaṇa should devote 12 years of his life to the study of each of the four Vedas,—*or as many years as may be necessary*. On the face of it, this appears to indicate an *Unlimited Option*, leaving it entirely at the option of the student whether he will finish the whole in 48 years or in 4 only; but by reasonings it has been shown by Kumārila that we have here an option of the 'limited' kind—the meaning of the text being that, 'if the student

is not going to take to the life of the Householder, he must devote 48 years to Vedic study; if however he is going to enter that life, then he should devote only 5 years to each Veda, 20 years in all; but if he is not able, under his peculiar circumstances, to devote more than 2 or 3 years, he should adopt this latter course, and so on.' (See *Ṭanṭravārṭika*, p. 112). The *fixity* of Options indicated by Direct Declaration is of seven kinds :—(1) with regard to *place*, —*e.g.* the 'consecration of fire' having been laid down as to be performed during the *Spring*, the question arises as to which of the two methods of counting seasons is to be adopted in this case—Seasons as a rule being counted by the 'lunar' month, and the lunar month being taken by some to begin with the New Moon, and by others with the Full Moon. The fixity of option in this case is due to the text that 'the lunar month should not be counted to begin with the dark half of the month.' (*Ṭrikāṇḍamaṇḍana*). With regard to *Time*;— in connection with the reciting of the *Vārṭraghnī* and the *Vṛiḍhanvaṭī manṭras* at the *Ḍarshapūrṇamāsa*, there being no rule as to which of the two is to be recited on the New Moon Day, and which on the Full Moon Day,—we have the decisive rule that the *Vārṭraghnī* is to be recited on the Full Moon and the *Vṛiḍhanvaṭī* on the New Moon Day. (3) With regard to *Agent*;—*e. g.* at the *Ḍarshapūrṇamāsa* the Sacrificer has to recite a *manṭra*; and in this connection three *manṭras* are laid down; from among which it would appear that any one may be recited; but we meet with the distinct rule to the effect that the first of the *manṭras* is to be recited by the *Brāhmaṇa*, the second by the *Kṣaṭṭriya*, and the third by the *Vaishya* sacrificer. (4) with regard to *action*;—for the *Varuṇapraghāsa*, two '*vihāras*' are laid down,—one to the right and another to the left; and a further rule lays down that the *māruṭi* material is to be placed to the *right*, and all others on the left. (5) With regard to *result*;—*e. g.* with regard to the many optional '*niḍhanas*' (the additional syllables added to the Sāman, by the exigencies of music) to be adopted at the *Jyoṭiṣṭoma*, we have a rule laying down that—'when the sacrificer desires *rain*, the *niḍhana* to be used is *hīṣ*, when he desires *food*, the *niḍhana urg*,' and when he desires *heaven*, the *niḍhana ū*.' (6) With regard to *cause* or *occasion*;—we have an example of this from the *Smṛiṭis*: We find the text—' in the case of the death of a *Sapiṇda*, the period of impurity is to be 10 days; or till after the day of the picking up of the bones (third day), or three days, or one day only;' and as this rule by itself would be a source of confusion, we have the additional rule that, ' when the dead *Sapiṇda* is one whose *Upanayana* has been done, the period is to be 10 days; if his *Tonsure* has been done (and not the *Upanayana*) 4 days, and so forth.........one day being the period in the case of the dead being a child who has just cut his teeth.' (7) with regard to the *limit* or *condition*;—*e. g.* the *Vrīhi* and the *Yava* being optional alternatives, we have the conditional rule—'*if one has begun with the Vrīhi*, he must continue with the same.'

5. In regard to *Options*, the following facts are noteworthy:—In many cases where there may be an apparent option, there is no real option at all; *e. g.* in cases where many details are laid down with regard to the same action,—each of these details being intended for a distinct purpose. In such a case, every one of the many details has to be used. (XII—iii—9). But in cases where the details are for the same purpose, we have *option*. (XII—iii—10 to 14). Similarly with regard to the many expiatory rites; if these are laid down in connection with the same *deficiency* or *discrepancy*, then there is *option* (XII—iii—16); but there can be no *option* when they are laid down in connection with distinct deficiencies—in which case all have to be performed (XII—iii—19). So with *manṭras*,—it is only when many are laid down for the same purpose that we have *option*

(XII—iii—29). But when of such *manṭras* one is found to be expressive of mere *recitation*, another of *praise*, and another of some *blessing*,—*all* have to be recited (II—iv—1,2). With regard to *gifts*, when several numbers—6,12, &c.,—are laid down, we have *option* (XII—iv—9).

CHAPTER IV.

SACRIFICES.

[*Books consulted* :—(1) Shaṭapaṭha Brahmaṇa (Berlin); (2) *Ibid.* Translated by Eggeling (Sacred Books of the East); (3) Shrauṭa-Sūṭras of Kāṭyāyana with the Bhāsya of Karka (Chaukhambha Sanskrit Series, Benares); (4) Shrauṭapaḍārṭhanirvachana ('Pandit', Benares); (5) Āpasṭambīya Ḍarsha-Pūrṇamāsā-Paḍḍhaṭi (Manuscript lent by Mahāmahopaḍhyāya Gaṅgāḍhara Shāsṭrin, Benares); (6) Kāṭyāyanīya Agnisṭoma-Paḍḍhaṭi (Manuscript lent by MM. Gaṅgāḍhara Shāsṭrin, Benares); (7) Bhāttabhāskara (Manuscript with the present writer); (8) Māḍhavāchāryas's Commentary on the Institutes of Parāshara (Bibliothica Indica); (9) Prakaraṇapañchikā (Chaukhambha S.S.).]

1. All Mīmāmsā discussions are based upon the interpretation of the rules and regulations laid down in the Vedas (pre-eminently in the Brāhmaṇas) bearing upon sacrificial ritual; hence for the due understanding of the reasonings employed, some knowledge of the ritualistic details becomes essential. We shall therefore devote this chapter to that subject.

2. Though as a matter of fact, the term '*ḍharma*' is applied to all such actions as *Yāga* (offering of Sacrifices); *Homa* (Pouring of libations); *Ḍāna* (giving of presents); *Snāna* (Bathing); *Ḍhyāna* (Meditation); *Japa* (Repeating of Manṭras), and so forth,—yet the principal forms of *Ḍharma* that constitute the subject-matter of the Mīmāmsā-Shāsṭra are *Yāga*, *Ḍāna* and *Homa* only (Shabara-Bhāṣya, p. 483, l.

18). Every one of these consists in the offering of a certain thing to some one else. The 'offering' common to all these has been defined as the 'resolution or making up of the mind to be indifferent to, or lose sight of, or give up, one's own proprietary rights over the thing that is offered' (Shabara-Bhāṣya, p. 484, ll.11-12). Then again, an offering becomes a '*yāga*' when the proprietary right is relinquished by means of words in favour of a Deity, (Mīm. Sū. IV—ii—27, also Bhāṣya p. 484, line 13), a personality who is not near the person making the offering. When it is relinquished and actually made to rest in, and transferred to, another person, who is near at hand, the offering becomes a '*ḍāna*' or 'giving' (Shabara-Bhā. p. 484, line 14). It is called 'Homa' when the thing offered is *thrown into*, and offered at, a particular assigned place (Mīm. Sū. IV—ii—28; *Prakaranpañchikā* page 105); it is not necessary for the offering to be thrown into the fire, in order to make it 'Homa' (as has been asserted in the *Bhāttabhāskara*, MS. pp. 92-93); because in many cases, the throwing of substances into water (as during the Avabhṛitha Iṣti, at the conclusion of the Agniṣtoma) is called 'Homa.'

The difference among *Yāga*, *Ḍāna* and *Homa* is thus briefly explained in the *Shabara-Bhaṣya*, p. 484—'The *relinquishing of one's proprietary right* is the factor common to all the three; the difference is only this—in *Yāga*, there is mere verbal relinquishment (the thing offered is not actually taken away by the recipient),—in *Ḍāna*, the thing is actually made over (to the recipient),—and in *Homa*, the thing offered has got to be thrown into some suitable receptacle (water or fire).'

3. The deity to whom sacrifices are offered is, for the Mīmāmsaka, a purely hypothetical entity, posited for the sake of the accomplishment of a Sacrifice. '*Yāga*' having been defined as 'offering to a Deity,' no *yāga* could be accomplished without a 'Deity'; hence the Deity is subordi-

nate to the Sacrifice; this is very clearly brought out in Mīm. Sū. IX—i—6-10; in which connection the *Bhāṣya* explains that the Deity has no body, it does not eat anything, it cannot be either pleased or displeased; nor can it award prizes or punishments, as results of sacrifices; hence it is that it cannot be regarded as the principal factor in the Sacrifice. Those Vedic passages that speak of certain gods having 'hands,' &c., all these passages must be treated as pure *Arthavāda*, even non-existent properties being attributed, in praise, to the gods.

The 'Deity' of a sacrifice is thus not necessarily a 'person' or 'being'; it is spoken of by means of some word or words in the injunctive sentences as one to whom the offering is to be made; and whose excellences are eulogised in the hymns; *e.g.*, in the sentence '*āgnēyo'ṣṭākapālo bhavati*,' the word '*āgnēyaḥ*' points to Agni to whom the *cake baked on eight pans* is to be offered. There are three sources of information as to the 'Deity' of sacrifices:—(1) Nominal affixes,—as in the instance cited, the nominal affix '*dhak*' added to the noun 'Agni' shows that Agni is the 'Deity'; according to Pāṇini's Sūtra, 4-2-24, which speaks of the '*dhak*' affix as indicative of the deity (see also *Mīmāmsa-Sūtra* (X—iv—25);—(2) The Dative termination,—*e.g.* in the sentence '*Agnīṣomābhyām yajati*,' the dative ending in '*Agnīṣomābhyām*' denotes that the pair 'Agni-Soma' is the 'Deity'; this is weaker in authority than (1), because the deity having no personal existence cannot, in the proper sense of the word, be the 'receiver' of a gift; and hence the '*receivership*' indicated by the Dative can be only figurative;—(3) *Mantras*,—in many cases it is some word or expression in the *mantra* that indicates the Deity, *e.g.* the word '*Kētu*' occurring in the *mantra* '*Ketuṅkriṇvannakēṭavē*, &c.' indicates Keṭu as the 'Deity.' (Vide *Bhātta-bhāskara*, pp. 92-93).

4. The main classification of Sacrifices is based upon the

difference in the substances offered. On this basis they have been classified under the following three heads :—

I. '*Iṣṭi*' (including also the *Haviryajñas*)—Sacrifices performed by the *Yajamāna* or 'Sacrificer' accompanied by his wife and helped by the four *Ṛitviks* or Priests—Aḍhvaryu, Brahman, Hoṭṛi and Agnīḍhra,*—consisting of offerings of milk, butter, rice, barley or other grains. The 'Prakṛiṭi' or 'Archetype' of this class is the dual sacrifice of the 'Ḍarsha-Pūrṇamāsa' (described in *Shaṭapaṭha Brahmāṇa*, I and II); and this, with the following six 'Vikṛiṭis,' 'Ectypes', forms the seven 'Samsṭhās' or 'forms' of the '*Iṣṭi*' :—(*a*) *Agnyāḍhāna* (described in *Kāṭyāyana's Shrauṭa-Sūṭra*, IV. 179, &c.); (*b*) *Agnihoṭra* with its ectype the *Māsāgnihoṭra* (described in *Shaṭapaṭha Br.* I. 7-1, &c., and also *Shrauṭa-Sūṭra* IV); (*c*) *Āgrayaṇēṣṭi* (*Shaṭapaṭha*, IV. 2-2); (*d*) *Chāṭurmāsya* (Shrauṭa-Sūṭra V); with its four sections, the *Vaisvaḍēva*, the *Varuṅapraghāsa*, the *Shākamēhḍa* and the *Shunāsīrīya*; (*e*) *Pashubanḍha* (*Shrauṭa-Sūṭra* VI and *Shaṭapaṭha* XI. 7·1); and (*f*) *Sauṭrāmaṇi* (Shaṭapaṭha XI). † Kaṭyāyana in his *Shrauṭa-sūṭra* deals in detail with the first five only. Even though without Agnyāḍhana, no *Iṣṭi* can be performed,—as these have to be offered into the fire consecrated by the Āgnyāḍhāna (*Shaṭapaṭha*, I. 6, 3, 20)—yet it is the *Ḍarsha-Pūrṇamāsa*, and not the *Agnyāḍhāna*, that is re-

---

* The *aḍhvanyu* is the most important among these; chosen before the rest, and operating from the beginning to the end of the performance. The *Brahman* is the second to be chosen; he is the general Superintendent or Examiner, well-versed in ritualistio details, and also in the three Vedas; he also performs the expiatory rites. The *Hoṭṛi* remains seated to the north of the altar, and recites all such hymns as the *Sāmiḍhenis*, the *Prayājas*, the *Ājyabhāgas*, the *Yājyās*, the *Puronuvākyās*, the *Sūkṭavāka* and the *Shamyuvāka*. The *Agnīḍhra* or the *Agnīḍ* holds the wooden sword and responses with the word '*asṭu*' to some of the acts done by the *Aḍhvaryu*.

† In this connection, we may compare the following passage from the Shaṭapaṭha Br. X. 1-5. यावन्मात्रं वा अमुष्मिंल्लोके ऽग्नि[?]याजी[?] ऽश्नाति अर्धमासे ऽर्धमासे दर्शपौर्णमासयाजी, चतुर्षु चतुर्षु मासेषु चातुर्मास्ययाजी षट्सु षट्सु, पशुबन्धयाजी, संवत्सरे संवत्सरे सोमयाजी, [?] [?] संवत्सरेऽग्निचित् काममश्नाति ।

garded as their 'Archetype;' firstly, because, as remarked by Karka, the *Shaṭapaṭha* itself begins with the *Ḍarsha-Pūrṇamāsa*, and secondly, because the *Agnyāḍhāna* is the consecration of the fire only, and so cannot be regarded as a 'sacrifice,' in the strict sense of the term, on whose model the other ectypal sacrifices could be performed. Other sacrifices of this class mentioned in the *Shaṭapaṭha* are the *Ḍākṣāyaṇa* (Shrauṭa-Suṭra IV, 104) and the *Ṭraiyambaka.*

II. *Pākayajñas*—consisting of the offering of cooked substances, not into the consecrated fire, but in the ordinary domestic fire. The seven principal '*samsṭhās*' of this class are:—(*a*) *Pañchamahāyajñas* (enumerated and described in Shaṭapaṭha X, 5, (6)—the 'Archetype'; (*b*) *Aṣṭakās* (*c*) *Pārvaṇashrāḍḍha*; (*d*) *Shrāvaṇī*; (*e*) *Agrahāyaṇī*; (*f*) *Chaiṭrī*; and (*g*) *Āshvayujī.* (See *Parāsharamāḍhava,—Vyavahāra-Kāṇḍā*, page 157, *Note*). These sacrifices are dealt with by the Gṛhyasūṭras, and not by the Shrauṭasūṭras. It is perhaps solely on this ground, and on that of their not being offered in the consecrated fire, that these sacrifices have been placed in a class apart from the *Haviryajñas* described above. Consisting of offerings of milk and grains, these are as much 'Haviryājña' (in the literal signification of the term) as the Ḍarsha-Pūrṇamāsa and the rest.

III. *Somayajñas*—Offerings of Soma-juice, also known under the name of '*Jyotiṣtoma*,' which however is a name that is given to the first of the following seven 'samsṭhās' of the Somayāga:—(*a*) *Agniṣtoma*—the 'Archetype'; (*b*) *Aṭyagniṣtoma*, (*c*) *Ukṭhya*; (*d*) *Ṣodashin*; (*e*) *Vājapēya* (*Shaṭa-paṭha* V, Shrauṭa-sūṭra XIV); (*f*) *Āṭirāṭra*; and (*g*) *Āpṭor-yamā.* All these are called "Ekāha,' as lasting for one day. There are some Soma-sacrifices that last from two to twelve days; these are called '*Ahīna*'; to this class belongs the *Ḍvāḍashāha* described in *Shaṭapaṭha* IV. 5. 1. Others again, called '*Saṭras*', are not 'sacrifices', but what have been called 'sacrificial sessions'; these last for more than twelve days, and are performed by many persons (generally seventeen) in combination (see *Shaṭapaṭha* IV. 4, 2, 12). Under this head, the *Shaṭapaṭha*, and also Kāṭyāyana, includes such elaborate and complex sacrifices as the *Gavāmayana* (*Shrauṭasūṭra* XIII), the *Rājasūya* (*Shaṭapaṭha*, V, and *Shrauṭasūṭra* XIII), the *Sauṭrāmaṇī* *Shaṭapaṭha* XI; *Shrauṭasūṭra* XIX); the *Ashvamēḍha* (*Shaṭapaṭha* XI—XIII, *Shrauṭasūṭra* XX); and also some minor sacrifices, such as—*Vasorḍhārā*, *Rāṣṭrābhṛiṭ*, *Vājaprasavīya*, *Payovraṭa*, *&c.* (*Shaṭapaṭha* IV). Almost all Soma-sacrifices involve the killing of an animal; hence older writers have included the 'Pashu' or 'Animal' sacrifices under 'Soma.' Later writers however appear to make some sort of distinction between the 'Soma' and the 'Animal' sacrifices; at least, such distinction is found in the *Shrauṭapaḍārṭhanirvachana*. There is however no authority for this either in the *Shaṭapaṭh t* or in the *Shrauṭasūṭras*.

5. We shall describe here, somewhat in detail, the performance of the two Archetypes:—The *Ḍarsha-Pūrṇamāsa* of the '*Iṣṭis*,' and the *Agniṣṭoma* of the Soma sacrifices.

THE ḌARSHA-PŪRṆAMĀSA.

6. This is the name given to two sets of sacrifices—the first set called '*Pūrṇamāsa*' consisting of the three sacrifices called the '*Āgneya*,' the '*Upāmshuyāja*' and the '*Agnīṣomīya*'; and the other set called '*Ḍarsha*' consisting of the three, called the '*Āgnēya*' the '*Anidraḍaḍhiyāga*' and the *Payoyāga*—offered on the Fnll-moon and New-moon days by one who has 'taken the fires.' That the sacrifices are to be performed every fortnight is laid down in the Shaṭapaṭha Brahmāṇa X—1. 5, अर्धमासे अर्धमासे दर्शपूर्णमासयाजी स्या 'Fortnight by fortnight one should perform the Ḍarsha-Purṇamāsa sacrifices. (See Bhāttabhāskara, *Ms.* p. 98.)

7. As these sacrifices can be offered only in the duly consecrated fire, and that also only after the daily Agnihotra offerings have been made, we shall preface an account of them by a brief description of the ceremony of '*Agnyāḍhāna*,' 'Fire-Consecration.' The salient features of this ceremony have been summed up by Eggeling (*Shaṭapaṭha Br.*, Sacred Books of the East, pp. 74-76), wherefrom we take the following extracts :—

8. "The Agnyāḍhāna......is performed on the first day "of the waxing moon........The normal performance requires "two days—the first of which is taken up with preliminary "rites, while the second is devoted to the chief ceremonies, "beginning with the production of the sacred fire by "friction.

"After the Sacrificer has chosen his four officiating "priests,* Brahman, Hoṭṛi, Aḍhvaryu and Agnīḍhra, he "proceeds with them to erect the 'fire houses' for the three "fires—'Gārhapaṭya,' Āhavanīya, and 'Ḍakṣiṇāgni'†........... "The Aḍhvaryu then procures a temporary fire......and after

* These four, with the Sacrificer, are the most important persons at the Sacrifice (Vide. *Shaṭapaṭha*, I. 1·1·15). Another important priest is the Uḍgāṭṛi, who chants the Sāman hymns. He is not required at the Agnyāḍhāna. We have an enumeration of the several priests in *Shaṭapaṭha* XII—1·1. A brief account of these is also to be found in the Journal of the Asiatic Society of Bengal, 1907, Vol. III, 4, 'Some Notes on Vedic Sacrifices.'

† The Agnihoṭra House is built on a flat level piece of gronnd, a regular square or oblong, with doors on the East and South. In this House, the centre of the Western half is called the 'Abode of the Gārbapaṭya,' which is a circle with a diameter of 27 *Aṅguls*, whereon there is the 'Kuṇda,' the receptacle of fire, the hearth surrounded by two raised boundaries, one six *Aṅguls* high and six broad, and the other six *Aṅguls* high and four broad. The fire deposited in this Kuṇda is called the 'Gārhapaṭya,' by reason of its special connection with the Sacrificer who is the *Gṛihapaṭi*, Master of the House. From the centre of this Gārhapaṭya Kuṇda, a tape called the 'Priṣthyā-Sūṭra' is drawn towards the eastern half of the house, where they have the 'Abode of the Āhavanīya, mapped out into a perfect aqnare. This being surrounded by two boundaries like those of the Gārhapaṭya Kuṇda, forms the 'Āhavnīya Kuṇda or Hearth.' The fire deposited in this hearth is called the 'Āhavanīya, on accouut of all offerings being made into this fire. Towards the South of the Āhavanīya Hearth, a space in the shape of the winnowing

"the four-fold lustration of the Gārhapaṭya Fire-place, he lays "down the fire thereon. Towards sunset the Sacrificer in-"vokes the Gods and Manes.........He then enters the "Āhavanīya House, passes to the Gārhapaṭya, and sits down "to the west of the fire; his wife at the same time entering "the Gārhapaṭya house from the south, and seating herself "south of him......Whereupon the Aḍhvaryu hands to the "Sacrificer two pieces of wood (Araṇī)......to be used next "morning for the production of the sacred fire by one of "them being rapidly drilled in a hole in the other......These "sticks are deposited on a seat. In the house of the "Gārhapaṭya a he-goat may then be tied up for the "night......to be presented to the Agnīḍhra.

"After sunset the Aḍhvaryu measures out four vessels "of husked rice-grains—each containing three handfulls—on "an ox-hide dyed red. With this rice the *Oḍana Chaṭuḥ-"prāshya* is prepared on the provisional Gārhapaṭya fire. "When it is ready, the Aḍhvaryu makes a hollow in the pap, "and pours clarified butter into it; he then takes three "kindling sticks, anoints them with some of that ghee, and "puts them on the fire one after another. Thereupon the "Sacrificer having paid due honours to the priests......bids "them eat.

"During the night, the Sacrificer and his wife have to "remain awake and keep up the fire. When the night clears "up, the Aḍhvaryu extinguishes the fire, or......takes it "southwards and keeps it in a safe place, till the Ḍakṣiṇāgni "fire is made up. He them draws with the wooden sword

---

basket is mapped out; this forms the 'Abode of the Ḍakṣiṇagni.' This surrounded by two boundaries forms the 'Ḍakṣiṇāgni-Kuṇḍa or Hearth'; the fire deposited herein is called 'Dakṣiṇāgni,' upon which rice is cooked for the four principal priests. That these names of the fires—'*Gārhapaṭya*'. '*Āhavanīya*' and '*Ḍakṣiṇāgni*'—are applicable only to duly consecrated fires, and not to the ordinary fire, is proved by Jaimini in *Mīm. Ṣūtra* XII—ii—1, where it is shown that the name 'vihāra,' which is given collectively to the three consecrated fires, cannot apply to the ordinary fire.

"three lines across the fire-place and proceeds with the "preparation of the hearth-mounds."

9. Eggeling stops short at these preliminary rites of the first day. An account of the rites of the Agnyāḍhāna proper, we take from the *Paḍḍhati* or manual based upon the Shrauṭa-Sūṭras of Kāṭyāyana (Adh. IV) and Āpasṭāmba, wherein we have, in a systematised form, what is described in *Shaṭapaṭha* II, 1·1 *et seq.*

On the hearth-mound, the Aḍhvaryu deposits a piece of gold, sprinkles the earth of the mole-hill, and surrounds it with pebbles (Shr. Sū. IV.210). Before or after sunrise, (Shaṭapaṭha II·1·4·8 and IV·1·2·11) the fire is produced by the drilling of the sticks (215), and after sunrise, is taken from the Gārhapaṭya to the Āhavanīya hearth. He takes a burning stick and deposits it on the Gārhapaṭya hearth,—the Brahman singing the Raṭhanṭara Sāman. From there the fire is taken to the Ḍakṣināgni hearth; and the Aḍhvaryu requests the priests to recite the *Shyaiṭa*, the *Vāravanṭīya* and the *Yajñāyajñiya* hymns. The Sacrificer then makes the Agnihoṭra offering, ending with the final offering, and pays the specified gifts to other Brāhmaṇas.

10. The above is an account of the Consecration of the Fire in which all sacrificial offerings are made. We shall now proceed with the details of the *Ḍarshapūrṇamāsa.*

11. Though both Kāṭyāyana's Shrauṭa-Sūṭra and the Shaṭapaṭha Brāhmaṇa begin with the 'Pūrṇāmāsa' Sacrifices, the later Manuals begin with the 'Ḍarsha.' We shall follow these latter, and note, in passing, all points where the the 'Pūrṇamāsa' differs from the 'Ḍarsha.'

12. On the morning of the day preceding the New Moon, (some of the lunar mansions are specially recommended in Shaṭapaṭha II·2), after the daily Agnihoṭra has been performed, the Sacrificer chooses his Aḍhvaryu, and with his help performs the five-fold lustration of the Āhavanīya

and Ḍakṣiṇāgni hearths in order to make them fit to receive the consecrated fire from the Gārhapaṭya hearth. This fire is then taken ont of the Gārhapaṭya and deposited on the other two hearths by the Aḍhvaryu (this being called the 'Agnyuḍḍharaṇa'), and two logs of fuel are placed upon each of these fires. Into the fire thus supplied with fuels, the Sacrificer makes certain offerings. Drinking a little water, he, along with his wife, imposes upon himself certain fasts and restrictions, preferring requests to Agni, Vāyu and Sūrya to help him in keeping these. The Aḍhvaryu taking up a knife heats it on fire; and with this and the water vessel in his hand, he goes a few steps either to the East or to the North, and picking up *Kusha* grass, throws one or two blades of it as an offering to cows; he holds the rest in his hand, holding the bundle tight on the point where the blades shoot off from the stem, and with the knife cuts the bundle at that point with a single stroke. Another handful is also similarly cut off for purposes of the *Prasṭara*, a bedding of *Kusha* grass npon the Altar, wherenpon the Juhū* is kept. Having cut off three more handfulls of *Kusha* (called 'Niḍhanas') he touches his own body. He prepares the *Shulva*,† lays down the stick, and keeps upon it the handfulls of *Kusha*, and upon one of these he deposits the *prasṭara*; he binds up the whole into a bundle, dedicating it to Inḍrāṇī, sprinkling water on the bundle. He takes up another supply of *kusha* and keeps it close to the place of the central *pariḍhi*.‡

13. At this point comes in the performance of the Pinḍapitṛiyajña. At this the Sacrificer makes an offering

* A full list with explanations of this and other things will be found later on at the end of the section.

† A rope of Kusha, with three knots in the middle, and one at the end, for the pnrpose of binding bundles of fuel.

‡ This is the name given to the three logs of wood that are kept along the Northern, Western and Southern sides of the altar, upon the first *mekhalā* or raised boundary.

of rice-balls to his three immediate ancestors*; and approaching the Gārhapaṭya hearth, hands over the ball offered to his grand-father to his wife; and throws the other two into the fire.

14. The Aḍhvaryu prepares another *Shulva*, and with this he ties up the three *pariḍhi*-logs into a bundle; and deposits it along with the bundles of fuel. He then prepares the *Veda*† and the *Upaveṣa*;‡ and the Sacrificer, assisted by his wife, sweeps the Sacrificial Honse and washes it thoroughly.

15. During the day, the Sacrificer shaves his head and chin, abstains from meat and from carnal pleasures (Kāṭ. Shr. Sū. II. 8-9). In the afternoon he, with his wife, partakes of the rice and barley mixed with ghee, called the '*Vraṭopanīya*' (Shr. Sū. II. 10); whereupon they take the vow of henceforward eating 'nothing but what grows in the forest, be it forest-herbs, or the fruit of trees' (Shaṭapaṭha, I—1·1·10, Shr. Sū. II·14). In the evening he offers the usual Agnihoṭra libations. The Aḍhvaryu, before retiring, spreads *kusha* on the *pariḍais* and around the three hearths, puts fuel on the three fires, separates the calves from their dames (this removal of the calves being called '*Vaṭsāpākaraṇa*, Shaṭapaṭha 7-I). The Sacrificer also spreads *kusha* round the fires, and invites the gods to lodge in his house; and then, with his wife, retires to rest, sleeping on the ground, in the Gārhapaṭya House or in the Āhavanīya House.

* At the '*Pūrṇamāsa*,' in place of this *yajña* they have the *Vraṭopāyana*, wherein the Sacrificer picks up two entire blades of *Kusha*, and sipping water three times, sprinkles water on the Āhavanīya fire into which he puts four pieces of fuel.

† A broomstick for the sweeping of the altar, made of Kusha grass donbled up and tied, with the ends lopped off;—the shape being similar to that of the thigh of a seated calf. ‡A piece of wood six inches long cut off from the root end of the branch of a tree..

16. This finishes the observances of the Previous Day, called the '*Upavasaṭha*'; 'because,' says the Shaṭapaṭha (I.—1-1-77), 'when the householder enters on his vow, he means to sacrifice to the gods the next morning; therefore, all the gods betake themselves to his house and *abide by* (*upa-vas*) him in his house.'*

17. On the next morning,—the morning of the New Moon—after the morning libations of the daily *Agnihoṭra* have been offered, the Aḍhvaryu, before the sun rises, † spreads Kusha round the fires, and prepares Kusha-seats for the Sacrificer and the Brahman; and then gets together the vessels, implements and all other articles, necessary for the performance.‡

18. The Sacrificer then proceeds to 'appoint' the Brahman; The priest accepts the post, and promising to perform his duty well, invokes blessings upon the Sacrificer and betakes himself to his assigned seat, called the 'Brahmasaḍana'. He takes from under his seat a blade of *Kusha* and throws it towards the South-East, thereby chasing away all undesirable elementals; and thenceforward, seated near the Āhavanīya, watches the performance. §

19. After the Brahman has taken his seat, the Aḍhvaryu gets in the Prīṇaṭā vessels, and filling them with water, sprinkles that water over his head with the *paviṭra* directing the Sacrificer to keep silent during the performance, he deposits the *praṇīṭā* vessels on *kusha* and covers them up with *kusha*. Taking up the *Agnihoṭra-havaṇi* and the

*At the Pūrṇmamāsa, the rites of the Previous Day are generally performed on the same day as the main Sacrifice.

†After sunrise, at the Pūrṇamāsa.

‡A list of these with brief descriptions, is given at the end of this account.

§At the Pūrṇamāsa, when it is being performed for the first time, the *Anvārambhaṇ ya* offering is made at this juncture; it consists of oblations of a rice-cake to Agni-Viṣṇu, boiled rice and grains to Sarasvatī, and a rice-cake to Sārasvaṭa ; the priest's fee in this case being an one-year old cow.

Shūrpa, he heats them over the Āhavaniya fire; and obtaining the Sacrificer's permission to prepare the offering, he proceeds to the cart which is full of corn, and takes out some corn in the *pāṭrī*; and ascending the cart, he washes the corn needed for the Sacrificial Cake, from which he removes all foreign substances. Having washed his hands, he puts the corn into the *Shūrpa* with the *Agnihoṭra-havaṇī* The Sacrificer then offers his invitation to the gods to be pleased to come to his house and accept the offerings; whereupon the Aḍhvaryu promises to prepare the cake for Inḍra-Agni *. Looking towards the East, he looks round the *vihāra* (ground mapped out for the Sacrifice), and descends from the cart; and deposits in their assigned places the handfulls of corn intended for the gods; and washes all the vessels. Taking up the skin of the black antelope, he shakes it up three times, and calling it the 'skin of Aḍiṭi', he spreads it, the hairy side uppermost, to the North of the Gārhapaṭya hearth, with its neck towards the East; on this he places the *ulūkhala*, and putting some corn into it, he takes the *musala*, and calls out loudly for the *Haviṣkṛiṭ*' or 'preparer of the offering;' whereupon the Lady (the Sacrificer's wife) begins to thump the corn.

20. Then follows the appointment of the *Agnīḍhra* or *Agnīḍ* priest. Having accepted the office and promised to perform his duty, he takes up the *Shamyā*, and strikes with it the *ḍriṣaḍ* and the *upala*. The Aḍhvaryu brings up the *Shūrpa* into which the corn thumped by the lady has been kept, and winnowing with iṭ, removes the husks, upon the *uṭkara* (the appointed place where all bits of grass and such other refuses are to be thrown); and then taking up the husks into the pan intended for the middle cake, throws them beneath the antelope skin, as an offering to the Rākṣasas. Having washed the pan, he cleans the grains

* For Inḍra-Vaimṛiḍha at the Pūrṇamāsa.

of all the husks, and keeps the cleaned rice in the *pāṭrī*; and being again thrown into the *ulūkhala* it is again thumped and cleaned by the lady aided by the Aḍhvaryu. The rice is then thoroughly washed, all the refuse being again thrown upon the *uṭkara* as an offering to Rākṣasas. The Aḍhvaryu takes up the *Shamyā* and keeping it on the skin, he places upon it the *ḍriṣaḍ*, and upon this latter the *upala*; taking the handfulls of corn set aside for each of the gods, one by one, into the *ḍriṣaḍ*, he pounds them, once forward once backward and then quickly, a number of times; whereupon he requests the Lady to finish the pounding, after which the flour is boiled eiher upon the Gārhapaṭya or on the Āhavanīya, fire. Taking a few live coals from the Āhavanīya the Aḍhvaryu puts them over the middle pan, and then over each of the other pans. He heats the *maḍanṭī* water, and having washed with this the *pāṭrī*, he puts into it the flour, naming the gods for whom the cakes are intended; and kneads it with the *Mekṣaṇa*; and having made it into a ball, he cuts this up into smaller balls of equal size, labelling each as intended for such and such a deity. With each of these balls he prepares a cake of the shape of the tortoise, not very high, and of the size of the horse's hoof. He then removes the live coals from the pans, and bakes the cakes upon these,—that intended for Agni upon eight pans, and so on*; repeating in each case the manṭra '*urupraṭhā urupraṭhasva...uru yajñapaṭiḥ praṭhaṭām*' (Shatapaṭha, I—i-6-8). When the Cakes have been baked, he sprinkles water upon them, and heats them again, by taking a burning

* The number of pans upon which the cake is to be baked, varies with the deity for whom it is intended. We shall note a few of these as mentioned in the *Shaṭapaṭha Brāhmaṇa*:—the cake intended for Agni is baked upon *eight* pans (I.—6-2-5; II—2-1-22; II-5-1-8; V.-2-1-4); that for Varuṇa on one pan (IV.—4-5-15); that for Inḍra-Agni on *twelve* (V-2-2); for Agni-Viṣṇu on *eleven* (V.—2-2-6); for Viṣṇu on *three* (V.—2-5); for Agni-Soma on *eleven* (V—2-4); for Vaisnvāhara on *twelve* (V.—2-4-13); for the Maruṭs on *seven* (V.—3-1-6); for Saviṭṛi on *twelve* or *eight* (V.—3-3 2); and for Indra on *eleven* (V.—4-2-10).

fuel round them three times. The cakes being ready, each is kept aside for use, being covered up with hot ashes.

21. Taking up the *sphya*, the Aḍhvaryu draws with it three lines on the ground, and proceeds to prepare an altar or mound 'of the size of the sacrificer.' The sacrificer having washed the altar, the Aḍhvaryu spreads Kusha over it, and directing the sacrificer to bring up the *prokṣaṇī* and other vessels, and to prepare the lady, he washes each vessel as it is brought in. The preparation of the Lady consists in the *Yokṭra* being tied round her waist, and seating her near the Āhavanīya. The ghee is then boiled over the Ḍakṣiṇāgni fire and poured into the Ājyasṭhālī over a *paviṭra*; and all ashes, &c., being removed from the ghee with the manṭra '*iṣē ṭvā*' the ghee is heated again on the Gārhapaṭya fire with the manṭra '*ūrjē ṭvā*' and then handed over to the Lady.* She looks into the ghee carefully, holding her breath (Shaṭapaṭha, I.—3—1-18). The ghee is again heated over the Gārhapaṭya, and is again examined by the Sacrificer and the Aḍhvaryu, who carries it to the altar and keeps it in the *ḍhruvā* and throws a few blades of Kusha towards the South as an offering to the Piṭrīs. Taking up the Kusha intended for the *prasṭara*, he hands it to the Sacrificer, who, in his turn, makes it over to the Brahman who prepares the *prasṭara*. The Sacrificer spreads some Kusha over the altar, taking special care to have the roots of one bundle covered up by the tips of the other. The Aḍhvaryu takes up the *prasṭara*, and, assisted by the Sacrificer, places the *pariḍhis* in their position,—the central one, that to the west of the hearth, having its top-end towards the North, presided over by the Ganḍharvas; the Southern one with its top-end towards the East, presided over by Inḍra; and

---

* *Iṣē ṭvā* &c., the first mantra of the Yajurveda Samhiṭā appears to have never been used, in its complete form, at any sacrificial performance. It is always spoken of in the Shaṭapaṭha as to be used in sections. See I-1.6-6-I-7-1-2; IV—3-117.

the Northern one, also having its top-end towards the East presided over by Miṭra-Varuṇa. Taking up two Kusha-blades, he keeps the *prasṭara* upon them. The *Sruk* having been placed upon the *prasṭara*, the Sacrificer consecrates the Juhū, the Aḍhvaryu doing the same with the *Upabhṛiṭ*, to the North of which he keeps the *ḍhruvā*, which, along with the *Sruva*, is consecrated by the Sacrificer. The Aḍhvaryu having kept the *Ājyasṭhālī* to the West of the *Sruk*, the Sacrificer consecrates the *Sruk*, takes up the *Veḍa*, the *ājyasṭhālī*, the *pāṭrī* and the *Sruva*. Taking the cakes out of the coals and reciting the words '*syonanṭē saḍanam kriṇomi, ghṛiṭasya ḍhāraā suṣēvam kalpayāmi*, he spreads *kusha* on the *pāṭrī*, and having removed the ashes from the cakes, and completing the *manṭra* '*ṭasmin sīḍa* &c,'. he deposits the cakes on the *pāṭrī*, and applies butter to the cakes with the *Sruva*, which are thereupon consecrated by the Sacrificer—each being called by its deific name as '*āgnēyā*' '*ainḍra*,' &c.

22. The seat of the Hoṭṛi—called the '*Hoṭṛisaḍana*' having been prepared with *kusha*, the priest-elect is called up and duly appointed by the Sacrificer; and wearing the sacrificial thread,* sits facing the East, to the North-East of the Āhavanīya. Being directed by the Aḍhvaryu, he recites the *Upāmshu manṭras* and also the *Sāmiḍhēnī* or 'kindling' verses†, the Sacrificer placing a fuel on the fire at the utterance of 'Om' accompanying each verse. The fire having been kindled, the Aḍhvaryu fans it with the *Veḍa*, and with the *Sruva* taking up ghee out of the *ḍhruvā*, he pours it along the fire, from one end of the hearth to the other,—

* From this it would seem that the 'sacred thread' was worn only during sacrificial performance, and not always; that this may have been the custom is also indicated by the name '*Yajñopavīṭa*' by which the 'sacred thread' is generally known. This view however is contrary to such well known texts as '*Saḍopavīṭinā bhāvyam, Saḍā baḍḍhashikhena cha*'.

† The number of these verses is variously mentioned in the Shaṭapaṭha; 'Fifteen' is mentioned in I—3.5.7; 'Seventeen' in I—3.5.10 and 6.2.12; and III—1. 3. 6; 'Twenty-one' in III—3.5.11. Eggeling has translated eleven verses in a footnote on page 102,—these eleven becoming fifteen by the first and the eleventh being repeated three times each.

all the while contemplating on Prajāpaṭi. Taking ghee out of the *Ājyasṭhālī* he fills the *ḍhruvā* again, to overflowing. The Aḍhvaryu and the Hoṭri thereupon repeat the names of the *Pravara-Riṣis*, and the Hoṭri offers his invitation to the deities of the Sacrifice. The Sacrificer handing over the *Sruva* to the Aḍhvaryu, the latter pours an offering of ghee to Inḍra; and taking ghee out of the *ḍhruvā* he pours it over the *juhū*, and also round the *ḍhruvā*; and drawing together the bundles of fuel with the *sphya*, he takes his seat behind the Agnīḍhra, and recounts his *pravara-riṣis*; the Hoṭri also doing the same, walks up to the Agnīḍhra and sweeps the ground three times, and then retires to his appointed seat.

23. The Aḍhvaryu takes up the *Juhū* and the *Upabhriṭ*, and requests the Hoṭri to make the following five 'Prayājas' or 'Fore-offerings' to the five seasons (*Shaṭapaṭha*, I-5—2 and 8):—(1) To the *Samiḍ*—*i. e.* the Spring, (2) to *Ṭanūnapāṭ*—*i. e.* the Summer, (3) to the *Iḍs*, *i. e.* the rains; (4) to the *Barhis*—*i. e.* the Autumn; and (5) to the *Svāhā*—the Winter. After these offerings, the Aḍhvaryu pours ghee into the *ḍhruvā* and the *upabhriṭ*; and cutting out short pieces out of the Kusha contained in the *prasṭara* he anoints these with ghee; and requests the Hoṭri to pour libations of ghee to Agni and Soma; and the Hoṭri pours a libation each to Agni and Soma, and another to the two combined. Whereupon the Sacrificer proceeds to perform the expiatory rites consequent upon the discrepancies that might have occurred during his previous day's fast and observances. This rite consists of the offering of libations to Agni and Prajāpaṭi. The Aḍhvaryu then cuts off five slices—each slice about an inch long—out of the cake dedicated to Agni; and pouring ghee over them, he hands them to the Hoṭri, who offers them to the following five deities:—(1) Agni, (2) Viṣṇu, (3) Agni-Soma, (4) Inḍra-Vaimriḍha, and (4) Inḍra-Agni.

24. After this come the two Pārvaṇa Homas ; the Aḍhvaryu taking ghee out of the *Ājyāsṭhālī*, with the *Sruva*, pours an oblation to the *Pūrṇamāsa* (the Full Moon Day) and one to the *Amāvāsyā* (the New Moon Day).

25. This is followed by the Nāriṣta Homas, at which offerings are made to Agni-Vayu, the Maruṭs, Brahman, the Ḍēvas, Paramāṭman, Agni-Sviṣtakriṭ and Agni-Vaishvanara. The Aḍhvaryu then cuts out a slice of the size of a grain of barley, out of the cake dedicated to Agni, and also from each of the other cakes; and puts these pieces into the Prāshiṭra vessel, which is made over to the Brahman priest who eats a little out of it. The Aḍhvaryu brings forward the *Idāpāṭra* and hands it over to the Sacrificer, who consecrates it and makes it over to the Hoṭri. While the Sacrificer recites the *Ḍēvagavī manṭras* (*Chiḍasi* &c. Vājasanēyi Samhiṭā IV.—19), the Aḍhvaryu permits the eating of the *Idā*, whereupon the four Principal Priests, along with the Sacrificer—'*Yajamānapañchamāḥ*'—eat it.

26. Dividing the Āgneya cake into four parts, the Aḍhvaryu keeps them on *Kusha* ; and the Sacrificer having assigned the shares of the four priests, has his own share assigned by the Aḍhvaryu. The Agnīḍhra and the Aḍhvaryu eat their shares.

The Aḍhvaryu cooks a large quantity of rice—called the '*Anvāhārya*.' When it is ready he smells it, and taking out a small quantity with his fingers, mixes it with the Brahman's share of the cake. The rest of the rice is then offered to the Brahmaṇas called in by the Sacrificer, who also gives them proper gifts.'

27. The Agnīḍhra selects some fuels and keeps them aside for the *Anuyāja* or the After-offerings (Shaṭapaṭha I—8-2); and the Aḍhvaryu throws the rest of the fuel into the fire, as an offering to Ruḍra.

28. The Aḍhvaryu now proceeds with the *Anuyāja* or After-offerings. (1) to the Barhis, (2) to Narāshamsa, and (3) to Agni. The Sacrificer sprinkles ghee on the *pariḍhis*; and assigning the central one to the Vasus, the Southren one to the Ruḍras and the Northern one to the Āḍiṭyas, he keeps the *juhū* on the *prasṭara*, out of which Kusha-blades anointed with ghee are offered to Agni, Soma, Viṣṇu, Agni-Soma, Inḍra-Vaimṛiḍha, the Ḍēvas, Agni-Sviṣṭakṛiṭ, Inḍra-Agni and Mahēnḍra. The *prasṭara* is then carried to the Āhavanīya hearth by the Agnīḍhra, who also carries to the same hearth, the *pariḍhis* one by one, and also fire in kindled sticks,—the Hotṛi all along reciting the *Shamyuvāka manṭra* (Shaṭapaṭha I—9-1-25; and Ṛigveḍa Sam 5—47—7). And into this fire, the Aḍhvaryu throws the *paṛiḍhis* as offerings to the Vasus, the Ruḍras and the Āḍiṭyas; and the Priests eat the remnants; and wash the vessels and implements.

29. Now follow the Paṭnīsamyājas (*Shaṭapaṭha* I—9-2). Led by the Agnīḍhra the priests move to the Gārhapatya hearth; the Aḍhvaryu sitting on its South and the others on its North. Offerings are then made to Soma, Ṭvaṣṭṛi, Rākā, Sinīvālī, Kuhū, the Ḍēvapaṭnīs (Wives of the Gods), and lastly to Agni-Gṛihapaṭi. The finger-joints of the Hotri being anointed with ghee, four drops of ghee are poured into his hand, and six drops in the hand of the Agnīḍhra. Being touched by the Aḍhvaryu, the Agnīḍhra, the Sacrificer and the Lady, the Hoṭṛi makes an offering of the ghee in his hand to Paramāṭman.

30. Then follow the *Piṣṭalēpa* and the *Phalīkaraṇa Homas*: Four drops of ghee being dropped into the *juhū*, the chaffs of the grain out of which the cakes were prepared are thrown into it. This mixture offered into the Āhavanīya constitutes the *Phalīkaraṇa* Homa ('*Phalīkaraṇa*' being the name given to the chaffs removed from the corn by the

Lady). After this comes the *Piṣtalēpa-Homa:* the Sacrificer having dropped four drops of ghee into the *juhū*, he puts into it the dough that may be found to be attached to the vessels, and offers it into the fire, as an offering to the Vishvēḍēvas. This offering is again repeated three times —(1) to Sarasvaṭī-Vishobhagīnā, (2) to Sarasvaṭī-Veshabhagīnā, and (3) to Inḍra.

The girdle-zone of the Lady is at this point unfastened and placed in her hands; after which she washes her face.

32. Betaking themselves to the Āhavanīya hearth, they perform the expiatory or Apologetic Homa, called the '*Sarvaprāyashchiṭṭa.*' This consists of the following offerings:—one to Brahman, one to Yajña, one to Varuṇa, two to Agni-Varuṇa, one to Ayas-Agni, one each to Prajāpaṭi, the Iṣtas, the Vaṣadiniṣṭha, Bheṣajanḍuriṣtī, Niṣkṛiṭi, Samṛiḍḍhi, the Ḍēvas, Agni-Jāṭavēḍas, Agni-Sviṣṭakṛiṭ, Inḍra, Inḍra-Abhayṅkara, Inḍra-Harivaṭ-Varḍhamana, Agni, Agni-Shraḍḍhā, Varuṇa-Inḍra-Saviṭri-Viṣṇu-Maruṭ, Agni-Ṭanṭumaṭ, Varuṇa, Agni, Vāyu, Sūrya and Prajāpaṭi. After these the Aḍhvaryu and the Brahman pour offerings to Prajāpaṭi, into each of the three fires; and finally the Aḍhvaryu filling the *ḍhruvā* with ghee, pours it as an offering to Yajña-Paramāṭman,—the Brahman reciting the *manṭra* '*Ayāshchāgue, &c.,*' (Maiṭrāyaṇī Samhiṭā I—4-3).

33. The Sacrificer now eats his share of the remnants. The Aḍhvaryu brings the Praṇīṭā vessel on to the altar; this is filled with water, with which the Sacrificer washes his face; and then the Aḍhvaryu pours the water on the altar. The Brahman eats his share of the remnants and retires.

34. The Sacrificer now performs the *Viṣṇukramā* (described in Shaṭapaṭha, I—9-3-8; I—12-13; IV—5-2-10; VI—6-4-1). That is, on the Southern side of the altar, moving his right leg foremost, he moves four steps to the

East, repeating the mantra '*viṣṇoḥ kramosi*, &c.'—Vājasaneya—Samhiṭa XII—5), invoking blessings upon himself and family, and destruction on his enemies. He then walks round the altar; offering salutations to Sūrya and Agni, he proceeds to the Garhapaṭya and salutes it with the *manṭra* '*Agnē gṛihapaṭē*, &c.' (Maiṭrāyaṇī Samhiṭā I—5-11). Proceeding to the Ḍakṣināgni hearth, he salutes it and sits down on the altar. Taking the *Vēḍa* on his lap, he pronounces the text '*Sūryasyāvṛiṭa anvāvarṭē !&c.*,' (Vajasanēya Sam II 27); whereupon he invites and feeds ten Brāhmanas; and divesting himself of his vow, retires. (Shaṭapaṭha, I—9-23).

---

35. List of the articles required at the *Ḍarsha-Pūrṇamāsa*,—arranged alphabetically :—

(*a*) *Anvāhāryasṭhālī*—the dish in which is strained the cooked rice intended for the four priests.

(*b*) *Agnihoṭrahavaṇī*—made of *vikaṅkaṭa* wood—15 inches long,—with one end shaped either like the lip of the elephant, or the beak of the swan, or the tail of the crow,—with a hollow 8, 5 or 4 *anguls* deep respectively,—the rest being kept as handle; this is used in making the Agnihoṭra offerings.

(*c*) *Ājyasṭhālī*—the vessel in which the boiled ghee is kept.

(*d*) *Iḍā-pāṭra*—a vessel made of Ashvattha wood,—with handle 4 *anguls* long attached to a hollow 4 *anguls* in circumference; in this is kept the Iḍā,—the remnants of the offerings.

(*e*) *Upabhriṭ*—a piece of Ashvaṭṭha wood similar to the *juhū*, kept by the Aḍhvaryu in his left hand while in his right hand he holds the *juhū* with which he makes the offerings.

(*f*) *Upala*—the piece of rounded stone with which things are ground upon the stone-slab.

(*g*) *Upavēṣa*—a two-inch piece cut out from the root-end of the *Palāsha* or *Shamī* branch shorn of its leaves. This is used for removing the live coals from the Gārhapaṭya fire.

(*h*) *Ulūkhala*—the mortar made of Palāsha wood, 12 *anguls* high, with a hollow in the lower half; used for the cleaning of the rice and other grains.

(*i*) *Kapāla*—Earthenware pans for the baking of cakes.

(*j*) *Kṛiṣṇājina*—skin of the black antelope, used as a seat for the mortar upon which rice and other grains are pounded.

(*k*) *Juhū*—a piece of *palāsha* wood similar in form to the *Agnihoṭrahavaṇī*; all principal offerings are made with this.

(*l*) *Ḍarbha*—Kusha grass.

(*m*) *Ḍṛiṣaṭ*—The stone-slab for grinding corns.

(*n*) *Ḍhruvā*—similar to the *juhū*, but made of *vikaṅkaṭa* wood; ghee is kept in this; and it is kept upon the altar from the beginning to the end of the sacrifice.

(*o*) *Pariḍhi*—Three sticks of fuel exactly of the length of the raised boundary of the *Āhavanīya*; they are placed upon the girdle, on the West, North and South of the hearth. These may be of the following woods—Palāsha, Vikaṅkaṭa, Kārṣmarya, Bilva, Khaḍira, Uḍumbara.

(*p*) *Paviṭra*—a blade of Kusha cut into two equal pieces and consecrated with a manṭra; used for sprinkling water.

(*q*) *Pāṭri*—a wooden dish in which the prepared cake is kept and cut up into slices for offerings and also for distribution among the priests.

(*r*) *Piṣtalēpaphalīkaraṇapāṭra*—Vessels for keeping the ground corns and the chaff thrown out from the winnowing basket.

(*s*) *Praṇīṭā*—Vessels made of *Ashvaṭṭha* wood; 8 *anguls* deep with handles 4 *anguls* long.

(*t*) *Prāshiṭra*—The remnant of the substance offered, kept aside in a vessel, called, on that account, the '*Prāshiṭra-pāṭra*,' which is made of *Khaḍira* wood, of the shape of the cow's ear.

(*u*) *Maḍanṭī*—The water heated in a vessel that becomes heated while the frying-pan is being heated.

(*v*) *Musala*—pestle made of *Khaḍira* wood, one and half times as long as the mortar.

(*w*) *Mēkṣaṇa*—a piece of *Ashvaṭṭha* wood 15 inches long; with one end flattened; used in mixing together the fried substances with *maḍanṭī* water.

(*x*) *Yokṭra*—a three-fold rope of Muñja, wound round the waist of the Sacrificer's wife (Shaṭapaṭha I-3—1—13).

(*y*) *Vēḍa*—a handful of Kusha grass, twisted and doubled up into the shape of the thigh of the seated calf; used in the sweeping of the altar.

(*z*) *Shamyā*—made of Khaḍira wood; 36 *anguls* long, having at one end eight knots, one *angul* apart from one another; placed under the flat grinding stone, when rice, &c., are ground; also used by the Agnīḍhra priest for striking the stone.

(*za*) *Shūrpa*—winnowing basket made of bamboo.

(*zb*) *Sphya*—a sword made of *Khaḍira* wood, 20 *anguls* long, 4 *anguls* broad.

(*zc*) *Sruk*—is the name given in common to the *Juhū*, the *Ḍhruvā*, the *Upabhriṭ* and the *Sruva*—the instruments for making offerings.

(*zd*) *Sruva*—a piece of Khaḍira wood, 15 inches long, with a hollow at one end, an inch in diameter; with this all offerings of ghee are made. It may be of *palāsha* or *vikaṇkaṭa* wood (Shaṭapaṭha V—2-3-15).

THE AGNIṢTOMA.

36. Having described the Archetypal *Iṣṭi,* we are now going to describe the Agniṣtoma (also called Jyoṭiṣtoma) which is the archetypal *Soma-yāga.* This sacrifice is dealt with in the Shaṭapaṭha Brāhmana, Prap. IV and IV, and in the Shrauṭa-Sūṭra of Kāṭyāyana, Adh. VII—XV. (*Chaukhambha Sanskrit Series,* pp. 417 to 601). It is upon these original texts, and upon the *Paḍḍhaṭi* or manual, by Yājñika Ḍēva—also based upon Kāṭyāyana—that the following account is based.

37. If the Sacrificer is a regular performer of the *Agnihoṭra,* he should perform the daily Agnihoṭra, and also the Ḍarsha-Pūrṇamāsa Sacrifices before he takes up the *Agniṣtoma.* But if he happens to be one who has had no 'Agni' in his family,—*i.e.,* who himself, or his two immediate ancestors have not been regular performers of the Agnihoṭra,—before he can be entitled to the Agniṣtoma, he has to offer a he-goat to the Ashvins,—this being an expiatory rite for cleansing himself from the character of the 'Bad Brāhmaṇa,' attaching to him on account of the non-performance of the Agnihoṭra, and the neglect of Vedic studies. After this comes the performance of the expiatory rite, if the Soma Sacrifice has not been performed in the family for three generations,—this rite consisting of the offering of a goat to Inḍra-Agni. Both the animals are sacrificed in the same manner as that to Agni-Soma, in course of the Agniṣṭoma (see below).

38. On the day preceding the one on which the Agniṣtoma is to be performed,—which generally is the day following the New or the Full Moon,—the Sacrificer performs the *Nānḍīshrāḍḍha,*—an offering to his ancestors. On the day of the Sacrifice, the Sacrificer and his wife, along with the sixteen priests-elect, have their bath early in the morning;

after which the priests are duly 'appointed.' Before the appointment of the *human* priests however, the *divine* oues are appointed: Agni being the *Hoṭṛi*, Āḍiṭya the *Aḍhvaryu*, Chanḍramas the *Brahman*, Parjanya the *Uḍgāṭṛi*, Apas the *Hoṭrashamsin*, and Rashmi the *Chamasāḍhvaryu*. The Sacrificer then announces his intention to perform the sacrifice in the following terms:—'I am going to perform the *Jyoṭiṣtoma-Agniṣtoma* in which the sacrificial gift shall consist of a hundred pieces of gold, aud 100 cows and clothes and horses,—it will be accompanied by the Raṭhanṭara-pṛiṣtha Sāman, and four *Sṭomas*; will you, Sir, *so and so*, of such and such a *goṭrā*, officiate as the *Brahman* priest.' This same formula is repeated with each priest, who accepts the place, aud receives from the Sacrificer the offering of *maḍhuparka*. The sixteen priests are:—(1) the *Brahman*, (2) the *Uḍgāṭṛi*, (3) the *Hoṭṛi*, (4) the *Aḍhvaryu*—these four are the principal priests, of the first class, called '*Mahartvik*';—(5) the *Brāhmaṇāchchhamshin*, (6) the *Prasṭotri*, (7) the *Maiṭrāvaruṇa*, (8) the *Praṭiprasṭhāṭṛi*,—these four belong to the second class, called *Ḍviṭīyin*';—(9) *the Poṭṛi*, (10) the *Praṭihartṛi*, (11) the *Achchhāvāka*, (12) the *Nēṣṭri*—these four belong to the third class, called '*Ṭṛiṭīyin*';—(13) The *Agnīḍ* (or *Agnīḍhra*); (14) the *Subrahmaṇya*; (15) the *Grāvasṭuṭ*, and (16) the *Unnēṭṛi*—these four belong to the fourth class called the '*pāḍin*'; the last twelve are also called "*Hoṭrāshamsin*.' The Soma is then handed over to the Sacrificer, who is thereupon anointed with a *ṭilaka* on the forehead, and receives blessings from the Brāhmaṇas.

59. The above having been done at the Sacrificer's house, he proceeds, with the priests, to choose a place for the Sacrificial House. The plot of land chosen should be higher thau all the land arouud, and should be sloping towards the east. Having cleared it of all vegetation, they build thereupon a house 20 *araṭnis* by 10, (an '*araṭni*' being nearly 15 inches), with three doors, on the East, South and

West. To the North of this house another house—5 *araṭnis* by 5,—is built facing the East, for the 'initiation' of the Sacrificer; and to the South, a similar house for the initiation of his wife. Returning home they pour a libation of ghee into the Āhavanīya fire,—this offering being called '*yūpāhuṭi*'; the remnant of the ghee is kept in a safe place.

40. Having consecrated the ground, they transfer into the *Araṇī* the fire from the Gārhapaṭya and Ahavanīya hearths of the Agnihoṭra; and placing the *Araṇi* on the cart, along with all other sacrificial implements and materials, they carry it with propitiatory songs and recitations to the ground chosen for the Sacrificial House. On reaching the place, the Sacrificer washing his hands, takes the *Araṇī* and the *Soma* in his hand and enters the House by the Eastern door; and deposits the *Soma* on a raised platform.

41. The Aḍhvaryu proceeds to the mound (4 *anguls* high, 24 *anguls* long, and 24 *anguls* broad), intended for the *Gārhapaṭya*, and having performed its lustration, he produces fire by the friction of the *Araṇī*, and keeps it on the mound. About 8 yards removed from this mound, he has the mound for for the *Āhavanīya*; and a little removed from this, the mound of the *Ḍakṣiṇāgni*. After the lustration of these mounds, he deposits fire on these also. The Sacrificer thereupon makes an offering of vegetables and grains to the Soma; and this finishes the morning functions.

42. In the afternoon, the Sacrificer and his wife may partake of rich food, consisting of rice and cakes and various kinds of meat; after which he makes over all sacrificial materials to a reliable person, requesting him to bring forward each thing at the proper moment.

43. After this comes the Initiation of the Sacrificer and his wife. In the Northern house, a jar full of water having been kept, the Aḍhvaryu, facing the North, pares the Sacrificer's nails, and shaves certain parts of his head,

proceeding from the right side. The razor is then made over to the barber, who shaves the rest of the head and the chin. The Sacrificer then takes his bath, for the purpose of purifying him of the barber's touch; and betaking himself to the North-east corner of the house, he wears a fresh silk cloth. In the Western house, the *Praṭiprasṭhāṭri* performs a similar ceremony for the Sacrificer's wife; the shaving of the head in this case bring purely optional; though the nails must be pared. The Lady also wears clothes similar to those put on by her husband. These two Initiations over, the Aḍhvaryu leads the Sacrificer by the hand to the Sacrificial House, by the eastern door, the Praṭiprasṭhāṭri leading the Lady by the other door. The Sacrificer and the Lady then repair to their appointed seats.

44. Then follows the *Ḍīkṣaṇīyā Iṣti*. A cake baked upon eleven pans is offered to Agni-Viṣṇu; and also an offering of *charu* is made to the *Āditẏas*. At this *Iṣti* no *manṭras* are recited loudly; nor is there any sacrificial gift. The remnants of the cake, &c., attaching to the *Sruva* are ultimately offered to the Vishvēḍēvas. The Ahḍvaryu spreads *kusha* grass on the eastern side of the Sacrificial House. The Sacrificer seated upon this receives *ghee* from the *Aḍhvaryu*, which he rubs all over his body, the parts he cannot himself reach being rubbed by the priest. With the pointed end of an arrow he applies collyrium to his eyes; the Aḍhvaryu sprinkles water over him; whereupon the Sacrificer closing his fist takes the vow of silence, and is led by the *Aḍhvaryu* into the House by the eastern door, and seated between the *Gārhapaṭya* and the *Āhavanyīa* hearths. The *Praṭiprasṭhāṭri* helps the Lady to go through the above procedure; and she is led into the House by the western door. Thus ends tbe Ḍīkṣaṇīyā Iṣti.

45. Next follows the *Oḍgrabhaṇa Homa*. With the *Sruva*, the *Aḍhvaryu* pours offerings of ghee to—(1) Ākūṭi—

Prayuj—Agni, (2) to Meḍhā—Manas—Agni, (3) to Sarasvaṭī—Pūṣan—Agni, (4) to Apas—Ḍyāvāpriṭhivī—Antarikṣa—Brihaspaṭi, and (5) lastly to Vishvēḍēva—Saviṭri—Miṭra—Brihaspaṭi—Pūṣan.

46. To the south of the Āhavanīya hearth, the Aḍhvaryu spreads two skins of the black antelope. The Sacrificer kneels ṭo the west of the skin, facing the east. Pronouncing the words '*Sharmāsi*' he places his right knee upon the skin; and binds round his waist a *muñja* rope twisted three-fold, pronouncing the words '*ūrgasi*'; and then he binds up the knot of his waist-cloth; covers his head with the upper garment, which, according to Āpasṭamba, he wraps round his head in the form of a turban; and to the free end of this turban, he ties the black horn, 6 inches long.* The *Aḍhvaryu* then hands over to the Sacrificer a stick of *uḍumbara* wood long enough to reach his face from the ground; and the Sacrificer raises it over his head, and finally places it on his right shoulder. While the *Aḍhvaryu* is doing this to the Sacrificer, the *Praṭiprasṭhāṭri* does the same to the Lady; with this difference that instead of the horn, a piece of wood is tied to the end of her upper garment, and in place of the turban, three folds of net are wrapped round her head; and in place of the *muñja* rope, the *yokṭra* is wound round her waist. With this ends the Initiation with all its details.

47. At sunset, the *Aḍhvarya* permits the Sacrificer and his wife to renounce the vow of silence; this is done by the Sacrificer uttering '*bhūḥ, bhuvaḥ, svaḥ*' while seated upon the black autelope skin. The *Aḍhvaryu* then milking the milk of two cows, gets some *yava* cooked in the milk; and with this the Sacrificer and his wife break their fast; the food intended for the Sacrificer is cooked over the *Gārhapaṭya* fire, and that for the Lady on the *Ḍakṣiṇāgni*.

* This horn is intended for scratching the itching parts of his body; this should not be done with the finger-nails. See *Shaṭapaṭha*, III—2-1-31.

Having partaken of the food, the Sacrificer requests the Fire to keep awake, and himself retires to sleep, on a bedding spread to the south of the Āhavanīya hearth; taking care not to lie upon his back or stomach; his wife sleeps in similar fashion to the South of the Gārhapaṭya hearth. The two cows are kept carefully guarded within an enclosure.

48. Towards the latter part of the night, the Sacrificer and his wife wash their faces and hands; whereupon the *Aḍhvaryu* offers to him milk in a *Kāṁsya* cup; and this milk he drinks, sitting upon the skin. The Lady also receiving the milk from the *Praṭirrasṭhāṭri* in a copper vessel drinks it. After this they ease themselves and go to sleep again if necessary.

49. At the break of dawn, the *Aḍhvaryu* makes the Sacrificer and the Lady to resume the vow of silence. The milk is then boiled and kept away. After this comes the Initiation; after which, if the Sacrificer happen to get angry, or to do any such improper thing as talking to a *Shūḍra*, telling a lie, uttering non-Sanskrit words, and so forth,—he has to recite the *manṭra*—'*agnē vraṭaḍā asi*, &c.' (Shaṭapaṭha, III.—4-3-9). From this point forward, till the concluding Bath, the Sacrificer has to observe certain restrictions. Some of these are as follows:—(1) not to mix with Shūḍras; (2) not to talk to the Shūḍras; (3) not to admit a Shūḍra into the house; (4) if it becomes necessary to talk to a Shūdra, this should be done through some person of the higher castes; (5) not to rise from the seat even on the approach of respected persons; (6) not to salute any person; (7) not to go into a tank; (8) not to touch rain water; (9) to talk sweetly and not harshly; (10) to talk Sanskrit only; (11) to observe strict veracity; (12) not to spit; (13) nor to laugh loudly, (14) uot to show his teeth; (15) not to ascend trees; (16) nor to wander out of the Sacrificial House; (17) not to cleanse the teeth; (18) not to bathe; (19) not to

make any such offerings as those of the *Agnihoṭra*, the *Vaishvaḍēva*, and so forth. Authorities are divided as to the number of Initiations to be adopted—they may be 12, 4, 3, or even one.

50. After the Initiation they proceed to do the *Yūpachchēḍana*—the cutting of the Sacrificial Post. Taking with them the remnant of the ghee and the fire-stick, they go to the place where they have kept the log of *khaḍira* wood intended for the Post. It is perfectly smooth and of even thickness all over. They produce fire by the friction of the sticks, into which they pour a libation of ghee, called the '*yūpāhuṭi*'; after which they cut out a piece of the wood, which may be 5, 6, 8, 9, 11, 12, 13 or 15 *araṭnis* long; and the piece of wood left behind is called tho '*Svaru*', and kept aside for purposes of the *Svaruhoma*.

51. After this follows the *Mahāvīrasambharaṇa*: The Brahman and the Sacrificer get together clay, anthill dust, the mud thrown up by the wild boar, the *puṭīkā* herbs, red flowers, goat's milk and the *gavēḍhuka* grass. Spreading the skin of the black antelope, they keep near it the scraper made of *uḍumbara* or *vikaṅkaṭa* wood, about 15 inches long. The Aḍhvarya takes up this scraper, and taking up in his hand the clod of earth, keeps it on the skin, whereupon he heaps, one by one, all the aforesaid things. To the North of the skin, the Adhvaryu chooses a square level spot; and covering it with a piece of cloth, keeping an opening to the east, he cleans the place and sprinkles sand over it; and accompanied by the *Praṭiprasṭhāṭṛi* the *Nēṣṭri*, and the *Unnēṭṛi*, he picks up the skin along with the things put upon it; and while the Brahman and the Sacrificer are reciting the *manṭra* '*praiṭu brahmaṇaspaṭiḥ* &c.' (Ṛigveḍa—I.—40-3) he carries the skin along with the things into the covered spot. Keeping the *gavēḍhuka* and the goat's milk aside, the Aḍhvarya mixes up the other things; and out of the lump

of clay produced by this mixture, he prepares three *mahāviras.* The *mahāvīra* is 6 inches long, with a cavity in the middle and a hole at the top, having a belt three inches below the upper end. Then he prepares the two *pinvanas*—which are similar in shape to the lotus on the *Sruk*—and also two circular pans of the size of the palm of the hand, which are called '*Rauhiṇakapāla*'. The clay left behind, called the '*upashayā*' is kept away in a safe place, for future use. The *mahāviras*, the *pinvanas* and the *rauhiṇakapālas* are then smoothed by being rubbed with the *gavēḍhuka.* Fire having been brought out of the *Ḍakṣiṇāgni* hearth, the priest throws it into horse-dung; and over the smoke thus raised, he smokes the *Mahāvira*, &c. Removing the antelope-skin, he digs a square pit, and spreading *Kusha* in it, and placing the three things over the *kusha*, he lights it with fire. After they have been thoroughly baked, he sprinkles goat's milk over them, and keeps them aside carefully in a safe place:—the breaking of these articles being considered inauspicious.

52. Next comes the *Prāyaṇīyā Iṣṭi.* At this there is no regular 'appointment' of priests; nor is there any distinct sacrificial fee. The priest cooks rice; and out of this cooked rice offerings are made to Agni, Soma, and Paṭhyā Svasṭi, and again to Agni, Soma, Saviṭṛi, Aḍiṭi and the Ḍēvas. These are followed by offerings of ghee to Paṭhyā Svasṭi; Agni, Soma and Saviṭṛi; all the *manṭras* being recited in a subdued voice.

With the same cooked rice, they next perform the *Aḍiṭi-yāga*; which consists of an offering to Aḍiṭi, and a concluding offering to *Sviṣṭakṛiṭ*; after which the remnant is distributed among the priests. The *prasṭara* is thereupon thrown into the fire, as an offering to Paṭhyā Svasṭi, Agni, Soma, Aḍiṭi and Saviṭṛi.

At this stage of the *Prāyaṇīyā*, the *Praṭiprasṭhāṭri* fetches the *Soma* from the House and deposits it on the reddish-brown calf-skin spread with its neck-end towards the east. The person who is to sell the *Soma*,—who must be either a *Shūḍra*, or a low-born person of the higher castes —then cuts the *Soma* into as many parts as there are joints in it. The *Aḍhvaryu* closes the door of the House, pours ghee four times into the *juhū*, and pours it as a libation, along with some fuels, into the *Āhavanīya*. Then he ties a blade of grass round a gold piece, and having tied it to a string, he puts it into the *juhū*. After which the remaining rites of the Prāyaṇīyā are performed.

53. After this comes the 'purchasing of the Soma.' The doors of the House are opened, and the *Aḍhvaryu* and the Sacrificer go out by the eastern door, and move towards the heifer that is to be given as the price of the *Soma*. This heifer is of tawny reddish-brown colour throughout, without any kind of mark on the body, without any ornamentations, not deficient in any limbs, nor with a distorted limb; and it is to be accompanied by a bull; and she must have tawny eyes; and must be one year old. The Aḍhvaryu having touched her body, she is led up to the *Praṭiprasṭhāṭri* and the other priests, the *Aḍhvaryu* and the Sacrificer following her. On the spot where the heifer puts her front right foot, in her seventh step, they all sit down, in the following order:—the *Brahman* and the Sacrificer on the South, the *Aḍhvaryu* on the West, the *Praṭiprasṭhāṭri* and the *Nēṣṭri* on the north, and the Lady further to the South. The *Aḍhvaryu* places the gold-piece that had been tied up in a string, on the exact spot where the heifer had put her foot; and makes an offering of ghee to Aḍiṭi. Upon the spot he draws three lines with the *sphya*, and taking up the gold-piece in his hand he puts it in the *Sṭhālī*. Having poured ghee upon the three lines he has drawn, he picks up the earth

bearing the foot-mark of the heifer, and hands it over to the Sacrificer, from whom it is again transferred to the Lady, who keeps it in a safe place: and ties the gold-piece to her ring-finger. The Sacrificer thereupon orders a servant to bring up piece of cloth for wrapping round the *Soma*, another as a 'bedding' for it, and a third as its 'turban.' One of these pieces is taken up either by the Sacrificer or the *Aḍhvaryu*, and the other two by the *Praṭiprasṭhāṭṛi*; and they go to the place where the *Soma* had been kept; and the Sacrificer and the Brahman seating themselves to the South of it, the Aḍhvaryu takes his seat on the North, and facing the east, touches the *Soma*; after which the 'seller' also is not permitted to touch it. All foreign substances having been removed from the *Somā*, the Aḍhvaryu folds up a piece of cloth four-fold, and spreading it on the skin, measures out, on to the cloth, ten handfuls of the Soma-chips; and then takes up the whole of it into the folded cloth; in which he wraps up the *Soma*, and ties up the knot on the top with the cloth intended for the 'turban'; and hands over this bundle to the 'seller.' Then proceeds the bartering for the *Soma*:—

Aḍhvaryu:—"Is your *Soma* for sale?"

Seller:—"Yes; it is for sale."

A.:—"I shall buy it."

Seller:—"You may do so."

A.:—"I shall pay for it the sixteenth part of a gold-piece."

Seller:—"My *Soma* is worth much more than that."

This goes on until the Aḍhvaryu offers a 'cow' as the price. This is accepted by the seller, who says—"The *Soma* has been bought by you." Directed by the *Aḍhvaryu*, the Sacrificer offers to the vendor a gold-piece and a she-goat which the Aḍhvaryu hands over to the vendor, with the right hand, receiving the *Soma* with the left. He then ties the *Soma*-bnndle to the right thigh of the Sacrificer, who therenpon gives the cow to the vendor, also gold and some other things. The Sacrificer and his wife therenpon nncover their heads, and belabonring the vendor with a bamboo-stick, wrest away from him the gold-piece that he had received. This bamboo-stick is thrown into the fire by the *Aḍhvaryu*, as an offering to Miṭra-Varnṇa. The Sacrificer takes np the Soma-bnndle and goes towards the cart intended for the carrying of the *Ṣoma*. On this cart the *Aḍhvaryu* spreads the black antelope skin, and places the *Ṣoma* npon it, and covers it np with the second piece of cloth. The skin on which the Sacrificer has beeu sitting is then fixed to a bamboo-pole and stnck into the gronnd in front of the cart. Two calves are then yoked to the cart; and they are driven with a *palāsha*-stick by the *Ṣubrahmaṇya*. The Aḍhvaryn goes ronnd the cart, and takes up a position behind it; and takes hold of the rope attached thereto; the Sacrificer and the resṭ proceed behind him. The cart is taken to the Honse.

54. The Aḍhvaryn on nearing the Honse, calls the Snbrahmaṇya, who therenpon calls the Brāhmaṇas to come forward. The *Praṭiprasṭhāṭṛi* brings the animal dedicated to Agni-Soma to the east of the Honse, and stands near the cart, holding the animal by the ear. This animal shonld be a deer either of black colonr with spots, or of reddish-brown colonr. The Sacrificer tonches this animal; and it is moved away. The Aḍhvaryn, helped by the *Praṭiprasṭhāṭṛi*, the *Nēṣṭṛi* and the *Unnēṭṛi*, carry to the cart, the *āsanḍī* (a stool made of *Uḍumbara* wood, high enongh to reach the navel of the Sacrificer, bnt only abont 15 inches sqnare at the top, intended as a repository for the *Soma*); and spreading the black antelope skin on this the *Aḍhvaryu* places the Soma-bnndle npon it; and the fonr priests taking

up the stool carry it into the House by the eastern door. and keep it to the south of the Āhavanīya hearth.

55. Next comes the *Āṭiṭhyēṣṭi*:—They bake a cake upon nine pans, intended as an offering to Viṣṇu; after which the *maḍanṭī* water for the Sacrificer is boiled upon the *Gārhapaṭya*, and that for the Lady on the *Ḍakṣiṇāgni* fire; and from this point onwards for all purposes they use water out of these two *maḍanṭīs* only. The fire being churned out of the *araṇī* sticks, offerings of ghee are made to Agni, Soma, Viṣṇu and the Ḍēvas; after which the cake is offered to Viṣṇu,—all the *manṭras* being repeated in a low voice. The Sacrificer and the priests then take out ghee with the *Sruva* out of the *ḍhruvā* and the *sṭhālī* twice over, and keep it in a vessel hidden away in a safe place.* The Sacrificer puts fuel into the *Āhavanīya* fire, and the Lady into the *Ḍakṣiṇagni*; and they bind up the *muṣti* and the *mekhalā*. The *Brahman*, the *Uḍgāṭri*, the *Hoṭri*, the *Aḍhvaryu*, the *Agnīḍhra*, and the Sacrificer tie gold-pieces to their ring-fingers; and repairing to the east of the Āhavanīya hearth, untie the *Soma* bundle. Returning to their places they put their hands on the *prasṭara*, and repair to their seats. This is followed by the apportioning of the shares of the Brahman and the Sacrificer, the sweeping of the fire-places, the washing of the *juhū*, and the besmearing of the *pariḍhis* with ghee. Carrying the *prasṭara* along with the *pariḍhiṣ*, to the Āhavanīya hearth, and sprinkling over these the water of the *Maḍanṭī*, the *Aḍhvaryu* hands them over to the *Agnīḍhra* for safe custody. The *Vēḍa*, the *Yokṭra* and the *Praṇīṭā* being removed, a blade of *kusha* is thrown to the South-West as an offering to the *Rākṣasas*; and the *Subrahmaṇya* having called the Brāhmaṇas, they receive their dues from the Sacrificer and the Lady.

---

* This is called the *Ṭānūnapṭra ājya*; and those taking part in this should remain friendly to one another throughout their lives.

56. The *Ātiṭhyēṣti* is followed by the *Pravargyacharaṇa*:—The three doors of the House are closed, the Lady also being kept out, by reason of the law that the performance of the *Pravargya* should not be witnessed by persons not learned in the Veda. The *Brahman*, the Sacrificer, the *Hoṭṛi*, the *Aḍhvaryu*, the *Praṭiprasṭhāṭṛi*, the *Prasṭoṭṛi* and the *Āgnīḍhra* recite the whole chapter of the Veda, beginning with the words '*ṛicham vācham prapaḍyē*' (Vajas-Samh. 36). The Brahman thereupon takes his seat either to the West of the *Ḍakṣiṇāgni* or to the South of the *Āhavanīya* hearth; spreading *kusha* behind the *Gārhapaṭya* the Aḍhvaryu collects the articles needed for the sacrifice—all the vessels being of *Uḍumbara* wood, and all strings and ropes being of *muñja* twisted three-fold (for the list, see end of section) He prepares the *paviṭras*, and having set up the *prokṣaṇī* vessels, he assigns to the *Hoṭṛi*, the business of reciting the hymns, and to the *Prasṭoṭṛi* that of singing the *Sāmans*. He washes one of the *Mahāvīras* (see above), as also all the vessels got together. The *Praṭiprasṭhāṭṛi* then takes the peg and post out of the eastern door, and sticks them on the ground on the southern side of the House, in such a position as to be within view of the *Hoṭṛi* who sits near the *Gārhapaṭya* hearth; the post is intended for the tying of the cow and the peg for that of the goat. Coming into the House again, he prepares, to the North of the *Gārhapaṭya* hearth, a mound 15 inches square and 4 inches high, smears it with cowdung, and consecrates it; a similar mound is prepared to the North of the *Āhavanīya* hearth, and a third also to the south of this latter hearth, close to the wall of the House. On each of these mounds he sprinkles the sand kept in each of the three cups. Between the *Āhavanīya* hearth and the stool of the *Soma*, he places another stool, high enough to reach the neck; and spreading the black antelope skin upon this, he keeps upon it the *Abhri*, the *Unashayā* and the other two *mahāviras*; and covers up the

whole with a piece of cloth. Taking ghee with the *Sruva* the *Aḍhvaryu* smears with it the *mahāvīra* that has been washed; and taking the silver 'hundred-pieces' (*Shaṭamāna*) he hides it within the sand on the mound to the North of the *Gārhapaṭya* hearth. The Prasṭoṭri singing the *Shukra Sāman*, the *Aḍhvaryu* spreads *muñja* grass along side of the mounds and keeps the *mahāvīra* filled with ghee on that grass; and sprinkling ash over it, he covers it up with live coals from out of the *Gārhapaṭya* hearth, and surrounding it with 13 pieces of *vikaṅkaṭa* wood, places on the top of it 100-carat-pieces of gold. While the *Chanḍra-Sāman* is being sung, he fans the fire with three fans prepared out of the pieces of antelope skin with handles attached to them; after having fanned the fire himself, he hands one fan each to the *Praṭiprasṭhāṭri* and the *Agniḍhra*, whereupon all three fan the fire. When the fire blazes, he removes the gold-pieces and keeps them away; and taking ghee with the *Sruva*, he sprinkles it on the *mahāvīra*. The *Praṭiprasṭhāṭri* then prepares the *Rauhiṇa* cakes; he takes up the *Shūrpa* and the *Āgnihoṭra-havaṇī*, and warms them on fire. Looking into the dough that has been prepared, he removes all foreign substances from it, and kneading it thoroughly, divides it into equal parts, spreads out each part into the form of a cake; placing *pariḍhis* of *Uḍumbara* wood round the Āhavanīya hearth, he smears the pans with ghee, and bakes the cakes on them. The Aḍhvaryu thereupon takes up the cake on the right; and while the Prasṭoṭri is singing the *Soma-niḍhana*, he throws it into the fire, as an offering either to Ḍharma or to Ahan. After this he takes up the *Rajjusan-ḍāna* and the two *pinvanas*; and accompanied by the *Praṭiprasṭhāṭri* goes out and milks the cow tethered to the post,—receiving the milk in the *pinvanas*; the priests milking the she-goat. Both return to the House and keep the milk in a safe place. The *Aḍhvaryu* picks out the *mahāvīras* with a pair of tongs, and taking them out of the house deposits them in a large vessel which is then covered with a stone-slab. After a short time, he brings them in and sprinkling goat's milk on them, he dips them in the cow's milk, and keeps them on the monnd near the Gārhapaṭya hearth. Bringing up *ghee* in the *gharma* vessel, he ponrs it as libation, with the *Ṣruk*, to the Ashvins, and another to Agni; and then keeps the vessel on the monnd to the North of the *Āhavanīya* hearth. He takes np seven bits (of wood or cake) and offers one each to Pūṣan-Sharās, Grāvan and Praṭirava; the fourth, after being hidden in a bnndle of *kusha*, is offered to the Piṭris; the fifth is offered to Ḍyavā-Priṭhivī, the sixth to the Vishvēḍēvas; and the seventh is handed over to the *Praṭiprasṭhāṭri*, who throws it to the North of the Honse. The Aḍhvaryn then offers the second *Rauhiṇa* cake into the *gharma*, and throws into the *Āhavanīya* the five pieces of wood kept on the *pariḍhis*. Libations of ghee are then ponred to Sūrya and Prajāpaṭi; and the remnants are eaten by the Sacrificer and the priests; and the *Upayamanī* is kept on the third monnd. Propitiatory *manṭras* being recited by the Sacrificer and the priests, the door of the Honse is flnng open.

57. This is followed by the *Upasaḍ-Iṣti* :—The *Agnīḍhra* having boiled the ghee, and the Aḍhvaryn having lighted the fire, the latter goes to the altar, and takes np the *Vēḍa* along with some *Kusha*, and throws it aside. The *Kusha* having been got together, the *sphya*, the *juhū*, the *sruva* and the *upabhriṭ* are washed; and the Lady having the *yokṭra* tied round her waist, examines the ghee and having removed all foreign substances, keeps it on the altar. All Homa-materials are then brought np to the Āhavanīya hearth, and libations are poured to Agni, Soma and Viṣṇn. The *Brahman*, the *Uḍgāṭri*, the *Hoṭri*, the *Aḍhvaryu*, the *Agnīḍhra* and the Sacrificer putting gold on their ring-finger, go np to the *soma* and tonch it. Returning to the hearth, they take np ghee and ponr a libation to Agni. The

prasṭara having its top-end dipped in the *juhū*, its middle in the *upabhṛiṭ*, and the lower end in the *Ājyasthālī*, is made over to the *Agnīḍhra* for safe custody. The remnants of the materials are then offered up to the fire; and this closes the *Upasaḍ Iṣti*.

58. Towards evening they offer to the Sacrificer a drink of milk in the same vessel in which they had kept the *Ṭānūnapṭra* ghee (§ 55); whereupon the *Pravargya* (§ 56) and the *Upasaḍ* (§ 57) sacrifices are again performed with some changes. In the *Pravargya* the *Rauhiṇa* cake is offered to *Rūri* (and not to *Ahan* as on the previous occasion); and in the *Upasaḍ* the libation is poured into the fire with the *manra* '*yāṭē agnē harāshayā*' (instead of '*ayāshayā*' as on the previous occasion). Before the sun sets, the sacrificer is permitted to give up silence and also to break his fast. Milk being drawn out of the three teats of the cow, it is boiled over the *Gārhapaṭya* for the Sacrificer and on the *Ḍakṣiṇāgni* for the Lady; and they retire to rest. Towards the latter part of the night they partake of the milk; and before the sun rises, the Sacrificer is required to resume his silence till sunrise. The *Pravargya* (§ 56) and the *Upasaḍ* (§ 57) sacrifices are again performed,—in the former the offering being again to Ahan, and in the latter the *manra* employed being '*yā ṭē agnē rajaḥshayā*, &c.'

59. They then proceed to map out the *Vēḍi*. Beginning from the centre of the eastern door of the house, the priest takes three steps forward, and there sticks the first peg—called the '*Anāhpāṭya shaṅku*'; taking up a *two-foot* measure (a *prakrama* being equal to two *padas*) they measure out 15 *prakramas* from the aforesaid peg to the south, and there put another peg,—this forming the southern boundary of the Vēḍi; similarly moving 15 *prakramas* to the north of the central peg, they drive in another peg—which forms the northern boundary; moving 36 *prakramas* from the central

peg towards the east they put in a peg—the eastern boundary, where also the post is set up. From this last peg to the south, at a distance of ten *prakramas*, a peg is put in; and one also at the distance of 12 *prakramas* towards the North. Having set up these pegs, they prepare the *Vēḍī*; and towards the North of it they make the *ukara* (place for the throwing of all waste matter). The *aḍhvaryu* then measures out the *chātvāla*, three *prakramas* to the west of the northernmost peg of the *Vēḍī*. Beside the *Vēḍī* they prepare the *uṭṭaravēḍi*, which is 10 ft. square.*

60. In the afternoon, they again perform the *Pravargya*, the cake being offered to *Rāṭri*; and also the *Upasaḍ*, with the *manṭra*, '*yā ṭē agnē rajaḥshayā &c.*' The Sacrificer, having drunk the milk in the evening, retires to sleep as on the previous night.—Next morning, they again perform the *Pravargya* and the *Upasaḍ*.

61. The *Brahman* and the Sacrificer seating themselves near the southern door of the House, the *Aḍhvaryu* prepares the ghee and goes to the Āhavanīya hearth. The *Agnīḍhra* throws one piece of fuel into the *Āhavanīya*; and the fire having blazed up, the *Aḍhvaryu* pours into it the fourth part of the ghee as an offering to '*Gharmasya Divyā Shuk*'. The *Agnīḍhra* lights another piece of fuel in the fire and holds it in his hand, while the *Aḍhvaryu* pours into the fire another

* 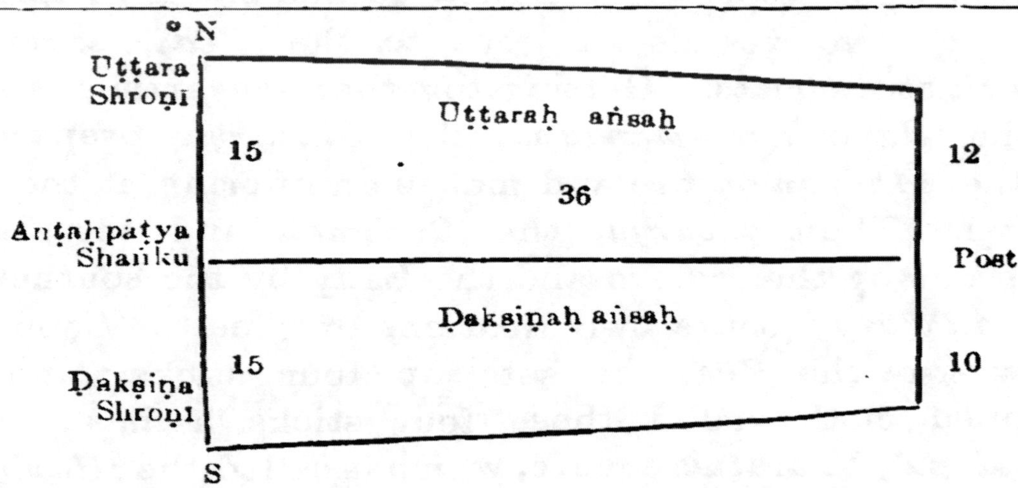

fourth part of the ghee as an offering to '*Gharmasya Antarikṣa Shuk*.' Similarly over the fire in the third stick, the third quarter of the ghee is offered to '*Gharmasya Pārṭhiva Shuk*.' Then placing the Lady before them, they go out of the House by the eastern door; and re-entering the House they go towards the *Uṭṭara Vēḍī*, on which they deposit the two *mahāvīras*, the two *parishās* being kept to the North and South of the third *mahāvīra*. While the *Prasṭoṭṛi* is singing the Vārṣāhara Sāman, the *Aḍhvaryu* sprinkles water upon the *Uṭṭaravēḍī*; the same being done by the other priests and also by the Sacrificer and the Lady, while the *Iṣṭāhoṭriya Sāman* is being sung. The Sacrificer puts some fuel into the *Āhavanīya*, and the Lady in the *Gārhapaṭya*; when the Sacrificer gives 100 carats of gold and silver to the *Brahman*, to the *Aḍhvaryu* he gives the cow that had supplied the milk for the *Gharma*; that which has given milk for the Sacrificer, he gives to the *Hoṭri*; to the *Udgāṭri* that which had given milk for the Lady; and lastly to the *Agnīḍhra* he gives a she-goat. This finishes the *Pravargyasāḍana*.

62. Next follows the *Agnipraṇayana*—*i.e.*, the fetching of burning sticks from the *Vēḍi* to the *Uṭṭaravēḍī*; and this is followed by the rigging up, close to the Vēḍī, of the '*Havirḍhāna*'—a room made up of cloth-pieces, in which the *Soma-juice* is kept. The *Aḍhvaryu* and the *Praṭiprasṭhāṭri* carrying two vessels of ghee to the *Vēḍi*, covers them up with straw mats. Getting together the articles necessary for the *Havirḍhāna-maṇḍapa*, the *Aḍhvaryu* prepares ghee on the *Āhavanīya* fire and makes an offering at the door to Saviṭṛi. The *Aḍhvaryu*, the *Brahman* and the Sacrificer going out by the eastern and the Lady by the southern door, the *Aḍhvaryu* pours two libations of ghee to Viṣṇu; and to the west of the *Vēḍī* he sets up four sticks; and having wrapped cloth round these four sticks, he has a 'room', a '*maṇḍapa*', 10 araṭnis square, which is called the '*Havirḍhāna*',

—which he dedicates to Visṇu. Generally two such rooms are rigged up—called the 'Northern' and the 'Southern' *Havirḍhāna.*

63. They now proceed to dig the *Uparava*, which on being dug, is examined by the *Aḍhvaryu* and the Sacrificer, who thoroughly wash it, and spread *kusha* over it. Spreading a circular piece of skin on the ground the Aḍhvaryu places 5 pieces of stone over it, and to the east of the *Uparava*, he prepares a mound.

64. After this they build the *Saḍas*—or place for some of the priests—and for those who come to witness the sacrifice. This place is six *prakramas* to the East of the *Anṭaḥpāṭya* peg of the *Vēḍī*,—measured out by means of a stick of the *Uḍumbara* wood, which is put iuto the ground, with its fifth part under the ground. Kusha being spread arouud this stick, the *Aḍhvaryu* takes up ghee with the *Sruva* and pours a libation over the stick, as an offering to *Ḍyāvā-priṭhivī*,—the quantity of ghee being large euough to smear the whole of the stick. The space for the *Saḍas* is mapped out 18 *araṭnis* by 9,—the *Uḍumbara* stick being at the centre; there are doors to the East and to the West; there are four pillars at the four corners; it is covered with a roof consisting of nine mats. It is guarded on all sides by six men.

65. This is followed by the *Agnīḍhranişpāḍana*—*i. e.* the preparation of the place called the '*Agnīḍhra*.' It is located to the North of the *Havirḍhāna*; it is 5 *araṭnis* square, with doors on the South and the East; it is built in such a manner as to make the inner end coincide with that of the *Havirḍhāna*. Half of it is to fall within the limits of the *Vēḍī*; it is dedicated to the Vishvēḍēvas.

66. After this comes the *Ḍhişṇyānivāsa*; that is to say, the preparation of the platforms for the sitting of the priests. At the centre of the *Agnīḍhra*, they make a flat platform 18 inches square; this is for the seat of the *Agnīḍhra* priest.

There are six other such platforms in the *Saḍas*—(1) one near the eastern door for the *Hoṭri*; (2) one at the central *Uḍumbara* stick, for the *Maiṭrāvaruṇa*; (3) one eighteen inches to the north of the Hoṭri's seat, for the *Brāhmaṇāchchhaṅsin*; (4) one to the north of this for the *Poṭri*; (5) next to this, one for the *Nēṣṭri*; and (6) the northernmost, for the *Achchhāvāka*. Every one of these platforms is besmeared with cowdung and has sand sprinkled over it. To the South of the *Agnīḍhra's* seat they prepare another called the '*Mārjalīya Ḍhiṣṇya*,' which is at one end of the *Vēḍī*.

67. All the above preparations having been made they proceed with the *Agnīṣomīya* offering :—

In the morning after the *Upasaḍ Iṣṭi* has been performed, the *Agnīḍhra* separates the calves from the cows *; and keeps the *praṇīṭā* vessels on the *Vēḍī*. The *Aḍhvaryu* picks up the *sphya*, and directs the *Agnīḍhra* to bring up *kusha* and fuels; and having washed the *Vēḍi*, he sprinkles water over the *kusha*. In the afternoon the *Aḍhvaryu* enters the House, and the *Agnīḍhra* brings up the fuel necessary for the *Agnipraṇayana* (§ 62), and sits down to the south of the Brahman and the Sacrificer. The *Aḍhvaryu* taking up the *sphya* ties the *yokṭra* to the Lady's waist. The Lady then examines the ghee and removes all foreign substances. The Sacrificer takes the *Soma* on his lap and sits at the door of the House. The *Aḍhvaryu* divides into four parts the clod of clay bearing the foot-prints of the cow given in exchange for the *Soma* (see above, § 53), throws one part over the *upayamanī* near the *Āhvanīya* hearth; another part being powdered and scattered at the door. The ghee having been got ready, the Sacrificer and his whole family—sons, brothers, grandsons, &c.—are seated together and covered with a piece of cloth; and the fire having blazed up, the *Aḍhvaryu* pours libations to Asu and to Soma.

* This is what is called the '*Vaṭsāpākaraṇa*, mentioned in the *Shaṭapaṭha Br.* 1-7-1-1, and 2-5-3-4, as to be done with a *palāsha* stick.

All of them then follow the *Aḍhvaryu* to the *Āhavanīya* hearth, the Sacrificer repeating the *manṭra*, '*Agnē naya*, &c'. (*Vājas. Samh.* 40.). All the articles being taken to the *Agnīḍhra* room, the priests enter the room by the southern door; and the *Aḍhvaryu* pours a libation of ghee to Agni; and then keeps the 5 pieces of stone and the stool of the Soma on the *Āgnīḍhra* mound; and all other things, except the Soma and ghee are then taken away to the *Āhavanīya* hearth; and all the preliminaries having been gone through, a libation of ghee is poured into the *Āhavanīya*, as an offering to Viṣṇu. Having washed his hands, the Aḍhvaryu receives the Soma from the hands of the Sacrificer, and accompanied by him enters the *Havirḍhāna*. Spreading the black antelope skin in the centre of the southern *Havirḍhāna*, he deposits the Soma upon this. The Sacrificer saluting the Soma, goes out and places fuel on the *Āhavanīya*, the Lady doing the same on the *Gārhapaṭya*. At this point ceases the restriction imposed on the Brāhmaṇas, not to eat anything at the house of the Sacrificer.

68. Having performed the *upākaraṇa* of the goat *—that is putting *kusha* between its horns,—they tie it up with a doubly-twisted rope, and tether it to the post, consecrating it to *Agni-Soma*, in virtue of which it is called the '*Agnīṣomīya Pashu*.' Making the goat lie down on a bedding of *kusha*, with its legs towards the North, and the head towards the West, the *Shamiṭris* (slaughterers) kill it,—this being called the '*sanjñapana*',—and recite over the body the *manṭra* '*aḍiṭiḥ pāsham*, &c.' The Lady pours water over the animal, and is taken away from the place. The *Aḍhvaryu* putting a bundle of *kusha* on the back of the dead body, cuts through the *kusha* into the skin; cutting out a piece of the skin, he throws it to the South-west, as an offering to the Rākṣasas

* That the *Agnīṣomīya* animal must be a *goat* is shown in *Mimāmsā Sūtra* VI—viii—30 to 42.

Enlarging the rent in the body, he draws out fat from about the regions of the heart, and makes a lump of it. Two offerings of this lump of fat are then made to Agni-Soma, with the *Juhū*. Fetching water from a flowing current, the priests and the Sacrificer sprinkle it over themselves. This finishes the *Vapāyāga*—the 'Fat-offering.'

69. After this comes the *Pashupurodāsha* Offering:—Having directed the *Prashamitṛi* to prepare the *Pashupurodāsha*, the *Aḍhvaryu* offers the *Shviṣtakṛiṭ* offerings. The *Pashupurodāsha*—*i.e.* offerings consisting of slices of the cake mixed up with certain parts of the body of the goat—having been got ready, they are offered to Agni-Soma; and the remnants are placed between the fire and the post. The hind-part of the goat is then carried into the *Saḍas*, and the thighs are kept near the *Agnīḍhra* mound, for use in the *Paṭnīsaṁyāja*, for doing which the *Aḍhvaryu* goes to the East of the House-door, and placing the Lady before him, pours libations, on her behalf, into the *Gārhapaṭya*, for Soma, Ṭvaṣṭṛi, Ḍēvapaṭnīs, Rākā, Kuhū, Sinīvālī and and Anumaṭi. All the priests going out of the House, the Lady sits at the door facing the East. The Sacrificer, sitting behind the *Uṭṭaravēḍi*, takes the Soma in his lap, having brought it out of the *Havirḍhāna*. The *Aḍhvaryu* takes two jars full of water and keeps one on each side of the *Uṭṭaravēḍi*, dedicating them to Inḍra-Agni. Taking the Soma from the Sacrificer, he keeps it on the stool, previously placed upon the *Agnīḍhra* mound; and during the night the Sacrificer keeps guard over the Soma there deposited. The milk-vessels are washed; the calves are separated from their dames; the Aḍhvaryu receives the gift of a house for sleeping, and all retire to rest.

70. Next morning comes the *Suṭyahā*—the Day for the extracting of the Soma-juice. Towards the latter end of the night, the servants of the Sacrificer wake up the priests.

They wash their faces and wearing washed clothes, proceed to their assigned duties. The Sacrificer resumes his vow of silence. The *Agnīḍhra* boils the gheè, and ties the *yokṭra* to the waist of the Lady, who thereupon examines the ghee and removes all foreign substances. The *pṛiṣaḍājya* mixture is then got ready; and all the things, except the ghee and the Soma, are kept near the *Āhavanīya*. The *Aḍhvaryu* accompanied by the Sacrificer enters the *Havirḍhāna*, and taking up the Soma-bundle loosens its knot; and placing five pieces of stone upon the skin, throws the pieces of Soma upon these stone pieces. The Hoṭṛi is then called up, and seated near the eastern door of the *Havirḍhāna*, recites the *Prāṭaranuvāka* or the Morning Hymn,—and then either retires to sleep again, or sits there watching the performance. The *Savanīya* cake having been prepared, of *Vīrhi* or *Yava* corns, upon eleven pans, for Inḍra, offerings of it are made to him. The Lady's share of the milk is boiled, and while it is hot, they put into it a little curd. They clean the barley grains, and pound them on the stone-slab; the dough is placed upon the *Pāṭrī*, kneaded, made into the shape of a cake, and baked and ornamented. The dishes for the various deities are then washed and kept in their proper positions by the *Unnēṭṛi*. Inside the *Havirḍhāna* they alos keep the cups made of *vikaṅkaṭa* wood,—each four *anguls* deep, supplied with a handle;—that intended for the *Hoṭṛi* being circular, for the *Brahman*, square-shaped, and so on, different shapes being laid down for the several priests. In the *Havirḍhāna*, they also keep an odd number of jars filled with water. By the time that the *Hoṭṛi* finishes the recitation of the Morning Hymn, the *Aḍhvaryu* takes ghee in the *Pracharaṇī*, and pours a libation into the *Āhavanīya* as an offering to Agni—Aḍhishuvana—Ḍēva and Saviṭṛi. Taking up ghee again, he asks the other priests to bring up the Lady; and then accompanied by her, the Sacrificer and the Brahman, he goes to the water-reservoir and pours an offering to Apas. Hethen fills oe jar nwith water. Returning to the House, they request the *Hoṭri* to repeat the Morning Hymn. The cup of the *Hoṭri* is then filled with water and handed over to the Sacrificer. Going over to the *Ahavanīya*, the *Āḍhvaryu* pours a libation to Agni.

71. The Sacrificer and the *Aḍhvaryu* seat themselves inside the *Havirḍhāna* upon the skin on which the Soma-juice is to be extracted, the other priests seating themselves all round. They collect all the articles needed for the 'extraction' ceremony; and each of the five priests takes up a stone piece in his hand. The Aḍhvaryu puts gold on his ring-finger and measures out five handfulls of Soma and puts each handful upon the stone-slab; and keeps aside one handfull for purposes of the *Kṣullakā.* The *Praṭiprasṭhāṭri* then picks up six shoots of the Soma. Then begins the *First* or the *Great 'Savana'* or '*Juice-Extraction.*' The *Aḍhvaryu*, the *Praṭiprasṭhaṭri*, the *Nēṣṭri* and the *Unnēṭri* wash their hands; and the *Aḍhvaryu* wets the Soma with water out of the *Hoṭri* cup. Dividing the wetted Soma into four parts distributed among themselves, the four priests proceed to 'extract' the juice by pounding it upon the stone-slab,—thinking all the time that each stroke of the stone-pounder is inflicted, not upon the Soma, but upon the enemy (on a blade of grass, in case the priest happens to have no enemy); this pounding is continued until the *Soma-bits* are reduced to a pulp; having rested a little, they make all the Soma-pulp into a lump, from which they extract the juice by pressure. This is the first 'round' of the extracting process. They collect all stray particles of Soma, and begin pounding again; when the whole is reduced to a pulp, they press out the juice again. The same proces is repeated once more. The three rounds of 'extraction' having been finished, they pour water over the squeezed pulp, in order to make it swell again with the soaking water; after

which they pound it again, going through the three rounds as before. Soaking the lump with water again, they go through the third 'three rounds' of the 'extraction'. This finishes the First Extraction, called '*Mahābhiṣava*'.

72. This is followed by *Kṣullakābhiṣava.* This is done by the *Aḍhvaryu* alone. He takes up the sixth handfull of Soma that had been kept aside, and puts it on the pounding slab, and strikes it eight times with the pounding stone. Having pressed out the juice, he picks out three shoots from the squeezed pulp and puts them into the *Hoṭri*-cup; and putting the *paviṭra* over it, he presses the shoots and extracts a little juice into the cup.—He pounds the pulp again with eleven strokes, and extracts the juice. The third time, he extracts the juice after twelve strokes. He then covers up the mouth of the cup, thereby closing up the life of his enemy whom he names. The *Aḍhvaryu* comes out of the *Havirḍhāna*, and is followed by the Sacrificer who gives to him any present that he asks for. They both go to the Sacrificial place, and standing at the middle of the Southern *pariḍhi*, they pour into the fire the Soma-juice in the cup, as a libation to Sūrya.

73. After this they go through their morning prayers, and await sunrise; in the meantime, the Sacrificer and his wife finish all their necessary ablutions, &c. The *Ūḍgāṭri* priest takes up the *Ḍroṇakalasha*, and keeps it upon the stonepieces on the skin on which Soma has been pounded; over this jar a *paviṭra* is kept, and upon this a gold-piece. The *Unnēṭri* brings up the Soma, and the Sacrificer fills a number of cups with Soma-juice. At sunrise, they take up one of these cups, called the '*Anṭaryāma*' and pour the juice as a libation to Sūrya. The *Aḍhvaryu* takes up the cups dedicated to Indra-Vāyu, to Shukra, and to Manṭhin,—and fills them with Soma-juice. Bringing up the *Āgrayaṇasṭhālī*, the Aḍhvaryu fills this also

with Soma-juice, and covering it up with the *paviṭra*, offers it to the Vishvēḍēvas. He then brings up the *Ukṭhyasṭhālī* and filling it with *Soma-juice*, offers it to Inḍra; similarly filling the *Ḍhruvasṭhālī*, he offers it to Vaishvānara. The *Ḍroṇakalasha* is then half-filled with Soma-juice; and the *Aḍhvaryu* pours a libation of ghee to Soma; similar libations being poured by others also. They then go out of the *Havirḍhāna*,—the Aḍhvaryu leading, and being followed by the others in the following order—the *Praṭiprasṭhāṭri*, the *Prasṭoṭri*, the *Uḍgāṭri*, the *Praṭiharṭri*, the *Brahman* and the Sacrificer; each touching the one in front of himself. They take their assigned seats; and the *Uḍgāṭri* sings the prescribed hymns,—the Sacrificer leading. When two hymns have been sung, the *Aḍhvaryu* directs the *Agnīḍhra* priest to bring up the cakes and adorn them; and also the *Praṭipasṭhaṭri* to come up with the animal. The former brings out the cakes from under the ashes and keeps them on the mound; to the East of the fried barley, and to the South of the *Karambha* (a preparation of *Sakṭu* mixed with ghee) to the North of the milk and the *Vājina* (the water passed off from curdled milk); after which the cake is dedicated to Inḍra, the fried barley to Inḍra-Harivaṭ, the *Karambha* to Inḍra-Puṣanvaṭ, the curd to Inḍra-Sarasvaṭivaṭ, the *Payasyā* to Inḍra-Miṭrāvaruṇa, and the *Vājina* to the Vājins. The *Praṭiprasṭhāṭri* brings up the *Savanīya* animal and stands near the *Uṭṭaravēḍī*. The *Aḍhvaryu* enters the *Havirḍhāna*, takes up the *Āshvina* cup, and having washed it, keeps it in its place; and points out each of the other cups to the Sacrificer. Going up to the post, he puts some *Kusha* between the horns of the *Savanīya* goat tethers it to the post, and dedicates it to Agni. The seat of the *Hoṭri* is then placed in tbe *Saḍas*, and the *Hoṭri* priest duly appointed to his task; the other priests and the Sacrificer having their duties duly assigned, each of them pours libations into the *Āhavanīya*, in the same order in which they had come out of the *Havirḍhāna* ;—these libations being offered to Vāk, Vāchaspaṭi and Sarasvaṭı. The animal is then killed and its fat extracted in the same manner as in the case of the *Agnīṣomīya* animal (see above § 68); and this fat is offered to Agni; after which the Priests take their usual dinner.

74. Then follows the *Savanīyapurodāshaprachāra*. The *Savanīyas* having been brought up near the *Uṭṭaravēḍi*, and the *Vājina* placed upon the *uṭkara*,—the first halves of the five cakes are then cut up into five slices, which are offered to the five deities just mentioned—and a slice offered also to Agni-Sviṣṭakṛiṭ; a portion of the remants of these offerings being thrown into the *prāshiṭra* and made over to the Brahman, and the rest of the remnants is then distributed between the Brahman and the Sacrificer. The *Aḍhvaryu* now proceeds to make the *Ḍviḍēvaṭya* offerings. He enters the *Havirḍhāna* by the Eastern door, and picking up the Inḍra-Vayu cup, and requestiug the Miṭrāvaruṇa priest to sing the appropriate hymns, offers small quantities of the juice in the cup to Inḍra-Vayu, in two instalments, handing over the cup to the *Hoṭṛi*. Going into the *Havirḍhāna* again, he comes out with the Miṭrāvaruṇa cup, and pours a libation to Miṭra-Varuṇa. Similarly bringing up the *Āhsvina* cup, he pours a libation to the Ashvins. The remnants of these three offerings are kept carefully in the *Āḍiṭyasṭhālī*. The cups of the Sacrificer and the priests except those of the *Achchhāvāka* and the *Unnēṭṛi*,—are filled by the *Aḍhvaryu* with Soma-juice, in three instalments—first from out of the *Ḍroṇakalasha*, then out of *Upabhṛiṭ*, and then again out of the *Ḍroṇakalasha*. The *Aḍhvaryu* and the *Praṭiprasṭhāṭṛi* take up the *Shukra* (a cup of *bilva* wood) and the *Manṭhin* (a cup of *Vikaṅkaṭa* wood) respectively, and cover them up with pieces of the post. They bring out these from the *Havirḍhāna* and keep them on the *Shroṇi* of

the *Uttaravēḍ*; whereupon the pieces of wood with which the cups had beeu covered are thrown into the *Āhavan,ya* fire. The nine priests whose cups have beeu filled with Soma-juice,—and who are on that account called '*Ohamasāḍharyus*',—come forward holdiug in their hands their own cups, and take their seats near the *Aḍhvaryu* hearth, facing the East. The *Aḍhvaryu* and the *Praṭiprasṭhāṭri*, standing to the North and South of the post, pour out the juice iu their cups as libatious to Iuḍra, whereupon the other niue also pour out libatious to the same deity. The *Aḍhvaryu* theu calls for the cup of the *Hoṭri* and pours into it the remuauts of the *Shukhra* and *Manṭhin* cups; and the *Hoṭri* with three priests retires into the *Saḍas*. The other priests fill up their cups with Soma-juice out of the *Ḍroṇakalasha*, and the *Aḍhvaryu* pours libatious, out of the *Prashasṭri* cup to Miṭra-Varuṇa and Agui, out of the *Brāhmaṇāchchhansin* cup to Iuḍra aud Agui, out of the *Poṭri* cup to the Maruṭs and Agui, out of the *Nēṣṭri* cup to Ṭvaṣṭri and Agui, out of the *Āgnīḍhra* cup to Agui, aud theu again to Agni. Retaining in his hand this last cup, the *Aḍhvaryu* goes into the *Saḍas*, sits before the *Hoṭri*, and with him eats the remnants of the *Ḍviḍēvaṭya* offeriugs. *

75. After this, the priests proceed to drink the remnants out of the Soma-cups. The Aḍhvaryu drinks the remnaut of the *Shukra* cup, out of the *Hoṭri* cup; out of which also the *Praṭiprasṭhāṭri* driuks the remnaut of the *Manṭhin* cup; the Hoṭri drinks the remuants of both the *Shukra* and the *Manṭhin*, and also out of the *Brahman*-cup; out of which also the *Brahman* himself drinks; the *Uḍgāṭris* drink out of their owu cup; the Hoṭri having druuk a little out of the

* With regard to this *eating* there is a difference of opinion among the *Mīmāmsakas* and the *Yājñikas*. According to the former, who rely upon the text '*Vaṣatkarṭuḥ praṭhamo bhakṣaḥ*' (see *Mīm-Sū.* III—V—31 to 35), it being the *Hoṭri*, who being the pronouncer of the syllable '*Vaṣat*' with each libation, eats first; while according to the latter, precedence is given to the *Aḍhvaryu*. The *Paḍḍhatis* naturally adopt the latter order.

Sacrificer's cup, the Sacrificer himself drinks out of it; similarly the *Hoṭṛi* having partaken of the cups of the other priests, each of them drinks of his own cup;—the *Hoṭṛi* being entitled to a share in every cup, by reason of his having helped in all libations, with the uttering of the 'syllable '*vaṣat*' (Mīm. Sū. III-v-31). This finishes the 'drinking' in connection with the first set of offerings.*

76. The *Unnēṭṛi* akes up Soma-juice with the *uḍañchana* out of the *Upabhṛiṭ*, and enters the Saḍas; whereupon the nine *Chamasāḍhvaryus*, having poured out into the cup brought by the *Unnēṭṛi*, all the juice left in their cups, keep their cups within the *Havirḍhāna*. (These cups are henceforward called the *Nārāshaṁsa* cups). The *Aḍhvaryu* takes up the cake-slices that had been kept aside, and approaching the *Achchhāvāka* in the *Saḍas*, makes over the slices to him. The cup of the *Achchhāvāka* is then filled with Soma-juice out of the *Ḍroṇakalasha*; and the *Aḍhvaryu* takes up the cup and pours a libation to Inḍra-Agni; and after having drunk a little of the remnant, he hands it over to the *Achchhāvāka* who then drinks his own share. The *Brahman*, the *Hoṭṛi*, the *Agnīḍhra* and the *Miṭrāvaruṇa* entering the Agnīḍhra room, eat of the remnants of the cakes; and the Sacrificer also partakes of the remnants of the *Ḍviḍēvaṭya* offerings; and the Lady in her own room partakes of sweet cakes and pastries cooked on the ordinary *smārṭa* fire (she apparently being not entitled to the 'remnants').

77. This is followed by the offerings of the *vājina*, and also of the dough, &c. attached to the several vessels and implements. The *Achchhāvāka* having seated himself in the *Saḍas*, the *Aḍhvaryu* and the *Praṭiprasṭhāṭṛi* take up the *Riṭu-cups* and fill them with Soma-juice out of the

* In this connection, it may be noted that the priests drink out of each other's cups, and no difficulties are raised in regard to the '*Uchchhiṣṭa*' which occupies a very prominent place in the bearing of individuals towards one another, in modern Hindu society.

Dronakalasha ; whereupon going to the Sacrificial House, the *Adhvaryu* pours the juice as a libation to Indra ; and enters the *Havirdhāna* for bringing up another cup ; and the *Pratiprasthatri* coming up with another cup, libation out this is poured by the *Potri* to the Maruts ; then comes the *Adhvaryu* with another cup of juice which is poured as a libation to *Tvastri* by the *Nēstri*; the *Pratiprasthātri* bringing up another cup of juice, this is offered by the *Agnīdhra* to Agni. Thus alternately, the *Adhvaryu* and the *Pratiprasthātri* bringing up the cups one by one, libations are poured to Indra by the *Brāhmaṇāchchhaṁsin* and to Indra-Varuṇa by the *Prashāstri*, and so on; and lastly the *Adhvaryu* and the *Pratiprasthatri* bringing up the two original cups, libations are poured to the Ashvins and to Agni-Grihapati. Finally the *Adhvaryu* brings up the thirteenth *Ritu-cup* and pours a libation to Indra-Grihapati; and collecting the drippings of the cups into a vessel, goes to the *Sadas* ; and the *Pratiprastāthri* enters the *Havirdhāna* with another *Ritu-cup*, and placing into this the cup originally dedicated to Indra-Agni, keeps it on the mound near the *Āgrayaṇasthālī*, and goes out to the *Sadas* ; where they thereupon drink the remnants of the *Ritu-cup* offerings. While the *Shastra* hymns are beiug recited, the *Adhvaryu* enters the *Havirdhāna*, and taking up the Indra-Agni cup, and accompanied by the *Chamasādhvaryus*, who hold their own cups in their hands, pours libations to Indra-Agni ; whereupon they go to the *Sadas* and partake of the remnants. The Adhvaryu again fills the *Shukra* with Soma-juice out of the *Dronakalasha*, and keeps the Vishvēdēva cup on the spot where the *Shukra* was. Pouring out all the Soma-juice out of the *Dronakalasha* into the *Upabhrit*, he sets aside the former.

The *Agnīdhra* now prepares the four *Pashupurodāshas*—*i.e.*, cakes prepared of flour mixed with the lard of the animal. The first of these is for Agni, the second for Indra, the third for Indra-Harivat, and the fourth for Indra-Pusanvat. The

Aḍhvaryu cuts up the body of the goat, and with certain preliminary rites, slices the cakes; which are thereupon offered to the aforesaid four deities. The *Aḍhvaryu* picks up the Vishvēḍēva cup and pours libations to the Vishvēḍēvas and to Agni; and the other priests holding their cups in their hands shake them over the fire twice. They retire to the Saḍas and partake of the remnants.

78. After this come the three *Ukṭhyavigrahas*; the first performed by the *Aḍhvaryu* aud the other two by the *Praṭiprasṭhāṭri*:—The *Aḍhvaryu* takes up the *Ukṭhya* vessel, and pours into it the third part of the Soma-juice coutained in the *Ukṭhyasṭhālī*, and dedicates it to Miṭra-Varuṇa. The *Unnēṭri* takes up the cups of the priests aud keeps them on the *Uṭṭaravēḍī*; and pours into each of them the Soma-juice out of the *Upabhriṭ*. While the *Uḍgāṭris* are singing hymns, the *Aḍhvaryu* takes up the *Ukṭhya* vessel, whereupou the other priests also take up theirs. The *Aḍhvaryu*,—aud after him all the priests—pour libatious,—one to Miṭra-Varuṇa, and another to Agni. They repair to the *Saḍas* and drink the remuants. The above process is repeated twice by the *Praṭiprasṭhāṭri*,—the libations in this case being to Inḍra, aud Inḍra-Agni respectively. After this all the priests are permitted to go out and rest.

This finishes the *Prāṭaḥ-savana*.

79. Next comes the *Māḍhyanḍina*, or Midday *Savana*:—The Sacrificer seated to the west of the *Agnīḍhra* mound sings the *Lokaḍvārīya Sāman*. The *Aḍhvaryu* pours water into the *Hoṭri* cup and hands it over to the Sacrificer aud removiug the covering of the Soma, he hands it to the, *Grāvasṭuṭ*; whereupon the *Aḍhvaryu* and the other priests, as in the Morning Savana, extract juice from the Soma-bits; and puts these in water to soak and swell. The *Unnēṭri* pours the juice into the *Hoṭri* cup in the Sacrificer's hand, through which it is made to flow to the *Shukra*

and the *Manṭhin* cups, as also into the *Āgrayanasṭhālī*, the *Riṭupāṭra* and the *Ukṭhyasṭhālī*. The remaining juice is thereupon poured into the *Ḍroṇakalasha*. After this they all go out of the *Havirḍhāna* in the same order as in the Morning *Savana*. The *Udgāṭris* having suing the *Pavamāna* hymns, the *Agnīḍhra* is requested to bring out the cakes and bedeck them. The cakes having been brought up, the first offering out of them is made to Agni-Svisṭakrit; and then the cake is cut up into slices, which are offered to Agni, Inḍra, Inḍra-Harimaṭ, &c., as in the Morning *Savana*. Libations out of the *Shukra* and *Manṭhin* cups are made to Inḍra and Agni, and the remnants are drunk by the priests The dough, &c. attaching to the vessels are offered into the fire.

80. Then follows the paying of the Sacrificial Fee—*Ḍakṣiṇā*:—The *Brahman* and the Sacrificer enter the house; the *Aḍhvaryu* taking ghee in the *Pracharaṇī*, and tying to it the cloth and the gold intended for the Fee, pours the ghee as a libation to Sūrya,—repeating it three times; finally offering up the gold bound up in the cloth into the fire; out of which it is picked up by the Sacrificer who thereupon takes his stand on the East of the Vēḍi. A hundred cows are collected in the space between the House and the *Saḍas*, where also are brought certain grains. Advancing towards the *Saḍas*, the Sacrificer looks upon the persons therein seated, and goes to the *Agnīḍhra* mound, whereupon seated, he pronounces the formal words of the 'gifts'—promising to divide among the priests in accordance with the shares prescribed in the scriptures, gifts of gold, 100 cows and clothes,—all for the fulfilment of the sacrifice he has performed; the Lady adding the words—'this is given by me also'; when each thing is offered, the priests receive the gold as for Agni, the cow as for Ruḍra, and the clothes as for Brihaspaṭi. The shares have been assigned as follows:—12 cows and 12 gold pieces, each, to the *Brahman*, the *Uḍgāṭri*,

the *Hoṭṛi* and the *Aḍhvaryu*; 6 cows and 6 pieces of Gold each, to the *Praṭiprasṭhāṭṛi*, the *Prasṭoṭṛi*, the *Maiṭrāvaruṇa*, and the *Brāhmaṇāchchhamsin*; 4 cows and 4 pieces of gold each, to the *Poṭṛi*, the *Nēṣṭri*, the *Achchhāvāka*, and the *Agniḍhra*; and 3 cows and 3 gold pieces each, to the *Unnēṭṛi*, the *Grāvasṭuṭ*, the *Subrahmaṇya* and the *Praṭihartṛi*. Some more gold pieces are distributed among the *Upagāṭṛis*. Nothing is to be given to those *Brāhmaṇas* who may be there, simply clamouring for gifts.

81. After the *Praṭihartṛi* has received his fee, the *Aḍhvaryu* enters the *Havirḍhāna*; and taking up the *Maruṭvaṭ-cups* pours libations to Inḍra-Maruṭvaṭ and to Agni. Entering the *Havirḍhāna* again, he takes up the *Mahāmaruṭvaṭ* cup and filling it with Soma-juice, keeps it near the *Āgrayaṇa* vessel. After a little time he takes up this cup, and pours libations again to Inḍra-Maruṭvaṭ and Agni. They retire to the *Saḍas* and drink the remnants. Taking up the *Māhēnḍra* cup, they fill it with Soma-juice, while the *Priṣtha-Sāman* is being sung; and hands over the cup to the Sacrificer.

82. The *Aḍhvaryu*, accompanied by the *Praṭiprasṭhāṭṛi* the *Unnēṭri* and the *Nēṣṭri*, proceeds to perform the *Third Extraction—Ṭriṭīya-Savana* As before they extract the juice out of the Soma-bits in three instalments. The *Agnīḍhra* in the meantime prepares the other offerings —*i.e.*, the *Charu* or cooked rice for Soma, a cake for Varuṇa baked upon one pan, as also those that were baked in the other *Savanas*. Taking the Māhēnḍra cup from the Sacrificer's hands, the *Aḍhvaryu* pours a libation to Mahēnḍra and to Agni; and accompanied by the *Hoṭri*, drinks the remnant; the other priests drinking out of their cups as usual. After this follow the three *Ūkṭhyavigrahas* (see above, § 78) as in the morning *Savana*; after which the priests retire to rest. This finishes the Second—the *Māḍhyanḍina—Savana*.

83. Then comes the *Third Savana*: The Sacrificer and the four chief priests enter the *Havirḍhāna* by the eastern door, the Lady entering by the western door. The two doors are closed. The *Aḍhvaryu* takes up the *Āḍiṭya Sṭhālī* and filling it with Soma-juice, hands it to the *Praṭiprasṭhāṭṛi*, who mixes up curd and *kusha* with the juice, and hands it to the *Unnēṭri*, who keeps it on the skin, and covers it up with his hand. The doors are now opened; and the Sacrificer and the *Aḍhvaryu* going out with the vessel pour libations to the Āḍiṭyas; the Sacrificer also singing the *Lokaḍvārīya Sāman* and also pouring the libations. The *Aḍhvaryu* takes up the Soma in the *Āgrayaṇa-sṭhālī* and keeps it in its appointed place. Coming out of the *Havirḍhāna*, they go to the *Saḍas*, and request the *Uḍgāṭri* to sing the *Pavamāna* hymns. Offerings of cakes are then made to Soma, Inḍra, Varuṇa, Inḍra-Harimaṭ, &c. as in the previous *Savanas*;—the *Pashupuroḍāsha* in this case being made up of the dough mixed with the heart of the goat. After this the Soma-juice in the cups is offered to Mitra-Varuna Agni, Inḍra-Agni, Maruṭs-Agni, Ṭvaṣṭṛi-Agni, Inḍra-Viṣṇu-Agni, and Agni. Retiring to the *Saḍas*, they partake of the Soma remnants. The Sacrificer and the Priests take the remnants of the cakes, and make offerings of *piṇdas* to the father, grandfather and great-grandfather of the Sacrificer,—the *piṇdas* being offered upon the cups. The four chief priests then eat the remnants of the cake, the Sacrificer eating the remnant of the ghee instead. Bringing up the *Saviṭṛi-cup*, and the *Vaiṣvaḍēva cup*, the *Aḍhvaryu* pours libations to Ḍēva-Saviṭṛi and Vishvēḍēvas-Agni respectively; and accompanied with the other priests eats the remnants in these cups.

84. Then follows the *Sauryacharuyāga*:—The *Charu* having been brought up, offerings are made to Agni and Soma; a libation of ghee is poured to Viṣṇu or to Viṣṇu-Agni. Pouring ghee into the *Charu*, the *Aḍhvaryu* takes

it to the *Sadas* and gives it to the *Hotri*. Coming back he takes up ghee in the *pracharaṇī*, and pours libations in eight places :—

(1) On the *Agnīḍhra* mound, to Vibhu-Pravahaṇa, (2) on the *Hoṭri's* seat, to Vahni-Havyavāhana, (3) on the post to Shvāṭra-Prachēṭas, (4) on the *Brāhmaṇāchchhamsin's* seat to Ṭīrṭha-Vishvēḍēvas, (5) on the *Poṭri's* seat to Ushiṭri—Kavi; (6) on the *Nēṣtri's* seat, to Aṅghāri—Vambhāri, (7) on the *Achchhāvāka's* seat to Ambasyu-Ḍuvasyu ; and (8) at the centre of the *Saḍas*, to Shunḍhyu-Mārjalīya. The *Praṭiprasṭhāṭri* brings up the *Pāṭnīvaṭa* cup and pours a libation to Agni-Paṭnīvaṭ. The *Agnīḍhra* taking up the cup and going to the *Saḍas*, sits upon the lap of the *Nēṣṭri*, where he and the *Aḍhvaryu* drink the remnant of the *Pāṭnīvaṭa* The *Unnēṭri* goes to the *Uṭṭaravēḍī* and pours all the Soma-juice into the cups of the priests ; and while the *Yajñāyajñīya Sāmaṉ* is being sung, the Lady is led by the hand to the Saḍas, where she uncovers her right thigh and sprinkles water over it, after which, with the *Uḍgāṭri's* permission, she retires to her own room. Thereupon the *Aḍhvaryu* and the other priests take up the Soma cups and pour libations to Agni-Maruṭs, and to Agni ; and returning to the *Saḍas*, drink the remnants.

85. All the articles are then washed and set aside ; the *praṣṭara* is thrown into the fire as an offering to Agni, Vanaspaṭi, &c. The *Aḍhvaryu* enters the *Havirḍhāna* and pours all the Soma-juice he can find into the *Ḍroṇakalasha* ; and mixing up some grains with it, pours it as a libation to Inḍra-Hariamṭ and to Agni ; and keeps the *kalasha* in the *Saḍas*. The Sacrificer and the sixteen priests each pick up three grains out of the *kalasha*, and having smelt them, throw them, away upon the *Vēḍī*. Each of them throws six pieces of fuel into the *Āhavanīya* fire. Having filled the cups with water, and covering them with green grass, they touch their own, or

their neighbour's, cups ; and retiring to the *Agnīḍhra* mound eat curd.

86. Then follows the *Paṭnīsamyāja*, at which after the offerings have been made, the *Vēḍa* and the *Yokṭra* are removed. The *Aḍhvaryu* takes up nine pieces of fuel and offers them respectively to Vishvēḍēvas, Ṭvaṣṭri, Ḍhāṭrin, Saviṭri, Prajāpaṭi, Agni, Tvaṣṭri (again), Viṣṇu, Ḍēvas, Agni, Agni, Vāṭa, Yajña, and Yajñapaṭi. Taking up the Stool and the Post, all the vessels and implements that may be smeared with Soma-juice, the black horn and the *mekhalā*, the *Yokṭrā* (removed from the Lady's waist),—and while the Prasṭoṭri is singing a Sāmau, the closing notes of which are taken up by the Sacrificer, —all of them go to the riverside, or to a lake, for the *Avabhriṭha* or Final Bath. When gone halfway on the road, Sāman hymns are sung, all of them joining in the chorus. Reaching the river, the *Aḍhvaryu* leads the Sacrificer by the arm into the water ; after which follows the *Avabhriṭha Iṣṭi*:—Standing in the water, the Sacrificer and the priests take up their assigned places, holding in their hands the ghee, cake aud other things. The *Aḍhvaryu* takes ghee and ponrs into the water oblations to *Agni*, *Varuṇa*, *Ḍēvas* and *Ājyapās*. Taking up the cake, he offers it to Varuṇa and Agni-Varuṇa ; after which he sets the jar afloat on the water. Having washed the black antelope skin and handed it over to their son, the Sacrificer aud the Lady take their bath,—the Sacrificer washing the Lady's back, and the Lady doing the same to her husband. The *Aḍhvaryu* throws into the water all the things smeared with Soma-juice, whereupon all take their baths. The *Unnēṭri* leads by the arm the Sacrificer and his wife out of the water. Returning to the Sacrificial House, the Sacrificer puts fuel on the *Āhavanīya* and the Lady on the *Gārhapaṭya* fire. An offering of *kusha* having been made, the Sacrificer enters the Lady's Room, and sits down taking the antelope skin on his lap. The *Aḍhvaryu* pours a libation of ghee to Agni.

87. Then comes the *Uḍayanīyēṣti* :—All the minor details having been performed, rice is cooked, out which an offering is made to Aḍiṭi.

88. This is followed by the *Anubanḍhyā* :—at which offerings of ghee are made to Miṭra-Varuṇa; and the *Pashupuroḍāsha* having been got ready, it is offered to Miṭra-Varuṇa.

89. Then comes the *Payavyēṣti* :—the *Payasyā* and the *Vājina* being prepared, the former is offered to Miṭra-Varuṇa and the latter to Agni-Soma, Miṭra-Varuṇa-Agni-Hoṭra —Vājin.

90. After this comes the *Uḍavasānīyēṣti* :—A cake having been baked upon five pans, it is offered to Agni.

91. One thousand Brāhmaṇas are now fed; and the performance concludes with appropriate rejoicings; after which the Sacrificer performs the daily rites of the *Agnihoṭra* and makes the other necessary offerings.

ALPHABETICAL LIST OF THINGS REQUIRED AT THE AGNIṢTOMA, IN ADDITION TO THOSE NEEDED AT THE ḌARSHA-PŪRṆAMĀSA.

Abhri—Wooden scraper.

Abhyupashaya—Name given to two Mahāvīras.

Anṭarḍhānakata—Wooden partitions to screen off the wives of the gods.

Āsanḍī—Wooden stool.

Upayamanī—An earthenware vessel.

Ukhā—Boiling pot.

Uḍumbara—Fuel.

Chamasas—Earthenware cups.

Ḍhaviṭra—Fau made of deer-skin.

Parishāsa—Tongs.

Pānnējani—Jars filled with water for the washing of feet.

Pinvana—Made of clay.

Rajjusanḍāna—Rope-noose.

CHAPTER V.

THE BEARING OF THE MĪMĀMSĀ-SHĀSṬRA ON HINDU LEGAL LITERATURE.

1. The Mīmāmsa Sūṭras, as we have seen, have evolved a set of principles of interpretation of texts. They have based their discussions upon texts dealing with the details of sacrificial ritual; and this for the reason that at the time that the *sūṭras* were written, and the principles of Mīmāṁsā systematised, the performance of elaborate sacrifices was regarded as the *summum bonum* of life for the ordinary Hindu. At a later age, when these sacrifices dropped into disuse, the study of Mīmāṁsā proper fell in popular estimation; but it was soon discovered that though the examples chosen in Mīmaṁsā literature, for the application of the goueral Priuciples, did not appeal to the scholar, the Principles themselves were as useful as ever; specially in the study of Law. This branch of study had to deal with a number of original texts; whose range extended from the Vedas down to the most recent *Smṛiṭi* compilations; and as there were several discrepancies in these texts, on many points iu regard to the practices of men,—the only reasonable basis for the explaining away of these discrepancies lay iu the Principles of interpretation that had been worked out by ṭhe old *Mīmāmsā* writers, in reference to similar discrepancies in regard to Vedic texts bearing upon the details of sacrificial ritual. We accordingly fiud all-writers of Legal Digests making free use of the said Principles of interpretation.

2. The Legal Digests are as a rule divided into three sectious :—*viz.*, (1) *Āchāra*', Religious Practices; (2) Vyavahāra', 'Law' in the modern sense of the term, dealing with *worldly* 'business;' (3) '*Prāyashchiṭṭa*,' Expiatory Rites. The first and the last of these are likely to be as uninteresting

to the modern reader as the Sacrificial Ritual itself. Therefore we shall confine our present study to the '*Vyavahāra*' section of the Legal Digests; though, it has to be admitted, this limits the scope of our study to a great extent; specially as we have chosen for our study only the *Miṭākṣarā* (Vijñaneshvara's 'Comment' on the *Smriṭi* of Yayñavalkya) and the *Vyavahāramayūkha* of Shrikantha,—the two digests that are still recognised as 'authoritative' in the greater part of India.

3. The cases of application of Mīmāṁsā Principles in the *Miṭākṣarā* may be roughly grouped under the heads of—(a) *Evidence*, (b) *Joint Concern*, and (c) *Inheritance*.

(*a*) *Evidence.*

(1). 'In a criminal case against any person belonging to the four castes, when one is called to give evidence for the prosecution,—if his evidence is likely to bring about such conviction as would lead to capital sentence being pronounced on the accused,—the witness should either not give evidence at all, or should give false evidence.' (*Yājn̲av̲alkya*, II. 83). Though the ordinary rule (*Ibid* II. 82) is that a witness giving false evidence intentionaliy should be punished with fine or banishment, yet, in the particular case, the suppression of evidence, or the giving of false evidence, is permissible. But even thus the 'sin' of the act remains; and in expiation of this, the witness has to perform the *Sārasvaṭa Iṣṭi*, laid down in Mim. Sū. III—vi—18, 19. (*Miṭākṣarā*, Bombay, pp. 159-60).

(2) When a party has produced witnesses whose evidence goes against his case,—then, if at a later stage, he can produce other witnesses who are more reliable than the former batch, the evidence of the previous witnesses must be discredited. The mere fact of the later appearance of the witness does not militate against his reliability; because 'a person has to be regarded a *unreliable* only when either his

assertions are actually found to be false, or his means of knowing the facts of the case are not sufficiently valid'; as has been declared in Shabaras's *Bhāṣya*, page 8, line 15. In the case in question, until there is something to show that the later witness is unreliable, his deposition must be believed to be true ; but if it can be shown by proofs adduced by the other party that what he said was actually *untrue*, or that he had no means at his command whereby he could have any true knowledge of the facts in question, his evidence would fail to be accepted ; but until that is done, his evidence has to be reckoned with. In the case taken by the *Mimāṁsaka*, the fact is found to be that what is declared in the Veda must be accepted as true ; because statements can be regarded as false only when the person making the statement is found to be *untrustworthy* on the above mentioned grounds ; and in the case of the Veda, there being no 'person' making the statements, there can be no grounds for unreliability, (Miṭā. p. 156).

(*b*) *Joint Concern.*

In all joint concerns,—such as Trading and Theatrical Companies and Agricultural Bands,—the earnings are to be divided in accordance with the amount of capital invested by each partner ; just as at the Jyotiṣtoma sacrifice, the hundred cows that are prescribed as the 'sacrificial fee' for the priests employed, are to be distributed among the sixteen priests, in accordance with the amount of work done by each ; for instance, the four principal priests get 12 cows each, and so on, as laid down in *Mīm. Sū.* X—iii –53 to 55. (See above, Chap. IV, § 80). The general principle involved in this case is one of equity: 'Each person according to his dessert', 'the gains are to be in accordance with the pains'; the *Aḍhvaryu* gets more than the *Ūḍgāṭṛi*, because he does more work in connection with the Sacrificial performance than the other ; similarly in all joint concerns, the greater profit goes to the partner that works more and invests the larger amount of capital.

(c) *Inheritance.*

(1) '*Ḍāya*' or Inheritance has been defined as that wealth or possession which comes to a person simply by virtue of his relationship to its previous owner; the '*bhāga*' or 'division' of wealth is its distribution among a number of persons entitled to the ownership. This leads to the question—what is the 'title' or 'right' to a possession? Is the 'right' based purely upon *scriptural* authority or upon other, worldly, authorities also? It is argued that if it depended upon scriptural authority, then the ownership acquired under that 'right' would also be purely 'scriptural'; and as such could out be utilised in such purely *worldly* concerns as *buying*, *selling* aud the like; hence the 'right' under which ownership is to be acquired must be one that depeuds, not solely upon scriptural authority, but upon other authorities also. This line of argument has been borrowed from *Mimāṁsā-Sūṭra* IV—i—2 [*Vyāyamūlāvisṭāra*, page 219, 'fourth *varṇaka*' according to Kumārila, and 'third *varṇaka*' according to Prabhākara],—where in regard to the rules laid down in counection with the acquiring of wealth for the performauce of Sacrifices,—the question having been raised as to whether an infringement of those rules would cause a discrepancy in the sacrifice performed with the wealth thus wrongly acquired, or it would only produce some *blemish* or *sinfulness* in the Sacrificer—the *prima facie* argument of the Opponent propounded by Kumārila is that if the rules of acquisition pertained to the Sacrifice only, then the Sacrificer would have no *ownership* at all; inasmuch as *ownership* is something supernatural (based upon scriptures only). This statement of the *prima facie* argument however has been rejected by Prabhākara, as impossible, on the ground that, as a matter of fact, *ownership* is not something superna-

tural or spiritual, it is purely worldly or temporal; and the wealth acquired by temporal means can certainly be used in the performance of sacrifices. In delivering their final conclusion also, the writers have admitted the discussion on the understarding that *ownership* is something purely temporal; and hence if there has been anything wrong in the method of acquiring that ownership, it affects only the *man*, and not the *sacrifice*, which latter would be complete all the same; though the man will have to perform some expiatory rites for the employment of questionable methods. (*Miṭākṣarā*, page 181.) *

2. Yājñavalkya (II. 126) has laid down that after the regular partition is finished, if something is discovered to have been taken away surreptitiously by any partner, it should be recovered from him and divided among the partners in equal shares. In this connection the question is raised as to whether this surreptitious possession is reprehensible or not;—the argument for non-reprehensibility being that the partner who is in wrongful possession has also some right over the thing, and hence as he has been retaining the thing under the misconception that it is his own, his conduct is not blameworthy. The final conclusion however is that the wrongful possession has to be regarded as reprehensible. This conclusion is based upon the *Mīmāṁsā-Sūtra* VI—iii—20, where the question being raised as to the changing of the *muḍga* corn (that had been kept for the *charu*, and has become unfit for use) the opponent has argued that, if the Sacrificer substitutes an equal quantity of the *māṣa* corn, under the misapprehension that it is *muḍga*, his action cannot be regarded as a contravention of the rule that prohibits the use of the *māṣa*; because he has used the *māṣa* it is true, but he has used it *as muḍga*; and this view is rejected, the final conclusion being that even though done under a misapprehen-

*It is interesting to note that in this connection, the *Miṭākṣarā* quotes the very words of Prabhākara's *Bṛihaṭī* (Ms. p. 64b).

sion, the action must be regarded as an infringement of the rule wherely *māṣa, koḍravā*, and *chaṇaka* cannot be substituted for *muḍga*, at sacrifices. The principle underlying this is the maxim that Ignorance of the law is no excuse. (*Miṭākṣara*, page 193).

3. In regard to the rights of inheritance of widows, some writers have argued that, inasmuch as all property is primarily intended for sacrificial performances, to which the woman is not entitled, she can have no business to inherit any property; that women, apart from their husbands, are not entitled to sacrificial performances has been shown under *Mimāṁsā-sūṭrā* VI—i—17 to 21; though in the preceding *aḍhikaraṇa* it has been shown that she cannot be said to be absolutely *non-entitled* to such performances; as in the company of her husband she has her place at all sacrifices (see above).

This argument against the rights of women is met by another reasoning based upon Mīmāmsā-suṭras III—iv—26 to 30, where it is shown that the *wearing of gold* and such other things by the priests and the Sacrificer have no bearing on the sacrificial performance; on the basis of this principle it has been argued that, if *all* property were intended for sacrificial performances, from where could the gold be got? It is certainly 'property', and yet to does not have any bearing upon sacrificial performances. (*Miṭākṣarā*, pp. 200—1).

(4) With reference to the share to which the wife is entitled, we have the following texts:—

(*a*) यदि कुर्यात् समानोंशान् पत्न्यः कार्याः समांशिकाः ।

(*b*) पितुरूर्ध्वं विभजताम् माता ज्यंशं समं हरेत् ॥

(*a*) 'If the proprietor effects the division of his property during his lifetime, he should award to his wives shares equal to that of his sons.

(*b*) If the partition is effected after the death of the father, the mother should have a share equal to that of her sons.'

This text declares that the wife's share in the property of her husband is equal to that of each of her sons. Some writers,—who have held that the wife is entitled to a mere subsistance allowance,—interpret the texts to mean that, if the property is extensive, the wife is to have just enough to keep her; but in case the property is not much, she shares it equally with her sons. Against this it is argued that this interpretation would cause an incongruity in the above texts; as in that case, the first half of it would mean that she is to receive mere subsistence allowance; while the other half would give her an equal share with her sons; that such an incongruous interpretation of injunctive texts is not allowable has been shown under *Mīmāṁsā-sūṭra* VII—iii—19 to 25; wherein we have the following argument:——In connection with the *Chāṭurmāsya* sacrifice, the Veda enjoins '*Agni-Praṇayana*'; there are two such '*praṇayanas*'—that connected with the *Agniṣtoma*, which is accompanied by many other details, and the other related to the *Ḍarsha—Pūrṇamāsa*, which is simple and without accessory details; the question arising as to which of these two '*praṇayanas*' is to be employed at the *Chāṭurmāsya*, the conclusion is that it must be the latter. Upon this there arises a further question,—On which of the four sections of the *Chāṭurmāsya*—the '*Vaishvaḍēva*', the '*Varuṇapraghāsa*', the *Shākamēḍhīya* and the '*Sunāsīrīya*'—is this '*praṇayana*' to be done? The conclusion is that it should be done in connection with the *second* and *third* sections; though the *prima facie* argument is that is has to be done in connection with the *first* and *the fourth*, on the ground that the '*praṇayana*' has to be done on the *Uṭṭaravēḍi* and the use of this *Vēḍi* is implied in connection with the *first* and the *fourth* sections only,—this implication being deduced from the text which prohibits such use on the ground that it is only what is possible that can be *prohibited*; and hence the prohibition of the use of the *Uttaravēḍī* for the *first* and *fourth* sections implies the possibility of such use. In answer to this argument it has been shown that such an interpretation of the texts concerned leads to an incongruity in the text enjoining the use of the *Uttaravēḍī*; viz: with regard to the *first* and *fourth* sections its use is implied by the prohibition, and hence could be intended for *partial* acceptance only; while with regard to the *second* and *third* sections it is pointed out as to be used *permanently*; thus the same text laying down two entirely divergent courses of action. The priuciple of interpretation involved in this is that so long as a text affords one coherent meaning, there is no justification for breaking up its meaning into two incoherent parts. (*Miṭākṣarā*, pp. 201—2).

(5 In connection with the rights of the parents over the property left by their childless son, the question arises as to which of the two parents—the mother or the father—has the prior claim. The texts bearing on the question mention the word '*piṭarau*', 'parents'; and would therefore appear to leave the matter doubtful; but it has been argued that, inasmuch as the word '*piṭarau*' has been etymologically explained in authoritative grammatical works as equivalent to '*Māṭāpiṭarau*',—and as in this the 'Māṭā (mother) is mentioned first—hers should be the prior claim. This reasoning is based upon the *Mīmāmsā-sūṭra* V—i—4 to 7—where it has been shown that the *Prayājas*—*Samiḍ*, *Ṭanūnapāṭ*, &c.——are to be performed in the order in which they are mentioned in the injunctive texts,—in accordance with the accepted principle that the priority of mention gives the priority in action. (Miṭāksarā, p. 203).

4. The cases of application of Mimāmsā principles to law, in the *Vyavahāramayūkha** may be grouped under the following heads :—

* Lithographed Edition—Benares.

(a) *Sources of Proprietory Right.*

All proprietory right has its origin in the ways of the world, and has nothing to do with scriptures. It proceeds only from such sources as *purchase, gift* and the like. If it proceeded from the Scriptures, there would be nothing to establish one's right over the calf born of the cow that he may have purchased; as such right is established by ordinary usage only. Then again, the analogy of the said right over the calf cannot be extended to the case of the child born of one's own wife; because no person has any proprietory right over his child,—indicated either by usage or by the scripture; it is for this reason that in the *Vishvajiṭ* sacrifice, whereat the Sacrificer has to give away *all his belongings*, the children are *not* given away; this has been shown under *Mīmāṁsā-Sūṭra* VI—vii—1 (*Vya-ma.* p. 38, line 20) where it is shown that, the son, father, sister and such other persons do not come within the category of one's 'belongings', which word must be taken to be restricted to what is called '*ḍhana*', 'property.'

(b) *Adoption.*

* (1) In regard to adoption we have the text '*ḍauhiṭro bhāginēyashcha Shūḍrasyāpi cha ḍīyaṭē*', *i. e.*, 'the *Shūḍra* can also adopt the son of his daughter or the son of his sister'—following upon the general rule that the *Brāhmaṇa* can adopt a child only from among his '*Sapiṇḍas*'; the *Kṣaṭṭriya* from among *Kṣaṭṭriyas* in general, or from among his own '*Sagoṭras*', the *Vaishya* only from among *Vaishyas*, and the *Shūḍra* only from among *Shūḍras*. In view of these two texts read together, the conclusion with regard to *Shūḍras* is that for them the best form of adoption is that of the daughter's or the sister's son. This conclusion is in accordance with the principle embodied in *Mim-Sūṭras* IV—ii—16.

(2) † The adoption, even by the *Shūḍra*, has always to be done with full Vedic rites and ceremonies;—in this partic-

* *Vyavahāramayūkha*, p. 47, l. 1. † *Vyavahāramayūkha*, p. 47, l. 11.

ular case the *Shūḍra* being entitled to the *Vedic* rites in accordance with the principle of the '*Niṣāḍasṭhapaṭi*' laid down in *Mīm. Sū.* VI—i—51, where it is shown that the *Niṣāḍa* chief, even though a *Shūḍra*, is entitled to some Vedic sacrifices,—the only difference being that the *Vedic mantras* (which he, as a *Shūdra*, can not pronounce) have to be recited for him by a *Ḍvija* proxy. These exceptional cases are not touched by the general law that the *Shūḍra* is not *entitled to Vedic rites* as propounded in *Mīm. Sū.* VI,—i—25.

(3) In regard to the woman, it is laid down that she can adopt only in the company of her husband, or when permitted by him; as she, alone by herself, is not entitled to the performance of Vedic rites and ceremonies; and such rites and ceremonies are inseparable from all regular adoption. The preclusion of woman from sacrificial performances on her own account is discussed under *Mīm. Sū.* VI—i—6 (*Vide* above, chap. III §2).

(4) * With regard to a child that has been adopted in another family, Manu has laid down that he cannot *inherit the property* of his progenitor, nor *perform his Shrāḍḍha*; and though the text directly prohibits these two things only,—yet it has been accepted to imply the prohibition of all cognate things, —*e. g.*. all relationships and connections due to the progenitor and so forth. This is in accordance with the principles laid down in *Mīm. Sū.* III—vii—13, and also I—iii—3 (*Shabara-Bhāṣya*, page 71, line 15),—wherein it is shown that the texts '*anṭarvēḍi minoṭi* and '*jāṭapuṭraḥ kriṣṇakēsho*'-*gnīnāḍaḍhīṭa*'—even though making specific mention of only certain definite characteristics, are to be regarded as implying any place within the Vēḍi (and not the exact centre of it), or a particular point in the man's age (and not exactly meaning that his hairs should be black, &c.).

THE END.

* Ibid. p. 49, l. 5.